O9-BUB-592

CHILD SOLDIERS

Selected Titles in ABC-CLIO's
CONTEMPORARY
WORLD ISSUES
Series

Autism Spectrum Disorders, Raphael Bernier and Jennifer Gerdts
Celebrity in the 21st Century, Larry Z. Leslie
Climate Change, David L. Downie, Kate Brash, and Catherine Vaughan
Domestic Violence, Margi Laird McCue
Education in Crisis, Judith A. Gouwens
Environmental Justice, David E. Newton
Genocide, Howard Ball
Global Organized Crime, Mitchel P. Roth
Latino Issues, Rogelio Sáenz and Aurelia Lorena Murga
Lobbying in America, Ronald J. Hrebenar and Bryson B. Morgan
Modern Homelessness, Mary Ellen Hombs
Modern Piracy, David F. Marley
Modern Sports Ethics, Angela Lumpkin
Obesity, Judith Stern and Alexandra Kazaks
Online Privacy, Robert Gellman and Pam Dixon
Same-Sex Marriage, David E. Newton
Sentencing, Dean John Champion
Sexual Health, David E. Newton
Space and Security, Peter L. Hays
Substance Abuse, David E. Newton
U.S. Border Security, Judith A. Warner
U.S. Space Policy, Peter L. Hays, Ph.D.
Virtual Lives, James D. Ivory
Women in Combat, Rosemarie Skaine
Women in Developing Countries, Karen L. Kinnear
Youth and Political Participation, Glenn H. Utter

For a complete list of titles in this series, please visit
www.abc-clio.com.

Books in the Contemporary World Issues series address vital issues in today's society, such as genetic engineering, pollution, and biodiversity. Written by professional writers, scholars, and nonacademic experts, these books are authoritative, clearly written, up-to-date, and objective. They provide a good starting point for research by high school and college students, scholars, and general readers as well as by legislators, businesspeople, activists, and others.

Each book, carefully organized and easy to use, contains an overview of the subject, a detailed chronology, biographical sketches, facts and data and/or documents and other primary-source material, a directory of organizations and agencies, annotated lists of print and nonprint resources, and an index.

Readers of books in the Contemporary World Issues series will find the information they need to have a better understanding of the social, political, environmental, and economic issues facing the world today.

CHILD SOLDIERS

A Reference Handbook

David M. Rosen

**CONTEMPORARY
WORLD ISSUES**

⊙ ABC-CLIO

Santa Barbara, California • Denver, Colorado • Oxford, England

Copyright 2012 by ABC-CLIO, LLC

Library of Congress Cataloging-in-Publication Data

Rosen, David M., 1944–
 Child soldiers : a reference handbook / David M. Rosen.
  p. cm. — (Contemporary world issues)
 Includes bibliographical references and index.
  ISBN 978–1–59884–526–6 (hardcopy : alk. paper) — ISBN 978–1–59884–527–3 (ebook)
1. Child soldiers. 2. Children and war. I. Title.
UB418.C45R67 2012
355.3'3083—dc23   2012000449

ISBN: 978–1–59884–526–6
EISBN: 978–1–59884–527–3

16 15 14 13 12   1 2 3 4 5

This book is also available on the World Wide Web as an eBook.
Visit www.abc-clio.com for details.

ABC-CLIO, LLC
130 Cremona Drive, P.O. Box 1911
Santa Barbara, California 93116-1911

This book is printed on acid-free paper ∞

Manufactured in the United States of America

Contents

Preface, xiii

1 **Background and History, 1**
   Defining the "Problem" of Child Soldiers, 1
   Where Are the Child Soldiers?, 1
     A New International Problem but a Very Old Situation, 3
   Curbing Child Recruitment: The Problem of Armed
        Groups, 4
     Using Law to End the Use of Child Soldiers, 6
     First Steps: The Geneva Conventions, 7
     Protecting Child Combatants: The 1977 Additional
        Protocols, 10
     The Rome Statute: Setting Equal Standards, 12
     Child Soldiers and International Customary Law, 13
   Who Is a Child?, 14
     Straight-18: The Human Rights Position in the Convention
        on the Rights of the Child, 14
     Moving toward Age 18, 15
     International Treaties, Children's Rights, and the Definition
        of Childhood, 18
   Common Assumptions about Child Soldiers, 19
     Assumption 1: Children Are Vulnerable, 19
     Assumption 2: All Child Soldiers Are Abused and
        Exploited, 20
     Assumption 3: Child Soldiers Are a Product of the New
        Barbarism of War, 22
   The Role of Humanitarian Groups and "Civil Society," 24
   References, 27

2 Problems, Controversies, and Solutions, 33
Ending the Use of Child Soldiers: Problems and Solutions, 33
The Issue of Exceptions: Wars of National Liberation, 35
The Complexities of Treaties and International Law, 37
When Treaties Bind Nonsignatories, 38
Using Customary Law: The Case of Sierra Leone, 39
Captured Child Combatants, 40
Children's Rights and the Straight-18 Position, 41
Inventing a Universal Definition of Childhood, 41
Human Rights and the Realities of International Law, 42
Who Is a Child?, 42
International Law and Local Understandings
of Childhood, 43
The Boundaries between Childhood and Adulthood, 44
Civil Society and Social Change, 46
Child Soldiers in Cross-Cultural and Historical
Perspective, 47
Who Is a Child Soldier? Expanding the Definition, 50
Putting Child Recruiters on Trial, 52
The ICC: Cases from the Congo and Uganda, 53
The Special Court for Sierra Leone: The Meaning of
Recruitment, 53
Voluntary Enlistment or Forcible Recruitment?, 54
Local Customs, International Interpretations, 55
What Constitutes Enlistment?, 58
The Implications of an Expanded Definition
of Enlistment, 60
Putting Children on Trial, 62
Age and the Culpability of Children, 64
Wrestling with Children's Culpability, 66
Age and Culpability in Domestic Courts, 67
DDR: Disarming, Demobilizing, and Reintegrating Child
Soldiers, 69
References, 76

3 Special U.S. Issues, 85
Grappling with the Child Soldier Problem: U.S.
Achievements and Failures, 85
The Recruitment of Child Soldiers, 86
The United States and the Optional Protocol, 86
U.S. Domestic Legislation, 88
Compliance with Domestic Legislation, 89

The Protection of Child Soldiers: The United States and the
Treatment of Child Captives, 91
Rules for the Treatment of Detainees, 92
Unlawful Combatants and the War against Terror, 93
Detaining Child Soldiers, 94
The Treatment of Child Soldiers: The Legal Context, 96
Presidential Orders, 96
Legal Challenges, 97
Putting Child Soldiers on Trial: U.S. Military Commissions, 99
The Case of Mohammed Jawad: Tortured for Sport, 99
Omar Khadr: The First Child Soldier Tried since World
War II, 104
Conclusion, 110
References, 110

4   Chronology, 115

5   Biographical Sketches, 137
Child Soldiers, 137
al-Akhras, Ayat, 137
Arafat, Yasser, 138
Beah, Ishmael, 138
Bevistein, Abraham (Aby), 139
Casabianca, Giancomo, 140
Clem, John Lincoln, 140
Cornwall, John Travers, 141
Dayan, Moshe, 142
Jackson, Andrew, 143
Jal, Emmanuel, 144
Jawad, Mohammed, 145
Joan of Arc, 146
Khadr, Omar, 146
Ladd, Luther C., 147
Lucas, Jack, 148
Mackenzie, Clarence, 149
Murphy, Audie, 149
Okafor, Ben, 151
Soldaderas, 151
Tsam, Herzl Yankl, 152
Tungwar, Lam, 152
Yurlova, Marina, 153
Prominent Recruiters of Child Soldiers, 153

Dyilo, Thomas Lubanga, 153
Farhat, Maryam Mohammad Yousif, 154
Kony, Joseph, 154
Taylor, Charles Ghankay, 155
Key Figures in the Movement to End the Use of Child
    Soldiers, 156
Becker, Jo, 156
Coomaraswamy, Radhika, 157
Dellaire, Romeo, 157
Machel, Graca, 158
Otunnu, Olara A., 159

6   Data and Documents, 161
Data Overview, 161
International Treaties, 173
    Articles Relating to the Protection of Children from the
        Fourth Geneva Convention Relative to the Protection of
        Civilian Persons in Time of War, 12 August 1949, 173
    1949 Geneva Conventions Common Article 3, 176
    Selections from the Third Convention Relative to the
        Treatment of Prisoners of War, Geneva, 12 August 1949, 177
    Protocol Additional to the Geneva Conventions of 12
        August 1949, and Relating to the Protection of Victims
        of International Armed Conflicts (Protocol I), 8 June
        1977, 179
    Protocol Additional to the Geneva Conventions of 12
        August 1949, and Relating to the Protection of Victims
        of Non-International Armed Conflicts (Protocol II),
        8 June 1977, 181
    Articles Relating to Child Soldiers from the Convention on
        the Rights of the Child (1989), 182
    Optional Protocol to the Convention on the Rights of the
        Child on the Involvement of Children in Armed Conflict
        (2000), 183
    Articles Relating to Child Soldiers from the Rome Statute of
        the International Criminal Court (1998), 190
    Statute of the Special Court for Sierra Leone (2000), 196
    African Charter on the Rights and Welfare of the Child
        (1990), 197
    Cape Town Principle and Best Practice on the Prevention of
        Recruitment of Children into the Armed Forces and

Demobilization and Social Integration of Child Soldiers
in Africa (1997), 198
International Labour Organization Convention 182
Concerning the Prohibition and Immediate Action for
the Elimination of the Worst Forms of Child Labour
(1999), 207
U.S. Legislation 208
The Child Soldier Prevention Act of 2008, 208
The Child Soldier Accountability Act of 2008, 213
Human Rights Enforcement Act of 2009, 216

7 **Directory of Organizations, 219**

8 **Resources, 263**
Child Soldiers: General Studies, 263
Child Soldiers: Studies of Children at War, 264
Policy and Advocacy, 268
Human Rights Reports, 270
Disarmament, Demobilization, and Reintegration, 274
Child Soldiers in History, 276
Child Soldiers and International Law: Key Treaties, 278
International Criminal Tribunals, 280
Child Soldiers: Legal Analyses, 280
Autobiographies and Biographies, 282
Memorial Books, 284
Child Soldiers in Fiction, 285
Film and Video, 288
Podcasts, 294

Glossary, 297
Index, 301
About the Author, 323

Preface

This book is about child soldiers and the efforts over the past several decades to end children's presence in the military across the globe. The elimination of children from armed forces and armed groups is no easy task. The presence of children and youth in armed conflicts has a long history. A list of the most well known individuals who by today's standards would be called child soldiers would include Joan of Arc, Andrew Jackson, Moshe Dayan, Yasser Arafat, and many others from all walks of life. Put simply, in decades past, it was not that unusual for children to be part of armed forces and armed groups. In the early nineteenth century, the U.S. Navy was permitted to recruit boys as young as age 13, while the U.S. Marine Corps was permitted to recruit youngsters as young as age 11. One of the best descriptions of life in the Continental Army during the American Revolution was written by Joseph Plumb Martin, who was only age 15 when he enlisted along with many of his age-mates. Of course, youngsters never made up the majority of those who served in the armed forces, but neither were they a rarity. Throughout the eighteenth and nineteenth centuries, children and youth were a regular presence in military life.

Beginning in the middle of the nineteenth century, most Western nations began to reduce or eliminate children from their armed forces. Changes in the age of recruitment accompanied fundamental changes in thinking about children and childhood. In the eighteenth century, the boundaries between childhood and adulthood were less clear than they seem to be today. Children occupied many roles that today are often seen as suitable only for adults. Children brought home wages, worked on family farms, and often had a great deal of practical personal autonomy. Even as late as World War II, children in many countries began full-time work by the time they were age 14. Nevertheless, it is clear that by the middle of the nineteenth century, cultural and social distinctions between childhood and adulthood were hardening. Childhood increasingly came to be regarded as a separate and distinct stage of life characterized by innocence, vulnerability, and the need for protection. Moreover, as ideas about childhood changed, so did the ideas about whether children should serve in the military. As children came to be seen as increasingly innocent and vulnerable, military service and childhood came to be seen as increasingly incompatible.

None of this happened overnight. Even as Western armies began to raise the age of both voluntary enlistment and conscription, the actual enforcement of the rules was inconsistent, sporadic, and often ineffective so that youngsters continued to make their way into the military. In the American Civil War and World War I, thousands joined up despite rules against their recruitment. Fewer youngsters served in the U.S. Army during World War II, but those determined to serve often found their own way. Audie Murphy, the most highly decorated soldier in American history and winner of the Congressional Medal of Honor, altered his birth certificate in order to be able to enlist at age 17. Jack Lucas, who at age 14 lied about his age to get into the military, became the youngest marine to ever receive the Congressional Medal of Honor. They were not alone. During World War II, thousands of boys and girls across eastern and western Europe fought in partisan units, armed groups that fought against the armed invasions, occupations, and mass murders carried out by Nazi Germany and its allies during the war.

Because of the large numbers of children killed in World War II, new attention was given to the need to protect children during wartime. The Geneva Conventions of 1949, which codified the laws of war, provided many new protections for children but made no mention of child soldiers. But by the 1970s, many human rights and humanitarian groups determined to eliminate the presence of children in armed forces and armed groups throughout the world. In the United States and Europe, this effort was built on ideas about childhood that had been around for more than 100 years, but bringing these ideas to the rest of the world presented a problem of directed social change. It required transforming social attitudes toward child recruitments from treating it as normal and acceptable into believing it to be deviant and criminal. It was in the 1970s that the term "child soldier" first began to appear in its modern sense, meaning a child too young to be lawfully recruited into the military.

The elimination of child soldiers has proven to be a difficult task. Treaties have been signed, agreements reached, and recruiters put on trial, but child soldiers are present in conflicts across the globe. Chapter 1 of this book gives a broad overview of the issue, showing how the child soldier problem has increasingly become one of children associated with armed groups such as rebels, insurgents, and terrorists. It examines the history of attempts to end the use of child soldiers and the underlying assumptions about children and child soldiers that inform efforts by the world community to end their use. Chapter 2 examines the complexity of the issue and how it has been influenced by political considerations. It also examines how Western ideas about children in the military may clash with those of local peoples. Chapter 3 focuses on how the United States has confronted the issue of child soldiers. It looks at the treaties that the United States has signed and the laws that it has put in place as well as how it has met and complied with its treaty obligations. It also investigates how the United States treated child soldiers captured during the wars in Afghanistan and Iraq. Chapter 4 gives a detailed chronology of events related to understanding of the presence of child soldiers in armed conflicts as well as efforts to end or curb their recruitment. Chapter 5 provides biographical sketches of many child soldiers who have served in wars both past and present. Chapter 6 provides important data on the situation of child soldiers in current and recent conflicts as well as excerpts from key treaties and policy documents that are central to an understanding of the situation of child soldiers today. Chapter 7 is a directory of the major organizations that deal with the issue of child soldiers. The websites of these organizations provide important information about their work, and they can be contacted at the email and telephone numbers provided. Chapter 8 is a bibliography that offers ample material for further exploration of the topic. Many of the books can be found or ordered through your local library and in many cases can be accessed on the Web.

Writing this book was made possible because of a release-time award provided to me by Becton College of Fairleigh Dickinson University. I want to thank the release-time committee and Dean Geoffrey Weinman for their interest and support for this project. I would also like to thank my colleagues in the

Department of Social Sciences and History for their generosity of spirit and willingness to help me reflect on an issue that has been central to my academic life and research interests for more than a decade. My family has been extremely supportive of my work. I would like to thank my daughter, Sarah Maya Rosen, for her cheerful and very skillful research assistance. Finally, I would like to thank my wife, Tori Rosen, who has tirelessly heard me out on these issues and whose good humor, skeptical eye, critical reading skills, editorial command, and "red pen" invariably keep me on the right path.

1

Background and History

Defining the "Problem" of Child Soldiers

Who are the children who are fighting in today's wars, and why do they fight? Can the international community find these children and protect them from playing what is increasingly seen as an aberrant role in the international arena? More fundamentally, who is a child anyway? Does everyone agree? This chapter begins our examination of these fundamental questions that underlie the problem of child soldiers. It includes a preliminary look at where children are playing a role in war, the attempts by human rights groups and legal organizations to limit children's participation in war and to protect them from its greatest dangers, and the underlying political and cultural questions that make this such a thorny issue.

Where Are the Child Soldiers?

Around the world, millions of people are involved in wars, rebellions, insurgencies, and civil conflicts. It is commonly estimated that there are between 250,000 and 300,000 child soldiers involved in war somewhere in the world at any given time. Thus, over the past several decades, many hundreds of thousands of children have experienced war as soldiers. Until the middle of the twentieth century, it was very common for the armies of the world's nations to recruit children into their ranks. This practice has been abandoned only in recent years, as nations have turned from using citizen armies to using professional armies to fight their wars. Today, almost no national army regularly and systematically recruits children into its ranks. The primary locus of the child soldier problem has shifted from recruitment by the armed forces of nation-states to recruitment of children by non-state armed groups, such as insurgents; militants; rebels; revolutionary movements; guerilla fighters; global terrorist networks; regional tribal, ethnic, and religious militants; and local defense organizations.

This shift becomes evident in a quick review of the UN list of the most persistent users and recruiter of child soldiers ("Children and Armed Conflict" 2010). In Asia, the key recruiters are Abu Sayyaf and the Moro Islamic Liberation Front, Islamic separatist groups in the southern Philippines, and the New People's Army, the armed wing of the Communist Party of the Philippines. In Myanmar (Burma), both the national army and two rebel groups seeking independence, the Karenni Army and the Karen National Liberation Army, are extensive recruiters of children. In South America, the key recruiters are the Revolutionary Armed Forces of Colombia and the National Liberation Army, rebel groups that recruit and use child soldiers in their fight against government forces and allied paramilitary groups. In Africa, the United Nations has named violators on both sides of the current conflict in the Democratic Republic of the Congo. These include the Congolese national army, known as the Armed Forces of the Democratic Republic of Congo; the rebel Congress for the Defense of the People; the Democratic Forces for the Liberation of Rwanda; the Nationalist and Integrationalist Front; the Lord's Resistance Army (LRA); and various militias that are known as the Mai-Mai, which formed in local communities to resist Rwandan and Rwandan-related militias. In the conflict in Sudan, the United Nations lists the progovernment militias in Darfur and the southern-based Sudan People's Liberation Army (a largely Christian resistance group that has opposed the Islamic government of Sudan). In Somalia, the Transitional Federal Government is also on the list.

Child soldiers are also common in conflicts in the Middle East and south-central Asia. Indeed, Sergeant Nathan Ross Chapman, the first American soldier to be killed by hostile fire in Afghanistan, was shot in ambush by a 14-year-old boy. In Afghanistan, the most persistent recruiters are the Afghan National Police, a paramilitary police force; the Taliban, the insurgency movement fighting a guerilla war against the government of Afghanistan; the Haqqani network, an insurgent group allied to the Taliban; Hezb-i-Islami, a group that developed out of the Muslim Youth organization and that seeks to create a unified Islamic state; Jamat Sunat al-Dawa Salafia, an Islamic fundamentalist group committed to violent jihad; and the Tora Bora Front, a Taliban-related group in eastern Afghanistan. In Iraq, the United Nations has named al-Qaeda in Iraq, a group that identifies with Osama bin Laden and seeks to create an Islamic state in Iraq. Finally, children have also figured prominently as suicide terrorists for Palestinian organizations such as Hamas and Islamic Jihad in the Israeli-Palestinian conflict (Human Rights Watch 2002). These groups, which are involved in most of the armed struggles taking place in the world today, have no single unifying cause or ideology. What they share is a kind of "outsider" status in the world community. They are usually rejected by governments and the international community and regarded as illegitimate armed groups.

A New International Problem but a Very Old Situation

The history of warfare shows that young people have always been on or near the battlefield. Indeed, the idea that childhood and military service are absolutely incompatible is relatively new, even in the West. In the United States and England, children in uniform were ubiquitous in the nineteenth century and through World War I. For example, large numbers of children served on both sides of the American Civil War. Exactly how many is an extremely difficult question to answer. It is generally accepted that about 2.1 million soldiers and sailors served in the Union forces during the Civil War and that about 882,000 soldiers and sailors served in the Confederate forces (McPherson 2003, 306 n. 4). During the war, Benjamin Gould of the U.S. Sanitary Commission undertook a statistical analysis of the ages of soldiers in the Union army as of 1864. He examined the recorded ages in military rosters of 1,049,457 soldiers. It showed that 1.2 percent of the soldiers were under 18 years of age (Gould 1869). But Gould's figures are believed to be unreliable because of the large numbers of volunteers who misrepresented their age. In 1905, George Kilmer reviewed Gould's data and pointed out a number of statistical anomalies that led him to assert that at least 100,000 boys who were listed as being age 18 were often not even 16 or 17. This did not include the thousands who were officially listed as 16 or 17 or less (Kilmer 1905). In 1911, Charles King asserted that the Civil War was fought by a "grand army of boys." He claimed that 800,000 soldiers were below age 17, 200,000 were under 16, and another 100,000 were no more than 15 (King 1911). King did not explain how he obtained these figures. King, however, had a long and distinguished career in the U.S. military. He was a West Point graduate who participated in the Civil War and retired from active service in 1879. He later continued on in military service through the Spanish-American War and World War I. Thus, while we have no way of fully judging the accuracy of his claims, it is fair to say that he had a good understanding of the general age, makeup, and composition of military units. Accordingly, even if it is impossible to pin down exact numbers, the presence of underage recruits throughout the army was a well-known and accepted fact of life throughout the Civil War.

From a historical perspective, the practice of child recruitment has only recently ended in many Western armies. It is important to recognize this because it enhances our understanding of the thorny problem of child recruitment. Rather than simply imagine a world of evildoers who abuse children with impunity (although clearly there are some of these), we need to recognize the reality that there are people who reject or who are indifferent to new and sometimes alien concepts of childhood, people for whom Western ideas of childhood simply do not jibe with their own understanding of the world. This does not mean that the world is a museum in which old ideas of childhood must be preserved in a diorama. But it tells us that the entire child soldier project, with its goal of universally separating children from military service, is not only a matter of finding and jailing a few bad apples but also an extraordinarily complex and ambitious project of directed social change.

Curbing Child Recruitment: The Problem of Armed Groups

At the signing of the Declaration of Independence in 1776, Benjamin Franklin is reputed to have said, "We must all hang together, or assuredly we shall all hang separately." Franklin was reflecting on the typical fate of rebels everywhere. Rebellion was a criminal act, and the fate of defeated rebels was the hangman's noose. Little has changed since Franklin's time. Nation-states across the globe regard rebels of every type to be criminal enemies of the state, whether they are militants, insurgents, guerillas, terrorists, or freedom fighters. Although the right of rebellion against oppressive governments was central to the Declaration of Independence, no such right exists in international law. Indeed, the post–World War II human rights regime recognizes no human right to engage in rebellion against nation-states for any reason (Dunér 2005).

Because rebel groups were considered to be criminal, they stood completely outside the framework of international humanitarian law, the so-called laws of war that developed over several centuries and largely govern conflicts between sovereign states. Every nation regarded rebellion as an internal matter for the nation to handle as it saw fit. Rebels and most other forms of so-called nonstate actors were unrecognized in international law; they had no internationally acknowledged rights or duties.

This situation has changed significantly since 1977. One important change is that a variety of international treaties now require that such nonstate actors, which are usually termed "armed groups" in the language of treaties, forgo the recruitment and use of child soldiers. However, it is difficult to enforce international law against armed groups that are already regarded as illegitimate and criminal by the nations in which they operate. Since sovereign states deem rebels and insurgents to be illegitimate actors, they do not ordinarily grant these groups recognition despite the fact that there is evidence that when they do recognize them, both sides to the conflict are more likely to observe the laws of war. Further complicating this situation, nation-states are zealous guardians of their own sovereignty and limit or reject attempts by the international community to "meddle" in their internal affairs. As a general rule, the official position of nation-states is that the actions of rebel and militants groups are internal criminal matters that merit the same kind of response as that given to murderers and thieves. When UN officials want to contact such rebel groups, they must first obtain permission from national authorities to engage these groups regarding their use of children as soldiers.

Nations can perceive even including a discussion of such groups in an international report as treading on a state's national sovereignty. For example, following the UN report on the most persistent violators of international laws against the recruitment of child soldiers, the government of India objected to the inclusion of the Maoist rebels in the report. India argued that the United Nations had exceeded its authority and had no mandate to investigate and report on the situation of the Maoist rebels in central India. ("Naxal Problem" 2010). In other words, India's view is that the Maoist rebel forces in their country were simply local criminals who should be treated as criminals and were not the legitimate concern of international institutions or international law.

In India, the Maoist insurgency is rooted in serious grievances of tribal peoples in the forested areas of eastern and central India, who are among the most economically deprived peoples of India. There are some 10,000 to 20,000 rebels spread across eastern and central India, and the avowed goal of the Maoists is the overthrow of the Indian state. The Indian government has not deployed its army against the rebels but rather uses the Central Reserve Police Force, the largest paramilitary police force in the world ("India's CRPF" 2009). About 50,000 members of the Central Reserve Police Force are involved in combating the insurgency ("Interview with R K Vij" 2010). The Indian human rights group Forum for Fact-Finding Documentation and Advocacy estimates that some 80,000 children are involved directly and indirectly in the armed conflict in Chhattisgarh State, a main center of the insurgency. The great majority of child soldiers appear to be part of the rebel groups, although there are also children in government-supported self-defense militias (Zemp and Mohapatra n.d.).

Using Law to End the Use of Child Soldiers

The vast majority of efforts to end the use of child soldiers have focused on the development of international laws banning the recruitment and use of children in armed forces and groups. The broad goal is to create a comprehensive worldwide ban on the use of children in the military. All these efforts have focused on the creation of treaties in which nations agree to abide by rules that restrict the recruitment of children. But, as we shall see below, treaties are tricky. As a general rule, the terms of a treaty are only binding on the nations that are "state parties" to the treaty, meaning that they have signed and ratified the treaty. The result can be a bit of a hodgepodge in which the rules of one or more treaties are binding on some nation-states but not on others. Treaty advocates, of course, hope that most nations will ultimately sign and ratify a treaty, thus making it fully international. But it is important to remember, as we examine the history of treaties banning the recruitment and use of child soldiers, that not every nation is legally bound to each and every treaty that follows. The United States, for example, is a state party to the Geneva Conventions of 1949, but it is not a state party to the 1977 Additional Protocols I and II of Geneva Conventions, which have special provisions dealing with child soldiers. The United States is a state party to the 2000 Optional Protocol to the Convention on the Rights of the Child on the Involvement of Children in Armed Conflict, but it is not yet a state party to the original 1989 Convention on the Rights of the Child. As a result, international law remains unevenly applied across the globe.

First Steps: The Geneva Conventions

The story of legal attempts to ban the use of child soldiers begins with the 1949 Geneva Conventions (1949). The Geneva Conventions are a set of four treaties that were developed over a period of many years and were finalized and reaffirmed in 1949 in the wake of the catastrophe of World War II. The Geneva Conventions form a key element of what are generally called the laws of war, also known as international humanitarian law. The Geneva Conventions address primarily the problem of international aggression between nation-states, the same issue that helped bring about the establishment of the United Nations only four years earlier.

The 1949 Geneva Conventions make no reference to child soldiers. The Conventions did not define childhood, nor did they lay down a minimum age for childhood despite the large numbers of child combatants in World War II. However, some provisions in the Third and Fourth Geneva Conventions indirectly provided protections for children who served as combatants. The Geneva Conventions draw a sharp distinction between soldiers and civilians; making these categories separate and distinct was intended to help ensure that civilians could be protected during wartime. The writers of the Conventions did not want to allow soldiers to disguise themselves as civilians or to enable civilians to take up arms and then fade back into the general population. The premise of the Conventions was that, in combat, if regular soldiers could not distinguish among regular enemy soldiers, enemy soldiers disguised as civilians, or civilians who took up arms at night while appearing to be civilians during the day, then all civilians would be put at risk.

Accordingly, the Geneva Conventions distinguished between what today are referred to as "lawful" and "unlawful" combatants, who are also sometimes called "privileged" and "unprivileged" belligerents, although the Conventions do not explicitly use these terms. The category of lawful combatants (privileged belligerents) refers to the regular armed forces of a party to an international conflict but may include other armed groups allied to a party to an international conflict, such as guerilla and partisan units. Article 4 of the Third Geneva Convention detailed the many requirements needed to be met in order to qualify as a lawful combatant. Fighters must openly identify themselves as soldiers and not disguise themselves as civilians. In particular, they must display fixed and distinctive insignia or signs that are recognizable at a distance. They must also carry arms openly, be under the command and control of an individual responsible for his or her subordinates, and fight according to the laws of war. Guerilla forces fighting in an international conflict may or may not be deemed lawful combatants, depending on whether they operate in a manner consistent with these criteria. Lawful combatants have a privileged and protected status under the Geneva Conventions (Third Geneva Convention, Article 4). As soldiers, they are "licensed to kill" other soldiers and cannot be punished for doing what soldiers do. Unless they commit war crimes, they may not be prosecuted for actions that would otherwise be serious crimes during peacetime or illegal if committed by civilians even in wartime (Dormann 2003). If captured by the enemy, lawful combatants are entitled to the status of prisoner of war (Third Geneva Convention).

In contrast, under the Geneva Conventions, anyone who is not a lawful combatant is not entitled to take up arms. Such persons may be guerillas or members of a resistance group, but unless they are clearly identifiable as soldiers, carry out their activities openly, and follow the other rules of the Geneva Conventions, they are deemed to be civilians illegally engaged in hostilities and are labeled as unlawful combatants or unprivileged belligerents (Dormann 2003). Unlawful combatants have only minimal protection under the Geneva Conventions. They can be attacked, and if they are captured, they have none of the privileges of prisoners of war. They can be treated as criminals and even be executed. Their only legal protections are found in Article 3 of the Geneva Conventions, which is contained in all four Geneva Conventions and is therefore often called Common Article 3. Common Article 3 outlines minimal standards of conduct toward such individuals, who are referred to throughout the Geneva Conventions as "persons" rather than prisoners. Even the protections afforded to these unlawful combatants are important, but they are largely the procedural guarantees found in Article 3 of all the Geneva Conventions. Most significant among these is that even captured unlawful combatants are persons who must be protected against "outrages upon personal dignity, in particular humiliating and degrading treatment." In addition, if and when they are tried for criminal offenses, it cannot be by some kind of irregular or kangaroo court. Article 3 requires that there shall be no "passing of sentences and the carrying out of executions without previous judgment pronounced by a regularly constituted court, affording all the judicial guarantees which are recognized as indispensable by civilized peoples" (Third Geneva Convention, Article 3). Military forces that fail to adhere to these important provisions are themselves committing war crimes.

The original Geneva Conventions did not prohibit recruiting children into armed forces or groups. Accordingly, children who served as lawful combatants in international conflicts were, like adult combatants, entitled to prisoner-of-war status. However, the Fourth Geneva Convention also prohibited imposing the death penalty on persons under age 18 for offenses against an occupying power, a provision that could protect even unlawful child combatants in international conflicts (Fourth Geneva Convention, Article 68). Beyond these protections, the provisions of the Geneva Conventions do not generally apply to internal conflicts within a state; these conflicts are treated, at least from each sovereign state's point of view, as treason or rebellion. Ordinarily, rebellions and insurgencies are criminal per se under the domestic laws of their states, and international law has relatively little application.

Treaties addressing international conflict are the product of negotiation among the many sovereign states that are parties to the treaty. The effectiveness of international treaties on noninternational conflicts is limited. Since only sovereign states sign and ratify such treaties, one party is always absent—the rebel groups and/or insurgents said to be bound by the treaty that has been imposed on them without their involvement. In keeping with this distinction, the Geneva Conventions offered virtually no protection to children who served as combatants in noninternational conflicts. The Conventions provided no prisoner-of-war status for belligerents, militants, rebels, or anyone else engaged in internal conflicts. All, including child combatants, are regarded as unlawful combatants or unprivileged belligerents. All are entitled the minimal protections of Common Article 3, but beyond this, they may be treated as criminals. Nothing in the Conventions prevented imposing the death penalty on such combatants, even if they were children. Virtually all the forces recruiting child soldiers today fall into the category of unlawful combatants.

Protecting Child Combatants: The 1977 Additional Protocols

In 1977, two amendments were added to the Geneva Conventions, known as Additional Protocol I and Additional Protocol II, which addressed many different issues related to the conduct of war, not simply that of child soldiers, but included the first systematic attempt to directly address the issue of child combatants (Protocols Additional I and II, 1949). Although child protection was the goal of the treaties, they did not provide the same protection for all child combatants. Instead, the Protocols distinguished between the two categories of conflict mentioned above: Additional Protocol I addressed international armed conflict (wars between sovereign states), while Additional Protocol II addressed noninternational conflicts (civil wars, rebellions, and insurgencies). In addition, the Protocols created two categories of children: younger children (below age 15) and older children (between ages 15 and 18).

The protection afforded to children by the Protocols is linked to the nature of the conflict and the particular age category involved. Additional Protocol I (international armed conflict) imposes the least restrictive requirements on sovereign states. The treaty language is not very strong. It does not actually prohibit child recruitment but only addresses the youngest category of children by requiring state parties to take all "feasible measures" so that children who have not attained the age of 15 years do not take a "direct part in hostilities" (Additional Protocol I, Article 77). It also requires that they "refrain from recruiting them into their armed forces." With respect to the older category of children, its only requirement was that if and when states recruit older children, they should "endeavor to give priority to those who are the oldest."

The restrictions on child recruitment contained in Additional Protocol I are far less strong than originally proposed in a draft treaty by the International Committee of the Red Cross (ICRC). The ICRC originally proposed that state parties "take all necessary measures in order that children under fifteen years shall not take part in hostilities and, in particular, they shall refrain from recruiting them in their armed forces or accepting their voluntary enrollment" (Additional Protocols Commentary, 898, n. 2). In the final treaty, however, "all necessary measures" was replaced with "feasible measures," and the complete ban against participation in hostilities was replaced with a ban only on "direct participation in hostilities." The term "direct participation in hostilities" usually means an active form of combat, such as firing at an enemy or blowing up a bridge, but does not include other important military activities, such as intelligence gathering or supply transportation. The term "feasible measures" means that the protection of children is less important than ensuring the success of military operations. In contrast, the phrase "necessary measures" is regarded as giving higher priority to the protection of children. The ICRC's draft treaty also required states to refrain from recruiting younger children or accepting their voluntary enrollment. The ICRC interprets the final language of Additional Protocol I as not permitting the voluntary enrollment of children under 15 years old (Delissen 1991). In fact, however, the final treaty says nothing about the issue of voluntary enrollment (Additional Protocols Commentary, 900 n. 26).

A number of factors contributed to softening the restrictions in Additional Protocol I. First, states were hesitant to adopt unambiguous and binding language. Vague terms in the treaty allowed each state to decide for itself the meanings of "all feasible measures" or "direct part in hostilities." The protections for children are much stronger in Additional Protocol II, which governs the use of child soldiers in internal noninternational conflicts. This is not surprising because by taking a hard line against insurgents and rebel groups that threaten state sovereignty, these restrictions on recruitment support the military goals of state parties. Additional Protocol II (noninternational conflict) applies to civil wars between the armed forces of a state and dissident armed forces or other organized armed groups. Its restrictions against child recruitment are clear. It states that "children who have not attained the age of fifteen years shall neither be recruited in the armed forces or groups nor allowed to take part in hostilities" (Additional Protocol II, Article 4). The treaty terms are strong. Additional Protocol II creates a comprehensive ban on the using as a soldier any person under 15 years of age in any internal conflict. It allows rebels no escape clause for children under the age of 15 (Additional Protocols Commentary, n. 26). State parties took this stricter view of child recruitment by rebel groups because they wanted to deprive armed groups of an advantage that states believed such groups often had—the ability to recruit youngsters to their cause (Mann 1987).

The Rome Statute: Setting Equal Standards

Among the most significant recent legal developments in curbing the use of child soldiers is the creation of the International Criminal Court (ICC) in The Hague in 2002, which was established by the 1998 Rome Statute of the ICC. The Rome Statute consolidates many of the traditional laws of war into a single international criminal statute. It makes the recruitment of children under 15 years old a war crime. It provides for both the trial and the imprisonment by the ICC in The Hague of persons charged and convicted of recruiting them. This treaty gives the newly created court jurisdiction over war crimes "when committed as part of a plan or policy or as part of a large-scale commission of such crimes" (Rome Statute, Article 8). The ICC is the only permanent international court where individuals charged with war crimes can be brought to trial. The Rome Statute defines the term "war crime" as including "grave breaches" of the Geneva Conventions as well as "other serious violations of the laws and customs" applicable to both international and noninternational armed conflicts. In the case of younger children, the treaty ends previous distinction between international and domestic conflicts and imposes an absolute ban on the conscription, enlistment, or use of children under the age of 15 by both nation-states and nonstate armed groups.

The Rome Statute comes the closest of any international treaty to establishing a universal legal standard that applies to the youngest of child soldiers, but its focus is solely on the problem of the recruitment and the use of child soldiers. The ICC has no jurisdiction over any person who was under age 18 who commits a war crime. The statute specifically says, "The Court shall have no jurisdiction over any person who was under 18 at the time of the commission of the alleged crime" (Rome Statute, Article 26). As a result, it fails to tackle the issue of the legal culpability of children who committed war crimes. Notwithstanding its universal ban on child recruitment, the Rome Statute has not as yet been as effective as its drafters hoped because like the 1977 Additional Protocols, it has not achieved universal acceptance by the world's nation-states. Many major powers, such as the United States, Russia, India, and China, are not parties to the treaty. Most of the countries of the Middle East are also not parties to the treaty. The reasons nation-states do not sign these treaties vary; sometimes there is one particular item to which a nation objects, and sometimes nations are wary of anything that might encroach on their national sovereignty. That does not mean that they do not, in fact, pay attention to the Protocols and indeed often follow their mandates, but, as we shall see, they do so as part of what they consider to be international customary law.

Child Soldiers and International Customary Law

Many of the laws of war were considered part of international customary law long before they were incorporated into the Geneva Conventions and other treaties. Customary law refers to the general practice of states even if it has not been written down in treaty form. The United States, which is not a party to Additional Protocol I to the Geneva Conventions, still recognizes some its provisions, including the restrictions on the recruitment of the youngest of child soldiers as a matter of international customary law (Matheson 1987, 428). For a rule of law to be considered binding under international customary law, there must be wide acceptance or consensus among nation-states. There must be evidence that states follow this rule of law as a matter of perceived obligation. Finally, there should also be a substantial history of state practice; that is, it must be demonstrated that states have a history of compliance with the rule of law. It is possible for the terms of a treaty to become international customary law. For example, if the vast majority of nations of the world become parties to a treaty, it might be argued that the terms of a treaty are so widely accepted that they are now binding on everyone, even those who were never parties to the treaty.

It is now a nearly universal principle of international treaty law to ban the recruitment of children below age 15 by armed forces and groups. But one court, the Special Court for Sierra Leone, has also ruled that the recruitment of children under the age of 15 is already absolutely banned as a matter of customary international law ("Prosecutor v. Norman" 2004). If this court's ruling becomes widely accepted, it will be a clear example of how a rule of law that was once binding only on state parties to a treaty has been transformed into a universal principle applicable to all armed forces and groups. The legality of recruiting young people between the age of 15 and 18, however, remains unresolved.

Who Is a Child?

As we have seen, one of the most difficult practical obstacles to ending the use of child soldiers is the inability of the international community to curtail recruitment by armed groups. But the problem of recruitment is also exacerbated by important differences of opinion about who, exactly, is a child. Indeed, there is little universal agreement about the definition of childhood or agreement as to what activities and roles are compatible or incompatible with the life of a child. Definitions and roles for children vary widely from culture to culture. As a result, despite international laws against using children as soldiers, not everyone agrees that the life of the child and the life of a soldier are incompatible. In the next chapter, we examine more closely the problem of establishing a universal definition of childhood and the political and social implications of this enterprise.

Straight-18: The Human Rights Position in the Convention on the Rights of the Child

Although the laws of war and international criminal law have focused on the recruitment of children under 15 years old, contemporary advocates of an international ban on child soldiers use a different definition of childhood. For them, childhood begins at birth and ends at age 18. From this perspective, a child soldier is any person below 18 years of age who is recruited or used by an armed force or armed group. Known as the "Straight-18" position, this view is based on the universal definition of childhood contained in the 1989 Convention on the Rights of the Child (CRC). The CRC is an international treaty that has been signed and ratified by most of the nations of the world (with the exception of the United States and Somalia). State parties to the CRC have committed themselves to advancing children's rights and to enacting legislation and policy in accordance with the doctrine of the "best interests of the child." Widely hailed as a milestone in the development of children's rights, the CRC did, in fact, create the first international definition of the child as "any person below the age of eighteen years" (CRC, Article 1). The CRC's definition of childhood is the basis of the commonly cited number of child soldiers in the world: 250,000 to 300,000. Clearly, if the term child soldier referred only to persons below 15 years of age, the number would sharply decline.

The CRC is one of a number of human rights treaties that seek to expand the restrictions found in the laws of war, although they do not provide for criminal penalties for violators. The emergence of the CRC illustrates the increasing power of nonstate organizations to shape the international legal definitions of childhood and, by extension, the definition of who is a child soldier (Banks 2003). Among the most important of these organizations are the ICRC, Amnesty International, Human Rights Watch, International Save the Children Alliance, Jesuit Refugee Service, The Quaker United Nations Office, Terres des Hommes International Federation, Defense for Children International, and World Vision International. With the exception of the ICRC, these organizations also make up the Coalition to Stop the Use of Child Soldiers, the principal advocacy organization in the child soldier issue. All these organizations have adopted the so-called Straight-18 position (Happold 2008).

Moving toward Age 18

The CRC was not a complete victory for the human rights activists because, though it declared a universal definition of childhood, the treaty still allows nations to define the age of majority as younger and to establish an earlier age for the attainment of the legal rights and duties of adulthood even though this is a departure from the general rule. In fact, even when it comes to child soldiers, the CRC only prohibits recruiting soldiers who are under 15 years of age. Anti–child soldier activists saw this is a major flaw in the treaty and tried to fix it with a supplementary treaty known as the Optional Protocol on the Involvement of Children in Armed Conflict to the Convention on the Rights of the Child of 2000. This treaty was the first major opportunity to comprehensively apply the Straight-18 position to child soldiers ("Optional Protocol" 2000). The Optional Protocol uses age 18 as a target goal for banning or restricting recruitment by both armed forces and armed groups. Many nations have signed on to this treaty, but, even though both the CRC and the Optional Protocol set important international children's rights standards for curbing recruitment, there are few ways to enforce them. Both treaties depend on the voluntary compliance of the nations that sign them.

The Optional Protocol grew out of widespread dissatisfaction with the CRC. The ICRC has pointed to the two main criticisms of the CRC's treatment of the child soldier issue. First, Article 38, the provision dealing with child soldiers, was the only provision of the CRC that did not contain the general age limit of 18 years in spite of the fact that it dealt with one of the most dangerous situations children face. Second, Article 38 merely repeated the language of Additional Protocol I and completely ignored Additional Protocol II so that it actually provided weaker standards than those contained in the laws of war (ICRC 1997).Accordingly, the ICRC and other nongovernmental organizations (NGOs) resolved to promote the basic principle of ending the recruitment and use of children under age 18 in situations of armed conflict. The result of their efforts, the Optional Protocol to the Convention on the Rights of the Child on the Involvement of Children in Armed Conflict, specifically focused on the recruitment or use of anyone under age 18 in armed conflicts.

The Optional Protocol requires that states "shall take all feasible measures to ensure that members of their armed forces who have not attained the age of 18 years do not take a direct part in hostilities" (Optional Protocol, Article 1). Much of the language of the Optional Protocol echoes Additional Protocol I but raises the age bar to 18. The weak language remains, but raising the age limit for recruitment strengthens the earlier ban on recruiting the youngest of children by making it more difficult for field commanders to claim that they were confused about the age of the youngest soldiers. States must also "ensure that all persons who have not attained the age of 18 years are not compulsorily recruited into their armed forces" (Optional Protocol, Article 2). In addition, it requires states to increase the minimum age of voluntary recruitment to be higher than the age 15 set forth for the CRC. It makes clear that under the CRC, persons who are under 18 are entitled to special protection (Optional Protocol, Article 3). As with most treaties, enforcement is not easily achieved, although state parties are required to submit a binding declaration setting forth a minimum age for voluntary recruitment. Paralleling Additional Protocol II, the strongest restrictions in the Optional Protocol are used to squelch rebellion. It provides that "armed groups, distinct from the armed forces of a State, should not, under any circumstances, recruit or use in hostilities persons under the age of 18 years" (Optional Protocol, Article 4). The Optional Protocol's double standard permits sovereign states to recruit child soldiers but bars rebel groups from doing the same.

At around the same time, the Straight-18 position gained strength by being included in two other treaties that applied the Straight-18 position to child soldiers. The 1999 African Charter on the Rights and Welfare of the Child unequivocally defined a child as "every human being below the age of 18 years" (African Charter, Article 2). Using age 18 as the benchmark age for limiting recruitment, it also required that state parties "shall take all necessary measures to ensure that no child shall take a direct part in hostilities and refrain in particular, from recruiting any child" (African Charter, Article 22). Here the use of the phrase "necessary measures" was used in place of "feasible measures," which made clear that states were required to take all steps needed to effect a ban on child soldiers and not merely those that involved circumstances of armed conflict. However, the African Charter was silent on the issue of nonstate actors.

Similarly, the Worst Forms of Child Labor Convention of the International Labor Organization ("ILO Convention" 1999) also defined as children as "all persons under the age of 18" (ILO, Article 2) and required all state parties to take "immediate and effective measures to secure the prohibition and elimination of the worst forms of child labour as a matter of urgency." It included among the worst forms of child labor the "forced or compulsory recruitment of children for use in armed conflict" (ILO, Article 3). Like the African Charter, the ILO convention made no specific mention of nonstate actors, although the language of the statute implies that states will have broad powers to criminalize all forms of forced recruitment by anyone, but it imposes no duty on nonstate actors.

International Treaties, Children's Rights, and the Definition of Childhood

Treaties signed by national leaders often tell us very little about how the peoples of the world actually experience and understand childhood. Many nations signed the CRC and other children's rights treaties because they want to be counted as part of the community of nations and not necessarily because the terms of the treaty actually reflect how people experience and understand childhood. From this perspective, treaties like the CRC are best seen as aspirational statements of how world leaders imagine an ideal childhood. In more practical terms, the CRC is an attempt to use international law to create a new universal definition of childhood and to provide children with certain basic rights. Some argue that the entire effort to redefine childhood according to the dictates of the Straight-18 position is a bureaucratic fiction with little applicability outside Western societies (Montgomery 2009, 14).

In enumerating children's rights under the CRC, it is common to speak of the Convention as embodying four basic sets of children's rights: the rights of participation, protection, prevention, and provision (Van Bueren 1995. In practice, however, the central focus of political and legal action has been protection and prevention, while participation and provisioning take a distant second place. Even more remote are such rights as freedom of conscience for children, which have been formally rejected by many state parties to the convention. This should not be surprising because the children's rights movement differs from other such movements in a significant way. The primary forces behind the CRC are not disenfranchised groups that are seeking to gain full participatory rights in society but rather enfranchised adults who seek to spread a protective mantle over the world's children. While ideas about children's rights have many sources, their translation into practice is rooted in the operations of civil society, where social change is sought largely through lawmaking and the courts. It is a movement led by advocates and lawyers, working in tandem with helping professions, such as psychology and social work, that are ancillary to the legal system.

Despite its complications and shortcomings, the CRC is a very important document. The idea of children's rights has come of age and is gaining momentum throughout the world. Its development offers an unusual opportunity to examine the ambition and power of law and of the ability of communities to accommodate to and to resist one of the most powerful social movements of our time—a movement that seeks nothing less than the global restructuring of age categories along with the rights and duties of children and adults. Notwithstanding the complexity of these issues, it is settled international law that recruiting children under age 15 is a war crime. As we shall see, how this law translates into actual situations can be quite complex and difficult.

Common Assumptions about Child Soldiers

Despite differences in outlook and policy among advocacy groups, virtually all humanitarian and human rights efforts on the child soldier issue are shaped by a common belief that children are particularly vulnerable and innocent and that modern warfare is especially horrific. Whether or not these assumptions are firmly rooted in fact, they profoundly shape the international conversation about child soldiers.

Assumption 1: Children Are Vulnerable

Advocates for banning child recruitment generally believe that all children are inherently vulnerable; this equation of childhood with vulnerability is central to understanding humanitarian views of the child soldier, and it is also a central element of the CRC, with its stress on the need to provide a mantle of protection for the world's children. From this perspective, the recruitment of child soldiers is first and foremost the product of the actions of abusive and corrupt adults who bring harm to innocent children. This model is designed primarily to affix blame and assign culpability, and it frames virtually all discussions of child soldiers.

The UNICEF report *Adult Wars, Child Soldiers* ties the problem of child soldiers to the worst forms of child sexual abuse, such as sex trafficking or child pornography (UNICEF 2002). All these are forms of criminality in which unscrupulous adults exploit immature, innocent, and impressionable children. Child soldiers are frequently described as "used," "manipulated," or "cheap and disposable" (Youth Advocate Program International 2004). The latter term likens them to cheap modern goods and products—disposable cameras, razors, plastic cups, or wristbands—that are easily consumed and discarded. The term "disposable" is also frequently used to describe "human goods," such as labor migrants, child miners, and modern criminal form of slave labor.

Assumption 2: All Child Soldiers Are Abused and Exploited

In tandem with this belief that children are vulnerable is the focus on the forced recruitment and abusive exploitation of children who are used as child soldiers. Forced recruitment of child soldiers is frequently described as being linked to specific acts of terror and horror, such as compelling new recruits to kill family, friends, or covillagers in macabre ritual acts to ensure that the child is permanently alienated and separated from family, home, and community life. In addition, once they are recruited into armed forces, child soldiers are said to suffer from the worst forms of child abuse, including forced labor, sexual slavery, the forced use of drugs, and outright murder.

The language of the U.S. State Department's Trafficking in Person's Report is typical, as evidenced by the following "Facts about Child Soldiers:"

> Child soldiering is a unique and severe manifestation of trafficking in persons. Tens of thousands of children under age 18 have been conscripted into armed conflicts, serving in government armies, armed militias, and rebel groups. Some children are kidnapped and forced to serve; others join in the face of threats, bribes, and false promises of compensation.
>
> Hoping in many cases for food, clothing, and shelter, a child's decision to join an armed group cannot be considered a free choice. Children caught up in armed conflict are desperately searching for a means of survival. Because of their emotional and physical immaturity, children are easily manipulated and coerced into violence. Many child soldiers are forced to use alcohol or narcotics as a way to desensitize them to violence or to enhance their performance. (U.S. Department of State 2004)

A similar example comes from Amnesty International: "Youth is no protection against torture . . . In armed conflicts, children of an enemy group are often targeted precisely because they represent that group's future. Children are sometimes tortured to coerce or punish their parents. In Uganda, thousands of children are recruited to the armed opposition group, the Lord's Resistance Army (LRA), and forced to take part in ritualized killing. While all children are forced to fight and kill, girls are allocated to LRA commanders and held as sexual slaves"(Amnesty International 2000). The result of this abuse, it is sometime argued, is the creation of whole generations of psychologically scarred children who contribute to long-term social instability (Kaplan 1994).

At times, child soldiers have been described as "harvested" by various armed factions, a kind of postapocalyptic metaphor that describes them as expendable feed or fodder. Children are frequently described as "cannon fodder." Historically, of course, critics of war have often used the term "cannon fodder" to describe raw untrained recruits, both young and old, who were deemed expendable and cynically thrown into the face of enemy fire with little regard for the loss of life. But contemporary critics of the recruitment of child soldiers have adopted this term as especially applicable to all children who are recruited into armed conflict, deeming them "the cannon fodder of choice" (Masland 2002). Parents are sometime accused of being immoral accomplices in their children's recruitment. From a group who said they were 15 to 17 years old and had volunteered for the Mai-Mai Patriotic Resistance in the Congo, one child soldier reported that he was encouraged by his parents to fight. Joseph N. Giza, of the Congolese NGO Heal Africa, responded that this was not unusual. "Can you imagine?" he said, "sending your children to a war you are busy running away from? The children were used as cannon fodder" (Faul 2009).

Child soldiers are routinely said to be "programmed" in both advocacy literature and media accounts in reference to their being trained to function like robots or being inducted into a cult. They are described as being "programmed to kill," "programmed to lie about their age," and "programmed to feel little revulsion for their actions and to think of war and only war" (Honwana 1998, 21). They are said to be "programmed to develop a mindset that resists any acknowledgment of injury and sickness, be it physical or psychological" (Jamail 2009). Taliban child soldiers have been describes as looking like "they're in a trance; they rock back and forth; it's as if they're reciting things that they have been programmed to recite" (Lakhani 2010). The idea of the child soldier as programmed is so deeply engrained in public consciousness that the Australian ethicist Robert Sparrow likens child soldiers to actual "autonomous robots," which he foresees as the weapons systems of the future—the next generation of smart weapons (Sparrow 2007, 62–77).

Some critics object to this mode of describing child soldiers, in part because it dehumanizes child soldiers and turns them into mere objects of criminal instrumentality. Clearly, there are situations in which children are brutally exploited, such as in the cases of the Palestinian child suicide bombers of Islamic Jihad, the kidnapped recruits of the Revolutionary United Front in Sierra Leone, or the LRA in Uganda. But even in Uganda, data from the *Survey of War Affected Youth* suggest that the picture is more nuanced than sensationalized reporting in the media would suggest (Blattman 2007).

Sensationalized accounts of scarred and damaged children, coupled with assumptions that former child soldiers suffer from extreme trauma, may actually impede reintegration of former child soldiers into civilian life. In situations where people are struggling to meet basic needs, counseling approaches to reintegration may not be very productive, and counseling in general should be less about "healing wounds" or mental illness than helping young people socially integrate into the practical rhythms of civil life (Wessels 2006). Various forms of counseling and help, whether psychological counseling, traditional healing, or exercises in nonviolent conflict resolution, need to be harnessed in support of the key goal, which is to enable former child soldiers to make decent lives for themselves in situations plagued by chronic poverty. Treating child soldiers as "damaged goods" blinds us to children's ability to take charge of their own lives. Humanitarian groups rarely respect children's ability to participate in decision making, even though these groups routinely make pro forma declarations in support of children's agency and empowerment.

Assumption 3: Child Soldiers Are a Product of the New Barbarism of War

UNICEF's official position is that the use of child soldiers is an illegal and morally reprehensible practice that has no place in civilized societies. This view reflects some deeply felt ideas that the use of child soldiers is an especially heinous factor of contemporary warfare. In fact, one of the principal tenets of contemporary views of child soldiers is that child soldiers exist because modern or "new" wars differ significantly from traditional European wars. This idea draws on a theme from Robert Kaplan's notion of the "New Barbarism," the underlying premise of which is that so-called traditional wars, or "old wars," were rule bound and limited, while "new wars" are anomic and chaotic (Kaplan 1994, 14–76; Richards 1996).

The idea that the use of child soldiers is an especially barbaric practice of new forms of warfare stems from the intense focus on African conflicts. While children have been recruited as child soldiers in wars all over the world, much of the contemporary gaze remains firmly fixed on Africa. Exactly why this is the case is unclear. Certainly, some contemporary examples of the use of child soldiers in Africa, such as the Revolutionary United Front in Sierra Leone and the LRA in Uganda, have provided chilling examples of the abuse of children. But these extraordinary cases have also come to serve as the archetype of children's experiences in both Africa and elsewhere.

There are strong links between the central concepts of the New Barbarism—that Africa and other places where child soldiers fight are inherently chaotic and apolitical—and nineteenth-century descriptions of Africa. We could ask how different are the reports of violence and the recruitment of child soldiers found in the advocacy literature from similar descriptions found in Joseph Conrad's famous novella about the Congo, *Heart of Darkness*. In his 1899 book, Conrad took Africans out of real history and politics and suspended them between the human and the animal. Like contemporary humanitarians, Conrad had an idealistic purpose in writing *The Heart of Darkness*—to offer a critique of the colonial exploitation of Africa. Yet the African novelist Chinua Achebe decried Conrad's stripping of Africans of their humanity as well as his description of Africa as a "metaphysical battlefield devoid of all recognizable humanity." As Achebe tells us, "You cannot diminish a people's humanity and defend them" at one and the same time (Phillips 2003). Contemporary treatments of child soldiers—almost all geared to Western audiences—have a lingering tendency to see Africa and the other conflict zones where child soldiers are found with Conradian eyes, seeing only a heart of darkness.

The neo-Conradian vision of the New Barbarism completely removes war from the world of politics. War appears virtually out of nowhere, usually as a result of adult perfidy, to engulf children and to turn them into victims and killers. It is almost as if war was a malevolent natural phenomenon akin to a tornado that lands on a country and destroys it. The description of wars that involve child soldiers connote a kind of random and feral meaninglessness to war that unmistakably echoes Conrad's representations of the near-riotous inhumanity of Africans.

Why is it that we often see only mindless barbarism in contemporary warfare, in the poorest places on earth? Some argue that the new wars are, in fact, much more horrible than the warfare of the past. Moreover, the fact that war often takes its grim toll on civilians adds to our sense of fear and outrage. The portraits of children at war that form the set piece of humanitarian and human rights descriptions of child soldiers have been harnessed to serve modern notions of the greater good—ending children's involvement in war. But despite attempts to lend the situation of child soldiers a universal "everyman" quality, humanitarian portraits of child soldiers draw on an earlier discourse about Africa that served to dehumanize Africans. In the end, we may be writing the story of child soldiers throughout the world in much the same way that Conrad did so many years ago.

The Role of Humanitarian Groups and "Civil Society"

From the perspective of humanitarian and human rights groups who have helped shape international law, the ban on child soldiers is consistent with what they believe are (or should be) universal ideas about childhood. Others, however, argue that these are relatively recent ideas about childhood, developed in the West over the past century, that are being exported and imposed on other peoples of the world. If we understand that the attempt to ban the use of child soldiers is a form of directed social change, we are better able to analyze the difficulties of achieving compliance with the ban under international law. We can also begin to better understand the role of humanitarian and human rights groups in shaping both the perception of the problem and the proposed solutions.

Humanitarian and human rights groups are part of the many thousands of NGOs that collectively define themselves as "civil society." There is a unique and important connection between the United Nations, its agencies and offices, and civil society. In many respects, the United Nations is also the political capitol of civil society, providing legitimacy and an international forum to NGOs and allowing them to influence the development of UN policy and participate in shaping UN-sponsored treaties and international legal instruments. UN policy allows the key organizations of civil society routine access to the preparatory and working groups that develop and follow international conferences.

Public awareness of child soldiers comes primarily from newspapers accounts and the reports of humanitarian and human rights organizations that report and advocate on the issue. The Coalition to Stop the Use of Child Soldiers is the predominant organization in the humanitarian and human rights efforts to end the recruitment of child soldiers. Its member organizations have invested considerable energy, passion, and resources to shape public awareness of the issue and to bring about changes in international law and policy to help curb the recruitment of children into armed forces and armed groups.

The leading organizations of civil society are deeply embedded in the work of the General Assembly and the administrative agencies of the United Nations. They regard themselves as partners in the UN system and are regarded as such in the United Nations despite the fact that they have no mandate from any political community.Most of these groups do not take any contributions from governments, but because of their newfound power in the international arena, humanitarian groups and other members of civil society often function as political actors, pursuing specific political agendas. The organizations of civil society regard themselves as caretakers and upholders of the moral values of transnationalism but are frequently accused of being partisan in particular conflicts. This is a significant departure from the more traditional model of humanitarian groups, in which they were perceived to be neutral and politically impartial (Weiss 1999).

An equally important way in which these humanitarian organizations are political is in their extensive use of political "spin" to interpret events and sway public opinion and sympathy, including techniques such as extensively cherry-picking facts, assuming the truth of things that have yet to be proven,

and shaping the interpretations of international law to meet advocacy goals. Without doubt, these organizations play valuable roles
in combating the use of child soldiers, but it is crucial for
researchers to recognize that these groups are first and foremost
advocacy groups, not necessarily objective reporters of facts,
law, or policy.

These are not necessarily underfunded organizations that are
seeking to get their voices heard. Many of these organizations
wield considerable economic power and influence. Human
Rights Watch, for example, has an annual budget of over $45 mil-
lion and net assets of more than $106 million ("Human Rights
Watch" 2009). Amnesty International has an international budget
of some $60 million, which represents about one-quarter of the
total funds raised by the organization's national sections. This
means that the group's annual budget is about $240 million. Com-
pare this to the budget of Sierra Leone, one of the poorest countries of the world, which saw widespread use of child soldiers
during its civil war (1991–2001). In 2009, Sierra Leone's total
domestic revenues were $96 million ("Government of Sierra
Leone" 2010; U.S. Central Intelligence Agency 2010). Because of
international aid, Sierra Leone spent more than it generated in
domestic revenues, but even this small example makes clear the
relative economic power of some international NGOs.

In addition, many poor countries like Sierra Leone are
heavily dependent on foreign aid, and advocacy groups often influence the direction and flow of aid. As a purely practical matter,
some countries may need to agree with the views of advocacy
groups into order to receive continued aid. All these factors shape
the way such countries view and respond to the child soldier
problem.

In the following chapters, we return to the themes that have
been introduced in this chapter, including the ways treaties and
international law have been used to shape the debate about child
soldiers and the ongoing discussion of who is a child, and what,
in fact, constitutes being a child soldier. We examine the long history of child soldiers to ask how and why children become
recruited into warfare. We examine some of the key conflicts that
involve child soldiers today, the modes of recruitment and use
of child soldiers, the experiences of children themselves, the culpability of children who commit war crimes, and the attempts to
reintegrate former child soldiers back into society. We look at

changing attitudes toward children and childhood to examine whether these have affected our understanding of child soldiers. Finally, and most important, we begin to separate fact from fiction by examining how our beliefs about child soldiers measure up against what is actually known.

References

African Charter on the Rights and Welfare of the Child 1990. Organization of African Unity Doc. CAB/LEG/24.9/49. http://www .un-eu.org/images/stories/pdf/African%20Charter%20on%20the %20rights%20and%20welfare%20of%20the%20child.pdf. Accessed February 6, 2011.

Amnesty International. 2000. "Campaign Against Torture Media Briefing." http://www.amnesty.org/en/library/asset/ACT40/016/ 2000/en/51e8fe04-d0d2-4dc8-96a5-06d8253746ff/act400162000en.pdf. Accessed December 20, 2011

Banks, Angela M. 2003. "The Growing Impact of Non State Actors on the International and European Legal System." *International Law Forum du Droit International* 5: 293–99

Blattman, Christopher. 2007. "Making Reintegration Work for Youth in Northern Uganda." *Survey of War Affected Youth.* http://chrisblattman .com/documents/policy/sway/SWAY.ResearchBrief.Reintegration.pdf. Accessed February 6, 2011.

"Children and Armed Conflict: Report of the Secretary General." 2010. General Assembly-Security Council A/64/742–S/2010/181. April 13. http://daccess-dds-ny.un.org/doc/UNDOC/GEN/N10/311/28/PDF/ N1031128.pdf?OpenElement. Accessed February 6, 2011.

Conrad, Joseph. [1899] 1999. *Heart of Darkness.* New York: Penguin Books.

"Convention on the Rights of the Child, Nov. 20, 1989." *United Nations Treaty Series* 1157, no. 3. http://www.icrc.org/ihl.nsf/FULL/540? OpenDocument. Accessed February 6, 2011.

Delissen, Astrid J. 1991. "Legal Protection of Child Combatants after the Protocols: Reaffirmation, Development of a Step Backwards." In *Humanitarian Law of Armed Conflict,* edited by Astrid J. Delissen and Garard J. Tangje. Dordrecht: Martinus Nijhoff, 1991, pp. 153, 160.

Dormann, Knut. 2003. "The Legal Situation of 'Unlawful/Unprivileged Combatants." *International Review of the Red Cross* 85:45.

Dunér, Bertil. 2005. "Rebellion: The Ultimate Human Right?" *International Journal of Human Rights* 9:247.

Faul, Michelle. 2009. "Traumatized Child Soldiers Return Home in Congo." *AP News*, March 7, 2009. http://www.newsvine.com/_news/ 2009/03/07/2517439-traumatized-child-soldiers-return-home-in-congo. Accessed February 6, 2011.

"Geneva Convention for the Amelioration of the Condition of the Wounded and Sick in Armed Forces in the Field, Aug. 12, 1949." 6 U.S.T. 3114, T.I.A.S. No. 3362, 75 *United Nations Treaty Series* 31.

"Geneva Convention for the Amelioration of the Condition of the Wounded, Sick and Shipwrecked Members of Armed Forces at Sea, Aug. 12, 1949." 6 U.S.T. 3217, T.I.A.S. No. 3363, 75 *United Nations Treaty Series* 31.

"Geneva Convention Relative to the Protection of Civilian Persons in Time of War, Aug. 12, 1949." 6 U.S.T. 3516, T.I.A.S. No. 3365, 75 *United Nations Treaty Series* 287.

"Geneva Convention Relative to the Treatment of Prisoners of War, Aug. 12, 1949." 6 U.S.T. 3316, T.I.A.S. No. 3364, 75 *United Nations Treaty Series* 135.

Gould, Benjamin. 1869. *Investigations in the Military and Anthropological Statistics of American Soldiers.* New York: Hurd and Houghton.

"Government of Sierra Leone Report and Annual Statement of Public Accounts for the Financial Year Ended 31st December 2009." Accountant General's Department. The Treasury, Ministerial Building Freetown, Sierra Leone (2010). http://www.mofed.gov.sl/index.php?option =com_docman&task=doc_download&gid=21&Itemid. Accessed February 6, 2011.

Happold, Matthew. 2008. "Child Soldiers: Victims or Perpetrators?" *University of La Verne Law Review* 29:56, 69.

Honwana, Alcinda. 1998. "*Okusiakala ondalo yokalye*: Let Us Light a New Fire: Local Knowledge in the Post-War Healing and Reintegration of War-Affected Children in Angola." http://www.forcedmigration .org/psychosocial/inventory/pwg001/pwg001.pdf. Accessed February 6, 2011.

Human Rights Watch, *Erased in a Moment: Suicide Bombing Attacks against Israeli Civilians.* New York: Human Rights Watch, 2002. Accessed at http://www.hrw.org/en/reports/2002/10/15/erased-moment.

"Human Rights Watch, Financial Statements Year Ended June 30, 2009." http://hrw.org/en/about/financials. Accessed February 6, 2011.

"India's CRPF Urges New Intelligence Wing." 2009. UPI, May 19. http://www.upi.com/Top_News/Special/2008/05/19/Indias-CRPF -urges-new-intelligence-wing/UPI-67201211222492/tab-listen. Accessed February 6, 2011.

"Interview with R K Vij, Inspector General of Police and Spokesperson, Chhattisgarh Police." *Rediff News*, April 8, 2010. http://news.rediff.com/report/2010/apr/08/chhattisgarh-igp-on-the-naxalites.htm. Accessed February 6, 2011.

"ILO Convention (No. 182) concerning the Prohibition and Immediate Action for the Elimination of the Worst Forms of Child Labor, June 17, 1999." S. Treaty Doc. No. 106-5 (1999), 2133 *United Nations Treaty Series* 161.

International Committee of the Red Cross. 1997. "Position of the International Committee of the Red Cross on the Optional Protocol to the Convention on the Rights of the Child on Involvement of Children in Armed Conflicts. August 12, 1997." http://www.icrc.org/eng/resources/documents/misc/57jnuv.htm. Accessed February

Jamail, Dahr. 2009. " A Morally Bankrupt Military: When Soldiers and Their Families Become Expendable." *Truthout,* November 11. http://www.truth-out.org/1111097. Accessed February 6, 2011.

Kaplan, Robert D. 1994. "The Coming Anarchy: How Scarcity, Crime, Overpopulation and Disease Are Rapidly Destroying the Social Fabric of Our Planet." *Atlantic Monthly,* February 1994.

Kilmer, George L. 1905. "Boys in the Union Army." *The Century* 70: 269–75.

King, Charles. 1911. "Boys of the War Days." In *A Photographic History of the Civil War*, vol. 8, edited by Francis Trevelyan Miller. Springfield, MA: Patriot Press.

Lakhani, Kalsoom. 2010. "Pakistan's Child Soldiers" *Foreign Policy,* March 29, 2010. http://afpak.foreignpolicy.com/posts/2010/03/29/pakistans_child_soldiers. Accessed February 6, 2011.

McPherson, James. 2003. *Battle Cry of Freedom: The Civil War Era*. Oxford: Oxford University Press.

Mann, H. 1987. "International Law and the Child Soldier." *International and Comparative Law Quarterly* 36:32, 50.

Masland, Tom. 2002. "Voices of the Children: We Killed and Beat People." *Newsweek,* May 13, 2002. http://www.newsweek.com/2002/05/12/voices-of-the-children-quot-we-beat-and-killed.html. Accessed February 6, 2011.

Matheson, Michael J. 1987. "The United States' Position on the Relation of Customary International Law to the 1977 Protocols Additional to the 1949 Geneva Conventions." *American University Journal of International Law and Policy* 2:419–36.

Montgomery, Heather. 2009. *An introduction to Childhood: Anthropological Perspectives on Children's Lives*. West Sussex: Wiley-Blackwell.

"Naxal Problem Not an Armed Conflict, India Tells UN." 2010. *The Times of India*, June 18, 2010. http://timesofindia.indiatimes.com/india/Naxal -problem-not-an-armed-conflict-India-tells-UN/articleshow/6063604. cms. Accessed February 6, 2011.

"Optional Protocol to the Convention on the Rights of the Child on the Involvement of Children in Armed Conflict." 2000. *United Nations Treaty Series* 2173:222. http://www2.ohchr.org/english/law/crc-conflict.htm. Accessed February 5, 2011.

Phillips, Caryl. 2003. "Out of Africa." *The Guardian*, February 22, 2003. http://books.guardian.co.uk/review/story/ 0,12084,900102,00.html#article_continue. Accessed February 7, 2011.

"Prosecutor v. Norman 2004. Decision on Preliminary Motion Based on Lack of Jurisdiction (Child Soldiers)." *Special Court for Sierra Leone*. Case No. SCSL-04-14-AR72E. May 31, 2004. http://www.sc-sl.org/LinkClick .aspx?fileticket=XSdlFGVsuTI%3d&tabid=193. Accessed February 5, 2010.

"Protocol Additional to the Geneva Conventions of 12 August 1949, and Relating to the Protection of Victims of International Armed Conflicts (Protocol I), June 8, 1977." 1125 *United Nations Treaty Series* 3.

"Protocol Additional to the Geneva Conventions of 12 August 1949, and Relating to the Victims of Non-International Armed Conflicts (Protocol II), June 8, 1977." 1125 *United Nations Treaty Series* 609.

Richards, Paul. 1996. *Fighting for the Rain Forest*. Portsmouth, NH: Heinemann.

"Rome Statute of the International Criminal Court." 1998. *United Nations Treaty Series* 2187: 3. http://untreaty.un.org/cod/icc/statute/romefra .htm. Accessed February 1, 2010.

Sparrow, Robert. 2007. "Killer Robots." *Journal of Applied Philosophy* 24:62–77.

UNICEF. 2002. *Adult Wars, Child Soldiers*. New York: United Nations.

U.S. Central Intelligence Agency. 2010. *World Fact Book: Sierra Leone*, October 4, 2010. https://www.cia.gov/library/publications/the-world -factbook/geos/sl.html. Accessed February 6, 2011.

U.S. Department of State. 2004. Trafficking in Persons Report http:// www.state.gov/g/tip/rls/tiprpt/2004/34021.htm. Accessed December 20, 2011.

Van Bueren, Geraldine. 1995. *The International Law on the Rights of the Child*. London: Martinus Nijhoff.

Weiss, Thomas G. 1999. "Principles, Politics, and Humanitarian Action." *Ethics and International Affairs* 13 (1): 1–22.

Wessels, Michael. 2006. *Child Soldiers: From Violence to Protection.* Cambridge, MA: Harvard University Press.

Youth Advocate Program International. 2004. "Children Affected by Armed Conflict." http://www.yapi.org/conflict. Accessed August 30, 2010.

Zemp, Ueli, and Subash Mohapatra. N.d. *Child Soldiers in Chhattisgarh: Issues, Challenges and FFDAs Response.* http://www.otherindia.org/dev/images/stories/feda_child.pdf. Accessed February 6, 2011.

2

Problems, Controversies, and Solutions

Ending the Use of Child Soldiers: Problems and Solutions

For more than 40 years, humanitarian and human rights groups have sought to ban the recruitment and use of child soldiers. Their efforts have produced mixed results. On the one hand, they have had a profound effect on the development of international law prohibiting the recruitment of children, but, on the other hand, such laws seem to have had only limited efficacy in reducing the actual number of child soldiers participating in conflicts throughout the world. This huge gap between the aspirations of law and the practical reality of child recruitment is one of the greatest problems in ending the recruitment of child soldiers.

International efforts to end the use of child soldiers first bore fruit in 1977. That year, for the first time in history, there were changes made to the so-called laws of war that placed restrictions on recruiting children into armed forces and groups. Since that first victory, the issue of child soldiers has developed and expanded in scope. What began in 1977 as a relatively narrow concern with protecting children under 15 years old from serving as armed combatants has evolved into an international effort to sever a broad range of connections between the military and any person under the age of 18. The entire concept of the "child soldier" has evolved to encompass a greater number of children engaged in a wider variety of activities than first imaged. This raises some powerful questions. Are there actually more child soldiers in the world today than in the past? Certainly, child soldiers have been integrally involved in the military for a very long time. Andrew Jackson, the seventh president of the United States, joined the armed forces of the American Revolution at age 13, and he was far from alone in doing so. How have changing definitions of child soldiers affected our perception of the actual number of child soldiers in the world? Are all children who are involved in the military coerced or abused? Is it always the case that children would be better off away from military involvement? And, finally, when children are involved in military activity, should they be held responsible for their actions in the same way as adult soldiers? This chapter examines some of these complicated issues and some of the modern-day attempts to find solutions to the problem of child soldiers.

It is important to remember that recruiting children to be soldiers has been treated as a criminal act under the laws of war only since 2002, with the creation of the International Criminal Court (ICC). Before then, treaties depended on voluntary compliance by the nation-states that were parties to the treaty. There was no strong means to compel compliance or deter potential violators. There were no courts that could legally enforce the terms of the treaty against violators. At most, violators could be shamed in the court of world opinion into living up to their agreements, a process widely known as "naming and shaming." Importantly, although eliminating the use of child soldiers is a central goal of humanitarian and human rights groups, the issue has been riddled with political considerations. For example, as we have seen, international treaties dealing with child soldiers are created by nation-states, but the treaties also attempt to impose rules of law on armed groups, such as rebels, insurgents, militants, and others who challenge the authority and legitimacy of the existing state. It is not surprising that in creating treaties against using child soldiers, nation-states have often imposed greater restrictions on the armed groups of rebels than they impose on themselves. In addition, treaties sometimes include exceptions that favor particular groups or positions.

The Issue of Exceptions: Wars of National Liberation

Wars of national liberation are anticolonialist wars fought by indigenous peoples against imperialist domination in pursuit of their right to self-determination. Many wars of national liberation were fought in the years following World War II, as peoples in Africa, Asia, and elsewhere sought independence from their colonial rulers. Among the most well known of these efforts were the Mau Mau Rebellion (Kenya, 1954–1962), the Algerian War of Independence (1961–1974) , and the Mozambican War of Independence (1964–1974). Regardless of the merits of their causes, many groups that sought national liberation used terrorist tactics such as urban bombings and murder of civilians and their families. Moreover, these groups used children in a wide variety of combatant and support roles.

During the period of the Cold War (1949–1991), Western states regarded wars of national liberation as civil wars, while countries in what was then known as the communist world considered these wars to be international conflicts. The latter view prevailed in 1977, when Additional Protocol I created a major exception to the distinction between international conflicts and noninternational conflicts as these were set down in the original Geneva Conventions. Additional Protocol I broadened the definition of international armed conflict to include "armed conflicts in which peoples are fighting against colonial domination and alien occupation and against racist regimes in the exercise of their right of self-determination" (Additional Protocol, Article 1). By defining "wars of national liberation" as international conflicts, the treaty increased the degree to which political considerations and subjective factors played roles in determining whether an armed conflict was deemed to be international or noninternational (Sandoz, Swinarski, and Zimmerman 1967, 40–56). With this broader definition of international conflict, Additional Protocol I instantly reclassified and transformed a host of unlawful combatants into lawful combatants. One of the most important consequences of categorizing wars of national liberation as international armed conflicts was that Additional Protocol I permitted guerilla movements engaging in wars of national liberation to enroll and recruit children below the age of 15 into their armed forces. This was important because virtually all insurgent forces in twentieth-century wars of national liberation used enormous numbers of child fighters (Edgerton 1989; Elkins 2005).

From one perspective, Additional Protocol II came too late because by 1977 most post–World War II wars of national liberation were over. Some continued, such as the Namibia War of Independence (1966–1988) and actions by the military wing of the African National Congress in South Africa. Many newly independent states faced internal insurgencies, sometimes from rival groups that continued to recruit child soldiers, but since these insurgencies were not considered wars of national liberation, these groups did not benefit from Additional Protocol I. They were prohibited from recruiting the very age-groups that their immediate predecessors were allowed to recruit.

Muddying the distinction between international and non-international conflict created a class of politically privileged insurgents by giving them combatant status based on the political motive for their insurgency. It gave politically privileged insurgent groups greater discretion and flexibility in recruiting child soldiers than was allowed to ordinary rebels. This was certainly not the goal of the International Committee on the Rights of the Child (ICRC) and the human rights groups that sought to end the participation of children in war. It may be overstating the case to suggest that the child soldier issue was hijacked by the weaker states of the United Nations to bolster their own sovereignty and squelch internal rebellion, but this trade-off seems to be at least part of the implicit compact struck between humanitarian groups and state powers in order to ensure the ban on child soldiers.

Contrary to the intent of the Geneva Conventions, Additional Protocol I put civilians who were caught up in wars of national liberation at great risk from cross fire from insurgent forces. Its rules of engagement favor privileged insurgents over civilians. Rather than requiring forces to carry their arms openly, it allowed them to conceal themselves among the civilian population just prior to launching an attack (Additional Protocol I, Article 44). A prime example is the African National Congress in its insurgency against South Africa (Malanczuk 1997, 333–53). Of course, when these groups came into power after successful wars of national liberation, they faced rebellions of their own, but they could treat these rebels as unlawful combatants with no privileges under international law and no right to recruit children.

The Complexities of Treaties and International Law

There are limitations to the power of treaties, the most significant being that treaties are signed by nation-states; insurgent groups are neither recognized as legitimate bodies nor treated as anything other than criminals by the governments against which they are rebelling. As we saw in Chapter 1, the Maoist rebels in India are a good example of this situation, and the Indian government's position regarding the Maoist rebels is typical of nation-states. India treats the Maoist insurgents as criminals and deems their insurgency an internal civil issue, not subject to international intervention ("Naxal Problem" 2010). But this case highlights the problem that although the laws of war require armed groups to forgo the use of child soldiers, it is difficult to achieve tangible results. Armed groups like the Maoists are considered criminals under domestic law and receive no international recognition of the legitimacy of their causes, even where they comply with international law. Because armed groups obtain virtually no benefits under international law, it is difficult to persuade them to comply with international standards. There is little leverage to be used against the rebels other than persuasion.

In other conflicts, UN negotiators have tried to persuade armed groups to comply by arguing that victorious armed groups that use child soldiers will have difficulty achieving international recognition because they used children as soldiers. The United Nations has found it very difficult to achieve real progress, but there have been some small successes. Recently, the United Nations brokered action plans by the Sudan People's Liberation Army, the Unified Communist Party of Nepal-Maoist and the government of Nepal, and the Moro Islamic Liberation Front. On another front, in both the war in Sierra Leone and the war in the Democratic Republic of the Congo, the captured leaders of armed groups that have recruited children have been handed over to criminal courts for trial, and several have been convicted and given lengthy prison sentences. But these are very small successes, and the broader failure of these efforts has prompted some to call for "sharper teeth" in the enforcement of criminal and political sanctions against recruiters of child soldiers (Webster 2007, 227). Despite the tough language of the international legal and human rights communities, it is by no means clear how armed groups will be convinced to curtail their recruitment of children.

Although many of the laws affecting the use of child soldiers are universal in spirit, they are not universal in practice. For example, the United States signed but did not ratify Additional Protocols I and II and therefore is not a party to the treaties. Similarly, the United States signed the "Rome Statute of the International Criminal Court" (1998) but later withdrew its signature, thereby clearly stating its intention not to be bound by the statute. Both India and China oppose the creation of the ICC as a violation of national sovereignty and have refused to become parties to it. Thus, some of the most important and powerful countries in the world are not parties to the Rome Statute and not subject to its criminal laws governing the use of child soldiers.

When Treaties Bind Nonsignatories

New treaties routinely impose their requirements on nonstate actors such as rebel groups, but nation-states are rarely subject to the terms of a treaty unless they have signed that treaty. However, there is one important exception, which is that the UN Security Council is empowered to refer a situation to the ICC and thereby place a state that is a not a party to the statute under the jurisdiction of the court. This recently occurred in regard to the conflict in the Darfur region of Sudan, where the situation was referred to the ICC by the UN Security Council. The issue did not specifically involve child soldiers. The ICC issued an arrest warrant for Sudanese President Omar Hassan al-Bashir for war crimes, crimes against humanity, and genocide. This was the first arrest warrant ever issued for a sitting head of state by the ICC (*Prosecutor v. Omar Al Bashir* 2009).

Although not directly related to the child soldier issue, the Arab and African reaction to the indictment and warrant of arrest is an indication of the political difficulties of enforcing the laws under the Rome Statute against nonparties. In this instance, the Arab League and the African Union forcefully condemned the warrant and Arab and African states generally have refused to enforce it against al-Bashir. Some African and Arab leaders have denounced the ICC itself as being a neocolonial entity (Voice of America 2009).

Using Customary Law: The Case of Sierra Leone

In the civil war in Sierra Leone (1991–2002), virtually all the parties to the conflict recruited child soldiers. In 2002, the Special Court for Sierra Leone was jointly established by treaty between the United Nations and the government of Sierra Leone in order to try leaders of the warring factions for war crimes. It had jurisdiction over war crimes committed in Sierra Leone beginning on November 30, 1996. In the war crimes trials in Sierra Leone, the issue arose as to whether the rule of law against recruiting children under age 15 into armed forces or groups is a matter of customary international law.

Although child soldiers were recruited throughout the Sierra Leone's civil war, the statute of the Sierra Leone Special Court that criminalized recruitment came into force only in 2002, after the war had ended. Similarly, the Rome Statute of the ICC became effective only in 2002 (although it was signed in 1998). The central question before the court was whether a rule of international criminal law that became effective in 2002 could be used to punish individuals for actions that had taken place many years before. Most legal systems ban laws of this type. In the United States, federal and state laws that retroactively criminalize and punish actions that were legal at the time they were committed are called ex post facto laws and are prohibited by the U.S. Constitution. Similarly, continental European law and international law have generally followed the principle of *nulla poena sine lege* ("no penalty without a law"), which prohibits retroactive punishment.

For this reason, the court could prosecute only acts of child recruitment that took place prior to 2002 if the court found that the Special Court statute did not create a new rule of law (i.e., the criminal ban on recruiting children under 15 years old) but merely incorporated and recited an already existing rule of customary international law. The problem was that while previous treaties had placed restriction on the recruitment of child soldiers, they had not imposed criminal penalties on recruiters. While it might be easy to argue that the forced recruitment of children was merely a form of kidnapping and abduction and that adults who engaged in this behavior were criminals under both international law and Sierra Leone law, the situation was not as clear when it came to child soldiers who had enlisted voluntarily, a widespread practice in Sierra Leone. It is unlikely that adults who participated in voluntarily enlisting child soldiers could have known that what they were doing would, in the future, be regarded as criminal. Nonetheless, the Special Court determined that the recruitment of child soldiers had evolved by custom into a violation of international criminal law prior to 2002 (*Prosecutor v. Norman* 2004). It could not, however, point either to a long-established consensus on the criminality of voluntary recruitment or to the established practice of states to criminalize such recruitment.

Thus, the court's decision remains a controversial one, based on relatively weak criteria. If other courts accept this analysis, then the recruitment of child soldiers under age 15 will universally be deemed a war crime, regardless of whether a state is party to any treaty that makes this action criminal. In this way, the prohibition against using children as soldiers would be similar to other criminal acts whose prohibition originated in customary international law, such as slavery, torture, and genocide (Bellinger and Haynes 2007).

Captured Child Combatants

The Additional Protocols provided a number of legal protections for child soldiers. Most important, child combatants of any age who were captured by enemy forces were to be afforded special protections, even if they were unlawful combatants and therefore not required to be treated as prisoners of war (Additional Protocol I, Article 77). It also prohibits imposing the death penalty for war crimes on any person who was not age 18 when he or she committed the offense. The Additional Protocols had an equally important impact on children who are unlawful combatants. Although these children are not considered "prisoners of war," they are placed in the category of "protected persons" and are immunized from the death penalty. The anti–death penalty provisions of the Additional Protocols generated sharp debate over whether giving children immunity from the death penalty might lead child soldiers to commit the most terrible war crimes. Another fear was that regular soldiers might kill underage perpetrators of war crimes rather than capture them if they knew that the children would be treated leniently when captured. Despite these concerns, the principle of protecting children prevailed (Sandoz et al. 1987, 904). Additional Protocol II also gives protected status to children under age 15 (Additional Protocol II, Article 6).

Children's Rights and the Straight-18 Position

As we have seen, the laws of wars generally ban recruiting children under 15 years old, but there have been major efforts on the part of human rights and humanitarian groups to extend this ban to any person under age 18. Their efforts have focused primarily on using children's rights treaties to expand the scope of restrictions on child recruitment (Banks 2003). All the organizations in the Coalition to Stop the Use of Child Soldiers and the ICRC have adopted the so-called Straight-18 position, which argues for a universal definition of childhood as beginning at birth and ending at age 18 (Happold 2008).

These groups have successfully helped shape a number of important children's rights instruments that, as part of a more general recognition of children's rights, specifically call for restrictions on using child soldiers. These documents include the "Convention on the Rights of the Child" (1989), the "Optional Protocol to the Convention on the Rights of the Child on the Involvement of Children in Armed Conflict" (2000), the "African Charter on the Rights and Welfare of the Child" (1990), and the International Labor Organization Worst Forms of Child Labor Convention ("ILO Convention" 1999).

Inventing a Universal Definition of Childhood

The Straight-18 position is a very ambitious agenda in that it attempts to create a single universal definition of childhood in a world where ideas about childhood and the legal rights of children vary significantly (Lancy 2008; Montgomery 2009). The attempt to create a universal definition of childhood is clearly ethnocentric, but it is crucial to keep in mind that international humanitarian law is not unthinkingly or unreflectively ethnocentric; rather, it is *intentionally* ethnocentric. Its focus is not to respect local norms but rather to alter them systematically.

The entire history of treaty making regarding the recruitment of child soldiers shows that human rights use law as a principal instrument of directed social and cultural change. The drafters of the Additional Protocols were keenly aware of significant cross-cultural variation in ideas about childhood, youth, and adulthood, but they declared the participation of children and adolescents in combat to be an "inhumane practice," which made such cross-cultural considerations irrelevant (Sandoz et al. 1987, 900). Their drive to create a universal moral standard trumped any concerns about local understandings of childhood, which are treated as deviant and inhumane practices under international law rather than as legitimate expressions of local culture. The drafters' only concern at that time was that age 15 seem "reasonable" to members of civil society; they excluded as irrelevant any consideration of what might seem reasonable in local practice (Sandoz et al. 1987, 899). Because the courts also work from this perspective, they have a powerful incentive to avoid grappling with cultural issues, essentially seeing them either as irrelevant or as threatening the extension of international law.

Human Rights and the Realities of International Law

The differences between children's rights treaties like the 1989 Convention on the Rights of the Child (CRC) and the Optional Protocol and international criminal law reflect a broader chasm between aspirations of humanitarian and human rights groups and the reality of legal processes. Generally, nations are far more willing to sign treaties that involve fewer enforceable provisions than those that create binding obligations. While children's rights treaties reflect humanitarian and human rights aspirations, they create only a set of international goals and standards that depend on voluntary compliance. Nations that sign such treaties but fail to live up to them may be subject informal sanctions—such as "name and shame," in which the identities of violators are made public—but little else. In contrast, nations that are party to the ICC have agreed to subject individual violators to serious criminal sanctions. The disparity between humanitarian aspirations and settled criminal law reflects the considerable ambiguity over the age at which children become adults.

Who Is a Child?

As we saw in the previous chapter, one major practical obstacle to ending the use of child soldiers is that armed groups continue to recruit children, and the international community has difficulty controlling the activities of these groups. The problem is further complicated because there is no universal agreement on the age at which a person moves from childhood to adulthood or even on what activities and roles are incompatible with being a child. Despite international laws against using children as soldiers, historically not everyone has agreed that the life of a soldier and the life of a child are incompatible (see Cox 2009; Quaifem 1930).

The use of children as soldiers, says Carol Bellamy, executive director of UNICEF, "has no place in civilized societies" (UNICEF 2002). This statement clearly reflects the goal of UNICEF and many other humanitarian and human rights organization to eliminate the use of children in the military. UNICEF's view, which is no doubt shared by many people in the West, is that recruiters of child soldiers are evildoers engaged in a practice that is both illegal and immoral.

The language used by UNICEF makes this position seem absolutely self-evident. But once we step away from bombastic rhetoric about uncivilized evildoers and examine the problem more dispassionately, we will see that what seems at first to be such a simple moral and legal issue is actually quite complicated. One of the first complications is the question of who, exactly, is a child? Clearly, if the world is to eliminate child soldiers, it must first decide when a person is a child, and this requires a more sophisticated understanding than the simple declaration of a universal principle.

International Law and Local Understandings of Childhood

That the CRC defines childhood as ending at age 18 tells us little about the experience of childhood throughout the world. Common sense tells us that childhood does not actually end and adulthood begin on a single specific date, such as a person's eighteenth birthday. Instead, the transition from childhood to adulthood is a gradual process that takes place over time, and it is not easy to draw a simple bright line between childhood and adulthood. The choice of age 18 is as much a matter of social policy as it is a gauge of natural development.

Although it has become increasingly common in the United States and western Europe to adopt age 18 as the beginning of adulthood, this has not always been the case. Historically, there has never been a single universally accepted age that served as the sole boundary marker between childhood and adulthood. Much depends on local context and experience. Fixing the age of legal majority has often been a bit of a piecemeal affair. Children assume adult roles and responsibilities at different ages, depending on the issues involved, and the appropriate age is frequently the subject of controversy and argument. At age 18, a person living in the United States may be entitled to vote but is not entitled to be served alcohol. But if he or she flew to London, he or she could be legally served. The age at which children are subject to compulsory education ranges from 16 in Iowa to 18 in California. The age at which children are permitted to begin to work ranges from 14 in Massachusetts to 16 in Washington. The age at which a person is allowed to drive varies from 14 in Montana to 17 in New Jersey. The right of a teenage to have an abortion also varies from state to state. In New York, any minor can have an abortion without parental consent or notification, while in Delaware, anyone under 16 must give notice to a parent, grandparent, or guardian. For generations, people in the United States and across the globe have held different views as to when and under what circumstances children move from childhood to adulthood and can assume adult responsibilities and engage in adult behaviors.

The Boundaries between Childhood and Adulthood

The political and social struggles over the boundaries between childhood and adulthood can often be bitter. One of the most powerful recent examples is the struggle over the age at which children are regarded as adults for the purpose of imposing criminal liability. Prior to the nineteenth century, in both the United Kingdom and the United States, juveniles and adults were generally treated identically and were subject to the same laws and punishments. Beginning in the middle of the nineteenth century, child welfare advocates were successful in promoting the idea that it was inappropriate to treat juveniles as adults (Carpenter 1856; Platt 2009). Many social and cultural factors contributed to the idea that juveniles were essentially children and hence not fully developed agents who should be subject to criminal law and its punishments. In the late twentieth century, there was a significant reversal of this late nineteenth-century understanding of the agency of juveniles. Beginning in the early 1990s, the idea was widely promoted in the press and in the popular imagination that young people were about to become a generation of so-called superpredators. Legislatures began to enact a variety of laws that would allow both children and juveniles to be treated as adults. In theory, these laws were to apply only to the most serious crimes, such as murder and rape. In practice, however, these laws have been applied to virtually the entire range of serious offenses under the criminal justice system.

There is no consistent principled position that guides legal and legislative thinking about agency with respect to children and the law. Indeed, teenagers are increasingly assumed to have adult capacity; that is, they are deemed responsible for the consequences of their actions for the purposes of punishment, but that does not mean they are accepted as having adult agency in other areas of life. What has happened is a "cultural and legal transformation of the construction of youth from innocent, immature and dependent children to responsible, autonomous and mature offenders" (Zimring 2005). Finally, there are myriad racial, ethnic, and social class dimensions of this problem that make it amply clear that large numbers of children are ascribed as adult agents solely for the purposes of control and punishment.

These examples suggest that although defining the end of childhood and the onset of adulthood at age 18 may be a legitimate aspiration of the world community, that definition tells us little about how these transitions are actually understood and practiced by many peoples of the world. The struggle over child soldiers is the current focus of a centuries-old dispute about where childhood ends and adulthood begins.

The questions of age, cultural norms, national identity, and the persuasive power of the international legal and human rights communities are elements of a complex framework in which the movement to ban the use of child soldiers is being played out. Humanitarian and human rights groups, which have helped shape international law, view banning child soldiers as a natural corollary of what they believe are (or should be) universal ideas about childhood. There are those, however, who argue that these conceptions of childhood are relatively recent Western ideas that are being exported and imposed on other peoples of the world. Whether or not we characterize the humanitarian agenda as an "imposition of Western ideas," it will enable us to better analyze the difficulties of achieving compliance with the ban under international law if we understand that the attempt to ban the use of child soldiers is a form of directed social change.

Civil Society and Social Change

The development of the children's rights movement in the international arena and its agenda of directed social change is tied to the explosive growth of the internationally oriented institutions of civil society and their close relationships with the United Nations and its agencies. By civil society, I mean the many nongovernmental organizations (NGOs) that the United Nations regards as its partners. These organizations are officially accredited by the UN to work with its offices, agencies, and programs; play a key role at major UN conferences; serve as agents and partners of the United Nations at the country level; and are important shapers of UN policies and programs (Kohler 1998). The increasing power and influence of civil society, their emergence as what Salamon (2002) has called a "third-party government," has led many organizations to abandon ideas of political neutrality that were once the hallmark of these institutions. These organizations are not nation-states, but they often serve as powerful gatekeepers to significant economic resources, especially in the poorest places in the world, giving them the ability to dictate conformity to particular ideas about childhood.

For example, Susan Shepler (2005) reports that in Sierra Leone, which has recently emerged from civil war, local access to resources was often contingent on villagers publicly embracing international concepts of childhood, including the idea that child soldiers were "victims" rather than perpetrators. This directly challenged the local experiences of child soldiers, experiences that frequently diverge significantly from the assumptions that underlie the aims of humanitarian groups (Rosen 2005).

In the past, scholars have tended to see domestic law as flowing from existing custom, especially in regard to family law with its focus on the welfare of children. At times, of course, there are notable exceptions to this in which law is used as an instrument of social change or even of oppression. But wherever there is a gap between law and the manner in which lives are actually lived, there is vast room for both conflict and resistance. In the international legal arena, there is often an enormous gap between legal norms and the experience of daily life, that is, between the kinds of children and childhoods the law recognizes and the real lives of children. The enormity of this gap arises in part because in the international arena, lawmaking is in the hands of the institutions of civil society and its so-called norm entrepreneurs, for whom the purpose of lawmaking is to create aspirational rules that are often developed outside the framework of any arguably democratic processes or cultural consensus. The effect is a chasm between new rules of law and the lived experience of childhood.

Child Soldiers in Cross-Cultural and Historical Perspective

When we examine the role of young warriors in traditional societies, the disparity between international law and the lived experience of childhood becomes clearer. In many traditional societies, there was no single fixed chronological age at which young people became involved in war as warriors. The Mende, a traditional ethnic group in Sierra Leone, provides a good example of how children were transformed into adolescents with the rights and responsibilities of warriors. Like many of the traditional ethnic groups of Sierra Leone, Mende society had secret associations (Ferme 2001; Little 1949, 1965). Some, like the all male Poro society, or the all female Bundu or Sande societies, initiated virtually all adolescent boys and girls into their secret rites and practices through elaborate and highly orchestrated ceremonies (Little 1951). Traditionally, there were no specific ages that determined when boys became men or girls became women; rather, children were generally regarded as adults only after being initiated into these associations. In the past, these groups did not use calendars or birth certificates to determine maturity; instead, they relied—and to some extent continue to rely—on external signs of mental and physical maturity. As a result, the locally defined category of "adults," especially as used in rural areas of Sierra Leone, includes many persons who would be regarded as children in Western societies.

For boys initiated into the Poro society, becoming a man meant protecting the community as a warrior and participating in raids and battles against others. There were no standing armies that were separate from the rest of society; instead, virtually all boys immediately became warriors. In societies like the Mende, war required the participation of every available man, meaning all men who are members of the Poro, regardless of their chronological age. Similar to the requirement that all boys in the United States must register for the draft at age 18, initiation into the Poro meant that boys could be rapidly called up as a military force when they were needed. It did not necessarily mean that they immediately joined an active military group as soon as they were initiated. In the past, the youngest of these boys, so-called war sparrows, often fought alongside more seasoned warriors (Little 1951).

The example of the Mende has parallels in many preliterate societies that had few ways and no compelling reason to keep track of specific birth dates. Boys usually became warriors and begin to help defend their communities as they transitioned into adolescence. In Sudan, Dinka boys were traditionally initiated into adulthood between ages 16 and 18 and immediately received gifts of well-designed spears that symbolized the military function of youth (Deng 1972). In nineteenth-century America, Sioux and Cheyenne boys joined their first war parties at about 14 or 15 years of age and slowly became experienced warriors (Hoebel 1978). In East Africa, Maasai and Samburu boys of many different ages were collectively inducted into age sets and became warrior after they were initiated (Spencer 2004). There was no simple rule in traditional societies for determining when the young were fit to be warriors, although in most cultures they did not become warriors until adolescence. Becoming a warrior depended in part of a variety of practical issues since youngsters would have to be able to demonstrate their physical and emotional fitness for the role. Further, in some societies, young people are taught to be highly aggressive, and individual and collective violence is highly esteemed, whereas in others, more stress is placed on the peaceful resolution of disputes (Hass 1990). The overall picture suggests that the boundaries between childhood, youth, and adulthood show great diversity and are rooted in the historicity of each society and culture.

Given this complexity, how likely is it that the ban on child soldiers will be effective? Right now the answer is unclear. While a number of so-called African rebel leaders and warlords have been successfully prosecuted, it is by no means evident that this has deterred recruitment more generally.

Those advocating the Straight-18 position often claim that presence of children in the military is something new, that it is a modern-day aberration that involves the criminal abuse of children. Others make even more far-fetched declarations that the modern-day use of child soldiers breaks some kind of traditional "taboo" against the involvement of children in the military. Although these declarations fly in the face of anthropological evidence, it is easy to see the appeal of this approach. It suggests that if individual abusers can simply be singled out for their wrongdoing, captured, and imprisoned, then the problem can be solved. Certainly some recruiters of child soldiers are terrible abusers of children. Joseph Kony, the so-called spokesman of God who leads the cultlike Lord's Resistance Army (LRA), which has been fighting in both Uganda and the Democratic Republic of the Congo, has been involved in kidnapping and abuse of children and in forcing children to serve as soldiers (Rice 2009; "Confronting the Lord's Resistance Army" 2010). But other cases are far more complicated, such as the Civilian Defense Forces in the civil war in Sierra Leone (1991–2001). Here children joined local defense organizations to defend their homes and villages from a murderous rebel army. Human rights and humanitarian organizations argue that even these children are vulnerable and brainwashed, but many people who have worked with them are clear that these children are much more astute about their choices than conventional human rights rhetoric would indicate.

Translating the international legal prohibition against using child soldiers into reality can be tricky. Take, for example, the case of Somalia. The Transitional Federal Government (TFG) in Somalia is listed by the United Nations as one of the most persistent offenders. Somalia is not a signatory to the ICC. Accordingly, under the rules of the Rome Statute, a case against Somalia could come before the ICC only if the case were specifically referred to the court by the UN Security Council. The Somali army is fighting against a rebel army whose stated aim is to bring about an Islamic state in Somalia. The main fighting force of the rebels is the Islamist Harakat al-Shabaab Mujahideen ("Movement of Warrior Youth"), which is a major recruiter of child soldiers, even though they are not yet included on the UN list. While there are no exact numbers available, the evidence shows that many child soldiers are under age 15. There is no indication that these Somali child soldiers are either kidnapped or systematically abused. They seem to be recruited by both sides because of a combination of factors, including manpower shortages, young children's desire for empowerment, and their need for economic stability in a war-ravaged society. Somali officials claim that in their rush to build an army, they simply did not address the problem of age (Gettleman 2010a).

The United States and the European Union are the main supporters of the TFG, which they regard as the legitimate government of Somalia. The United States backs the TFG because of its fear that a radical Islamic state in Somalia would provide a base for international terrorism. The United States has provided arms for Somalia's army and has paid the salaries of its soldiers. Moreover, the United States is aware that child soldiers are being recruited by the TFG. According to one report, young Somali soldiers were apparently trained in Uganda in a program supervised by the United States. All this places the United States in the uncomfortable position of supporting a government whose child soldier recruitment policies are in violation of U.S. laws, namely, the Child Soldiers Accountability Act, which makes the recruitment of child soldiers under age 15 a crime and provides for severe criminal penalties for recruiters in foreign wars that even enter the United States. The president of Somalia, Sharif Sheik Ahmed, is reported to be investigating the issue. The U.S. government claims that it has little leverage over the matter (Gettleman 2010b). This demonstrates the way in which the mix of law and political interests can make it difficult to translate international law into direct action.

Who Is a Child Soldier? Expanding the Definition

Human rights groups are wresting with the question of not only who is a child but also what actually constitutes being a soldier. As the movement to ban child soldiers has gained momentum, the definition of "child soldier" has expanded. Very early, the treaties dealing with child soldiers focused not only on raising the age of recruitment but also on limiting the ways children could be involved with the military. In some instances, children were formally recruited—either forcibly or voluntarily—into an armed force or armed group. In many other instances, however, there was no formal recruitment process, and children might simply attach themselves to an armed force or group and perform any of a variety of tasks. The law sought to limit recruitment and also to reduce the range of activities a child might be permitted to be engaged in as a soldier, so the laws relating to child soldiers deal with both recruitment and use. Here again, however, the law does not incorporated a single standard that is applicable to all circumstances.

Additional Protocol I, which deals with international armed conflicts, required state parties to refrain from recruiting children and also from allowing children to take a "direct part" in hostilities. Although the treaty bans children from participating in combat, it still may allow indirect forms of participation, such as gathering and transmitting military information, transporting arms and munitions, and providing supplies. Children's rights advocates were concerned that even these indirect activities posed a danger to children in that children who were informally connected to the military and engaging in such activities might be deemed unlawful combatants, spies, or saboteurs and be subject to severe punishment if they were captured by an enemy (Commentary on the Protocols Additional 1987). In contrast, Additional Protocol II, which deals with noninternational armed conflicts and applies only to armed groups, bans both direct and indirect participation. It requires that children in such rebels groups not be "allowed to take part in hostilities" (Additional Protocol 4, Article 4). In this sense, there was no "escape clause" for rebel groups—all participation in hostilities, both direct and indirect, was banned.

The Rome Statute of the ICC consolidated these two points of view and prohibited both armed forces and armed groups from conscripting and enlisting children under 15 years old as soldiers or using them to "participate actively in hostilities." The latter term has generally meant a prohibition against direct participation in combat as well as active participation in military activities linked to combat, including scouting, spying, sabotage, and using children as decoys and couriers or at military checkpoints. It also prohibits using children in direct support functions, such as acting as bearers to take supplies to the front line, or activities at the front line itself. However, the statute excludes activities that are clearly unrelated to active hostilities, such as food deliveries to an air base or the use as domestic staff in an officer's married accommodation.

Children rights treaties have developed rather unevenly. The CRC required that state parties ensure that children under 15 years old not take a "direct part in hostilities." The African Charter requires state parties ban children under 18 years old from taking a "direct part in hostilities." Similarly, the Optional Protocol requires that state parties not permit children to take a "direct part in hostilities," although nonstate actors are prohibited from using children "in hostilities" in any form, directly or directly.

The definition of "who is a child soldier" continues to broaden. Outside of formal treaties, humanitarian and human rights groups have sought restrictions that would set children apart from *all* connections with the military. At a 1997 symposium organized by UNICEF and the NGO Working Group on the Convention on the Rights of the Child, a large number of humanitarian and human rights groups adopted the Cape Town Principles and Best Practices on the Prevention of Recruitment of Children into the Armed Forces and on Demobilization and Social Reintegration of Child Soldiers in Africa ("Cape Town Principles" 1987). The Cape Town Principles expand the concept of "child soldier" to include any person under 18 years of age who is part of any kind of regular or irregular armed force or armed group in "any capacity." This definition goes far beyond the distinction between direct and indirect participation in hostilities found in the laws of war or children's rights treaties and would include cooks, porters, and messengers as well as anyone accompanying armed groups other than family members. The definition includes girls recruited for sexual purposes and for forced marriage.

While designed to protect children, the Cape Town Principles expand the concept of "soldier" far beyond what most people would intuitively recognize. In 2007, UNICEF organized a review of the Cape Town Principles that resulted in the 2007 Paris Principles and Guidelines on Children Associated with Armed Force and Armed Groups (Principles and Guidelines, 1987). The Paris Principles formally abandon the concept of child soldier in favor of the concept of "a child associated with an armed group or armed force." The Paris Principles are not yet formally part of international law, but they do reflect the transformation of the child soldier problem from a specific concern with the problem of child combatants to an attempt to create an absolute barrier between children and the military and barring children from being involved with the military in "any capacity." For humanitarian and human rights groups, the next step seems clear: to build these principles into international law.

Putting Child Recruiters on Trial

As part of the multipronged attempt to limit or eliminate the use of child soldiers, the international community has sought to pressure those who actually recruit children into armies and armed forces. One mode of this pressure is to bring legal actions against people who have recruited child soldiers. The ICC and the Special Court for Sierra Leone provided the first opportunities to apply criminal sanctions against child recruiters. Cases heard in these two venues have touched on almost all the issues discussed in this chapter, including who is a child, who is culpable for war crimes, and what exactly is recruitment as well as the limitations of treaties and international law in the face of the disparities between international and local understandings and needs.

The ICC: Cases from the Congo and Uganda

The ICC has before it several situations involving persons charged with recruiting child soldiers, including the recent conflicts in Uganda and in the Democratic Republic of the Congo. One of the significant trials in this court is the case of Thomas Lugbanga Dyilo, a rebel leader in the Democratic Republic of the Congo and the first person ever arrested under a warrant from the ICC (*Prosecutor v. Thomas Lubanga Dyilo* 2006). The Dyilo case focuses exclusively on the recruitment of child soldiers. In addition to the Dyilo case, an arrest warrant has been issued for Bosco Ntaganda, deputy chief of the General Staff of the Forces Patriotiques pour la Libération du Congo and chief of staff of the Congrès National pour la Défense du People (*Prosecutor v. Bosco Ntaganda* 2006). Trials began on November 24, 2009, for Germain Katanga, former commander of the Force de résistance patriotique en Ituri, and Mathieu Ngudjolo Chui, former leader of the Front des Nationalistes et Intégrationnistes. (*Prosecutor v. Germain Katanga and Mathieu Ngudjolo Chui* 2007) In the Uganda situation, the ICC has issued arrest warrants for Joseph Kony, commander in chief of the LRA; Vincent Otti, Vice chairman and second in command of the LRA; Okot Odhiambo, deputy army commander of the LRA; and Dominic Ongwen, brigade commander of the Sinia Brigade of the LRA. All but Ongwen have been charged with recruiting child soldiers (*Prosecutor v. Joseph Kony, Vincent Otti, Okot Odhiambo and Dominic Ongwen* 2005).

The Special Court for Sierra Leone: The Meaning of Recruitment

As of 2010, the Special Court for Sierra Leone has been the only legal venue in which convictions for recruiting child soldiers have been obtained. Accordingly, the decision of this court gives insight into how courts deal with and define the offense of recruitment. The court has heard cases against the leaders of all sides of the conflict. These include the rebel forces of the Revolutionary United Front (RUF); the Armed Forces Revolutionary Council (AFRC), a military junta in league with the RUF; and the Civil Defense Forces (CDF), a militia that fought to restore the lawfully elected government of Sierra Leone. Former Liberian president Charles Taylor has also been put on trial for his involvement in the war. All were charged with "conscripting or enlisting children under the age of 15 years into armed forces or groups or using them to participate actively in hostilities" (Statute of the Special Court for Sierra Leone, Article 4). The language of the charges is identical to that of the Rome Statute as applied to armed conflicts not of an international character. This makes it plain that the court applied current international law governing personal criminal liability for recruiting child soldiers in these cases (Rome Statute, Article 8). Like the Rome Statute, the Special Court Statute distinguishes among three forms of recruitment of child soldiers: enlistment, conscription, and use. "Use" is specifically defined in the statute as "using them [children] to participate actively in hostilities" (Statute of the Special Court for Sierra Leone, Article 4).

The Special Court for Sierra Leone convicted all the key leaders of the RUF and AFRC on the basis of evidence that they forcibly abducted children of a wide range of ages. Both the RUF and the AFRC factions committed some of the most horrible war crimes in recent history, including the abduction of children as part of a broader pattern of atrocities (Rapp 2008). As the court stated, "The only method [of recruitment] described in the evidence is abduction" (*Prosecutor v. Brima* 2007), which is easily encompassed by the statute as a form of forced conscription (*Prosecutor v. Sesay* 2009).

Voluntary Enlistment or Forcible Recruitment?

The CDF cases were more problematic because many children had voluntarily enlisted. In addition, because they were allied with the lawfully elected government of Sierra Leone, the CDF forces were lawful combatants. The CDF defendants were ultimately acquitted of charges of recruiting child soldiers, although they were convicted of other major war crimes. In all these cases, the Special Court had to contend with the legal distinctions between conscription, enlistment, and use as outlined in the statutes. The CDF trial brought these issues into sharp focus when the court initially found one of the defendants, Allieu Kondewa, guilty of enlisting young children into the CDF and actively using them in hostilities (*Prosecutor v. Fofana* 2007a). He was sentenced to seven years in prison.

The second defendant in the case, Moinina Fofana, was found not guilty of the same charges. In the case of Fofana, a CDF commander, the trial court found that his mere presence at commanders' meetings did not demonstrate that he encouraged anyone to make use of child soldiers or that he aided and abetted in the planning, preparation, or execution of the crime. It also found that his presence at a military base where child soldiers were also present was not sufficient by itself to prove that he had any involvement in the commission of the crime. The court found that evidence that the CDF as an organization was involved in recruiting children and that using them in active hostilities did not demonstrate that Fofana was personally involved in such crimes (*Prosecutor v. Fofana* 2007a)

When Kondewa appealed his conviction, the Appeals Chamber had the opportunity to further examine the meaning of "enlistment" under the statute. Kondewa, described as a senior leader and "high priest" of the CDF, was in charge of initiating recruits, including child soldiers, into local units of the CDF. These local units were known as Kamajors, a word in the Mende language of southern Sierra Leone meaning "hunter" or "traditional hunter." The Appeals Chamber had to decide whether the ritual of initiation into the Kamajors constituted "enlistment." This was a difficult issue to decide because local units of the CDF emerged from village associations of hunters that were not necessarily military in nature (Hirsch 2001). The court had to decide whether children who had been initiated were merely joining a special society of hunters or were really being recruited into an armed group.

Local Customs, International Interpretations

In order to resolve this issue, the predominantly non–Sierra Leonean judges had to examine issues of social organization with which they were entirely unfamiliar. In Sierra Leone, as in many areas of West Africa, traditional cultures abound with secret societies and associations. Some Sierra Leonean secret societies, like the all-male Poro society or the all-female Bundu or Sande societies, initiate almost all adolescent boys and girls into their secret rites and rituals. Initiation involves dramatic rituals (Ferme 2001; Little 1949, 1951, 1965). Traditionally, once children had been initiated into these societies, they were regarded as adults. There were no exact fixed dates that determined when boys and girls became adults. These cultures had no calendars or birth certificates. Instead, they relied on obvious signs of mental and physical maturity. As a result, many people classified as "adults" in these societies would, in Western societies and under international law, be regarded as children.

For boys, becoming a man also meant participating in the protection of the community as a warrior. Mende society had no separate army. Going to war meant that all men, that is, all who were members of the Poro, were called on to fight. Thus, we can see that initiation into the Poro was not the same as joining an armed group or necessarily tantamount to immediately joining a military group, although it could be if there were existing conflicts. The members of the Poro could be rapidly called up as a military force. The youngest warriors, often called "war sparrows," fought alongside more seasoned warriors.

The Kamajors were traditionally associations of hunters who themselves were members of Poro, but they also had distinctive rites and rituals of initiation into Kamajor membership. They are probably best regarded as a subset of Poro members (Fanthorp 2007). During the Sierra Leone civil war, groups of Kamajors organized to defend local communities against the forces of the RUF. These groups frequently modeled themselves on the Poro society. But the civil war in Sierra Leone transformed the traditional Kamajors, first into military scouts and finally into organized civil militia called the CDF (Ferme and Hoffman 2004). As in the Poro, recruitment into the Kamajors involved formal rituals of initiation. These rituals lent the aura of tradition to forms of military organization that were increasingly professional, urban, and highly integrated into the Sierra Leone government and military. Thus, in the end, unlike the Poro, initiation into the ranks of the modern Kamajors really signified membership in a distinctly modern military structure in which most of the initiated were not traditional hunters (Ferme and Hoffman 2004). Were the Kamajors really a traditional society of hunters, or were they a modern military force that only had the appearance of being traditional? The Special Court had great difficulty deciding whether the age of initiation was clearly proven and whether initiation per se into the Kamajors constituted recruitment into a group of traditional hunters or enlistment into a modern militia.

The Special Court heard testimony from three former child soldiers, but in convicting Kondewa, it relied solely on the testimony of only one of them, a witness identified only as TF2-021. This witness was initially abducted by the rebel forces of the RUF in 1995 when he was nine years old. He remained with the rebels until 1997, when he was captured by the Kamajors. Immediately after they captured him, the Kamajors required him to help carry property that had been looted in a Kamajor attack. Following this, he was initiated into the Kamajors at Base Zero, the main base of the Kamajor fighting groups, just north of the town of Kenema, in territory controlled by the Kamajors. The witness testified that he was age 11 when he and about 20 other young boys were initiated at the same time. All were initiated by Kondewa. Later, at age 13, he was again initiated into another group of Kamajors known as the Avondo society, a group directly led by Kondewa (*Prosecutor v. Fofana* 2004).

In sentencing Kondewa after his conviction, the Special Court noted the particular vulnerability of the witness and of child soldiers more generally, citing the commentary of the International Committee of the Red Cross that "child soldiers are deprived of a family, deprived of an education, and all the advantages that would otherwise help them be children and prepare them for adulthood" and also asserted that "child soldiers will suffer deep trauma, which persists, long after the fighting has stopped" (*Prosecutor v. Fofana* 2007b). The court also asserted that his role as high priest of the Kamajors, a position that placed him in charge of initiations and played an essential role in the leadership of the CDF, only added to his criminal liability. In the end, however, he was found guilty of recruiting only one child soldier: TF2-021.

Both the prosecution and the defense appealed the conviction and sentencing. Kondewa's attorneys argued that he had never recruited TF2-021. The prosecution argued that Kondewa should also have been convicted for enlisting the other child soldiers. (*Prosecutor v. Fofana* 2008). They pointed to TF2-021's testimony about the 20 other boys initiated with him. The prosecution argued that it was only reasonable to infer that some of these boys, if not all of them, were under the age of 15 and that the court had erred in ignoring this. The prosecution pointed to evidence that other child soldiers were present at Base Zero, where TF2-021 was initiated. But the Appeals Chamber ruled that without additional evidence of the actual ages of the boys, TF2-021's testimony alone was enough to convict Kondewa for enlisting any other child soldiers. This case highlights the fact that it is sometimes difficult to actually prove the ages of children in the absence of written birth records and therefore hard to convict adults of illegally recruiting them into the military.

What Constitutes Enlistment?

On appeal, the Special Court addressed the issue of the relationship between initiation and enlistment. The Trial Court originally held that initiation into the Kamajors did not necessarily mean enlistment. It implicitly accepted that the Kamajors were a society of "traditional hunters." Noting that there might be reasons other than enlistment for parents to want to have their children initiated into the Kamajors, the court held that it was necessary to examine all the facts and circumstances of the initiation of any specific child in order to determine whether it constituted actual enlistment (*Prosecutor v. Fofana* 2007a). Based on this factual examination, the Trial Court found that the initiation of TF2-021 was enlistment. The court pointed to the fact that initiates were given potions to rub on their bodies before going into battle, were told that the potions would make them strong, were given military training, and were sent into battle and concluded that these circumstance proved beyond a reasonable doubt that the initiation performed by Kondewa was an act analogous to enlistment into the military.

The Appeals Chamber dismissed this entire approach to the problem and acquitted Kondewa. While not directly disagreeing with the Trial Chamber's legal analysis of initiations, it reversed the conviction on the grounds that that TF2-021 had actually been recruited and enlisted *prior* to his initiation. The court noted that immediately after TF2-021 was captured by the Kamajors, they required him to carry their looted property, long before his initiation by Kondewa.

In his testimony, witness TF2-021 told the Trial Court of his capture by the Kamajors after an attack on the village of Ngeihun while he was a child soldier for the rebels:

Q. What events did you see in Ngeihun while you were staying with the rebels?

A. Well, when I was with the rebels, Kamajors came and attacked the village.

Q. How did you know that they were Kamajors who attacked the village?

A. Well, after they attacked the village, they captured seven of us little boys.

Q. When did this attack occur?

A. Well, from 1997 to 1998—by then AFRC was in power.

Q. What happened when the Kamajors attacked the town?

A. When they attacked the town, they captured seven of us little boys with three women.

Q. How old were the little boys?

A. We were all in the same age group. There was only one that was older.

Q. How old was the one who was older?

A. He was 15 years of age.

Q. What happened to the three women who were captured with you?

A. When they captured us in the town, we were gathered together in one place, they entered the huts and looted some properties and brought them outside and then set some houses ablaze and the things that they looted, they gave some to us to carry on our heads. They said we should come down to Kenema. On our way to Kenema the three women that were captured—

PRESIDING JUDGE: Not too fast.

MS PARMAR:

Q. Witness, I'll ask you again to go slowly so that everyone can follow what you're telling us.

PRESIDING JUDGE: You said they gave them the looted property to carry—to where, to Kenema? Take it from there, please.

MS PARMAR:

Q. Witness, what type of properties did you carry?

A. Well, the properties I saw were tape and some clothes—some clothing, some seed rice. That was what they gave to us to carry. (*Prosecutor v. Fofana* 2004, 33–34)

The CDF Appeals Chamber ruled that these events, which took place before TF2-021's initiation, constituted "enlistment" into the CDF. His testimony showed that he was used to carry looted property as the Kamajors retreated from the town of Ngeihun in Kono District back toward their base in Kenema.

The Appeals Chamber did not want to address the cultural issues tackled by the Trial Chamber. It rejected the idea that each and every instance of initiation into the Kamajors might require a full inquiry into the facts and circumstances to determine that an initiation ritual was simply initiation or constituted "recruitment." Instead, it wanted to find a single "bright line" that would establish whether TF-021 was recruited. There could be no mistake of fact that TF-021 was under the age of 15, but by finding that he was "enlisted" when he carried rice to Kenema, the court could avoid the questions of whether initiation constituted enlistment. However, this position also resulted in reversing Kondewa's conviction because if TF-021 was recruited when he was captured, he was already a Kamajor long before his so-called enlistment by Kondewa.

The Implications of an Expanded Definition of Enlistment

The implications of the Appeals Court's decision go far beyond this case, however, because in making this ruling, it also expanded the legal definition of enlistment as it applies to armed groups. The Appeals Chamber initially stressed that the different modes of recruitment detailed in the statute (i.e., enlistment, recruitment, and use) were distinct from each other (*Prosecutor v. Fofana* 2008, para. 139). It defined enlistment as "accepting and enrolling individuals when they volunteer to join an armed force or group" (*Prosecutor v. Fofana* 2008, para. 140). But the Appeals Chamber then immediately disregarded these distinctions and held that the "the act of enlisting presupposes that the individual in question voluntarily consented to be part of the armed force or group." However, a child under the age of 15 is not allowed to volunteer, so such a child's consent is not valid. Therefore, claiming that a child under the age of 15 years "volunteered" and then was allowed to join an armed force or group is not a valid defense against recruitment of children since children are not allowed to volunteer in the first place (*Prosecutor v. Fofana* 2008, para. 140). The court also said that "in the context of this case, in which the armed group is not a conventional military organization, enlistment cannot be defined as a formal process." The Appeals Chamber regards "enlistment" in the broad sense as including "any conduct accepting the child as part of the militia" (*Prosecutor v. Fofana* 2008, para. 144).

The court's interpretation of the idea of enlistment constitutes a very broad reading of a criminal statute. The statute clearly distinguishes between three different forms of culpability: (1) "conscription," which refers to involuntary recruitment by use or force or threat of force; (2) "enlistment," which may be voluntary and consensual on the part of the child but which is legally considered "involuntary" and "nonconsensual" because of the child's age; and (3) "use" which involves the child in active participation in hostilities. By redefining enlistment as "any conduct accepting the child as part of the militia," the court seems to be saying that virtually any "use" of a child by an armed group, including that which is not directly connected to fighting, is now a form of enlistment, which is a war crime. Moreover, the phrase "any conduct" makes clear that force is not a central element of the crime and that it can include a wide variety of activities in which children subjectively participate as volunteers.

Reviewing what actually happened in this case shows how "use" of a child became "enlistment." TR1-012 was never conscripted, nor did he volunteer to enlist. Neither was he used by the Kamajors in active hostilities. However, the court found that the fact that the Kamajors had used TR1-012 in any capacity constituted recruitment. Thus, in the court's logic, virtually any use of a child, in any capacity, constitutes recruitment of a child soldier—a war crime. The court's decision draws an ever-widening prohibition between children and their involvement with armed groups.

The Special Court's decision, without specifically saying so, seems very close to adopting a central element of the Paris Principles discussed above. Recall that the Paris Principles formally abandoned the concept of child soldier in favor of the concept of "a child associated with an armed group or armed force." It transformed the child soldier problem from a specific concern with the problem of child combatants to a concern with creating an absolute barrier between children and the military, prohibiting children from being involved with the military in "any capacity," not solely military ones. The Special Court's definition of enlistment as "any conduct accepting the child as part of the militia" seems, on the face of it, to be a virtually identical standard.

The Special Court's holding makes it hard to imagine any kind of activity that a child might do in connection with armed groups will not be deemed criminal. Legally, this has the biggest impact on rebels and other armed groups, which rely heavily on young people. It shows that while the rhetoric about child soldiers has focused on the most grievous cases, the most substantive changes are being made in legal decisions that separate children from participating in armed groups. The law is bringing about directed social change on an international scale.

Putting Children on Trial

One of the most controversial issues affecting child soldiers is whether child soldiers who commit war crimes should be punished for their crimes. Recall that lawful combatants, including child soldiers, are licensed to kill. That is, as long as they do not commit any war crimes, they, like all other lawful combatants, are entitled to fire on and kill enemy combatants and cannot be punished for doing so. But a lawful combatant can be punished for deliberately killing civilians, acting as a spy, committing rape, using civilians as human shields, or violating many of the laws of war. How should child soldiers who are lawful combatants be treated when they commit a war crime?

Unlawful combatants are in a different category. They are not entitled to kill anyone—neither soldiers nor civilians whom they may regard as their "enemies"—and if they do so, their actions are punishable as murder. In addition, they are considered criminals for merely being unlawful combatants. Humanitarian groups argue that since it is always illegal to recruit children under 15 years old, it is increasingly understood that no one under 15 years old, even if deemed to be an unlawful combatant, should be considered a criminal merely because he or she was recruited or used as a child soldier. We consider this issue in detail in the American context in the next chapter in the case of the U.S. Military Commission's recent conviction at Guantanomo Bay, Cuba, of Omar Khadr, a Canadian citizen arrested by the United States in Afghanistan in 2002 for crimes he committed as a child.

The general polemical position of advocacy groups is that the heart of the child soldier problem is adults' use of actual force—often horrific force—in recruiting and using child soldiers. The legal effect of this assumption is that it allocates criminal liability to child recruiters, but at the same time it relieves child soldiers themselves of any moral or legally relevant agency. All their actions, no matter how criminal or heinous, are attributed back to the adults who recruited them.

It is not always easy to reconcile this view of child soldiers with actual events on the ground. For example, testimony during the war crimes trial at the Special Court for Sierra Leone reveals that many children do, in fact, commit terrible war crimes. Indeed, the testimony before the court is filled with examples of children's agency and criminal culpability. One example is the recent and uncontested testimony of Alex Teh at the trial of former Liberian president Charles Taylor before the Special Court for Sierra Leone. Teh describes the gruesome murder of a young boy by other children, members of the so-called Small Boys Unit (SBU) of the rebel forces of the RUF:

> I saw some other SBU boys coming closer to me with another small boy and the boy was crying, screaming, he was screaming. He asked them, "What have I done?" They didn't say anything to him, but the boy was screaming. At first they had to put his right arm on a log. They took a machete and amputated it at the wrist. The boy was screaming and they took the left arm again and put it on the same log and sliced it off. He was still screaming and shouting. They took the left leg and put it on the same log and cut it off at the ankle. At last they took the right leg again and put it on the same log and cut it off with a machete. Some held him by his hand at that time now and I am speaking about the same SBU boys. They are the same people doing this. Some held his other hand, legs. They were swinging the boy. They threw him over into a toilet pit. I was there, I saw it myself. (*Prosecutor v. Charles Taylor* 2008)

Nowhere in Teh's testimony is there any evidence that these children were compelled or coerced to behave in this particularly horrible way or to act out what might be called a ritual of terror. Indeed, evidence from a variety of sources points to the joy that some children took in killing and murder. The contrast between humanitarian views of child soldiers and the reality of their activities frames the issue of how to deal with children who kill.

Age and the Culpability of Children

The question of whether children are culpable and therefore should be held responsible for their actions, even very terrible ones, is being settled with the same kind of wrangling and negotiation of treaties and laws as we have seen in the question of child soldiers in general. These issues generate similar debates about age categories, local customs and perspectives, and humanitarian concerns.

Although child soldiers have committed many war crimes and other atrocities, since World War II no child soldier has been put on trial before an international tribunal. The Special Court was the first that could have addressed the issue of the criminal culpability of child soldiers, but in fact it did not. As we have seen, the civil war in Sierra Leone involved large numbers of child soldiers, many of whom committed terrible atrocities. The president of Sierra Leone asked the UN Security Council to pass Resolution 1315, which required the secretary-general to negotiate an agreement with the government of Sierra Leone to create the independent Special Court. The resolution recommended that the Special Court address crimes against humanity, war crimes, and other serious violations of international humanitarian law as well as relevant crimes under Sierra Leonean law committed during the war ("Security Council Resolution 1315" 2000). The resolution recommended that the court focus its attention on "persons who bear the greatest responsibility for the commission of the crimes," particularly those leaders whose crimes threatened the establishment of and implementation of the peace process in Sierra Leone.

In its draft statute for the Security Council's consideration, the secretary-general focused closely on the issue of whether the Special Court should try child soldiers for war crimes under the Special Court ("Report of the Secretary General" 2004). Drafting the statute generated enormous and highly emotional diplomatic and political debate, pitting Western diplomats and international NGOs against African diplomats and civil society organizations (Cohn 2001; "UN Says" 2000). The essence of the controversy was that, with a few exceptions, such as Amnesty International,

a broad array of child protectionist and human rights groups lob-
bied hard to prevent the court from trying any person under
18 years old regardless of the severity of the war crimes the child
was accused of committing.

These groups' efforts to assure children of blanket immunity
for war crimes under international law goes well beyond anything in the CRC, which had, in fact, anticipated instances in
which children might be culpable (Cohn 2001, 7). The CRC permits the recruitment and conscription of child soldiers over age
15, so it seems highly unlikely that the creators of the CRC
intended to simultaneously extend them blanket immunity from
prosecution for war crimes. The NGOs also misrepresented the
idea that the Rome Statute of the ICC, which at the time had not
yet come into force, had also assumed that only those over the
age of 18 could be held criminally culpable. In reality, the Rome
Statute of the ICC did not apply to persons under the age of 18
precisely because the drafters did not want international criminal
law to usurp national law regarding offenses committed by children. They recognized that there is a high degree of national
variation in ideas about children's maturity and criminal responsibility and wanted these issues to be handled locally (Cohn
2001, 6).

However, both the United Nations and international NGOs
distrusted Sierra Leonean domestic legal institutions, especially
with respect to the treatment of children's offenses. The NGOs
hoped to prevent any kind of legal action or accountability in
Sierra Leone against children under 18 years old. They used a
very new and radical notion that all persons under age 18 must
be treated solely as the beneficiaries of rehabilitation and not as
the subjects of judicial accountability. Their proposed UN solution was to transfer judicial accountability to the Special Court
so that any prosecutions that might take place would be subject
to international standards.

Many of the claims made by NGOs seem in retrospect to
have been quite fanciful. For example, it was asserted that "the
prosecution of children would run counter to Sierra Leone's cultural values of healing and forgiveness" and that "local communities would doubt the legitimacy and effectiveness of a Special
Court that disregarded the traditional shared vision of the child
as a vital channel of peace and reconciliation" (Cohn 2001, 11).

Many Sierra Leoneans, in contrast, wanted some form of
judicial accountability by child soldiers for their actions.

Ambassador Ibrahim Kamara rejected the idea that all child soldiers were traumatized victims and stated that he feared the possibility of mob violence in the absence of judicial accountability ("UN Says" 2000, 107). The secretary-general of the United Nations took these views seriously and in his report noted that "the people of Sierra Leone would not look kindly upon a court that failed to bring to justice children who committed war crimes of that nature and spared them the process of judicial accountability."

Accordingly, the draft statute represented a compromise between these strongly held positions. The secretary-general tried to include accused children within the Special Court's jurisdiction by expanding the scope of personal jurisdiction from "those who bear the greatest responsibility for the commission of crimes" to "persons most responsible" for serious war crimes. This definition would include political and military leaders as well as persons down the chain of authority, not excluding persons ages 15 to 18. These children, if brought to trial, would be tried in a special juvenile chamber that would guarantee internationally recognized standards of juvenile justice, and, if they were convicted, they would not be subject to criminal penalties ("Report of the Secretary General" 2004, 5–7).

The statute finally adopted by the Security Council retained the secretary-general's proposal that the court extend its jurisdiction to include 15- to 18-year-olds and accepted in principle the concept of judicial accountability without penal sanctions. But it rejected the secretary-general's recommendation to expand jurisdiction to persons "most responsible." By doing so, it ensured that, as a practical matter, the Special Court would focus on the senior leadership of the warring armed forces and groups. Moreover, the final statute made no provision for a juvenile chamber, meaning that, in reality, no one under the age of 18 was likely to be tried. In fact, that is exactly what happened. David Crane, the first prosecutor in the Special Court, arrived in Sierra Leone and announced that he would not prosecute any person under 18 years of age. This decision guaranteed that no juvenile offenders would be subject to judicial accountability of any kind.

Wrestling with Children's Culpability

Aside from Sierra Leone, at least one other international court has had the authority to grapple with juvenile offenders. In East Timor, the court of the United Nations Transitional Administration in East

Timor (UNTAET) had the authority to try offenses committed by minors between ages 12 and 18. Minors between 12 and 16 years of age were subject to prosecution for criminal offenses in accordance with UNTAET regulations on juvenile justice—but only for the most serious offenses, such as murder, rape, or a crime of violence in which serious injury is inflicted on a victim. Minors over 16 years of age could be prosecuted as adults, but the rules provided that the court was required to safeguard the rights of the minor in accord with the CRC and to consider his or her juvenile condition. (UNTAET 2000). Thus, although it has been possible to try child soldiers in the Sierra Leone and East Timor courts, there have been no such trials to date.

Age and Culpability in Domestic Courts

The differences are striking in the ways in which international and domestic courts handle cases involving children. Child protectionism has prevailed in the international arena, while domestic courts that deal with child soldiers have been extremely harsh. In the wake of the 9/11 attacks, the United States held at least 12 juveniles at Guantanamo Bay. One of them, Yasser Talal al-Zahrani, hanged himself shortly after arriving at the prison camp. The most widely known case is that of Omar Khadr, a 15-year-old child soldier who was captured and detained as an unlawful combatant after a firefight with American troops in Afghanistan in which an American soldier was killed. Classified as an unlawful combatant, he was charged with murder and attempted murder under the Military Commissions Act (2006) and pled guilty in October 2010. The Military Commissions Act provides for the death penalty. The United States has not ratified Additional Protocols I and II to the Geneva Conventions, so Khadr's only legal protections as a child soldier come from Common Article 3 of the Conventions, which do not preclude the death penalty for child soldiers classified as unlawful combatants, and from the Optional Protocol. Nevertheless, because Khadr is a Canadian citizen, the government of Canada successfully pressured the United States not to apply the death penalty in this instance (Farley 2007; Human Rights Watch 2007). Chapter 3 includes a more comprehensive discussion of Khadr's case and other trials arising from the post-9/11 detainees at Guantanamo Bay.

The situation for child soldiers in the courts of other countries is also problematic. In 2002, the government of Uganda charged two captured boys ages 14 and 16 with treason. The boys were members of the LRA. Human Rights Watch urged the Ugandan government to immediately drop the treason charges and release them to a rehabilitation center. It also requested that Uganda issue a public statement that children would not be subject to treason charges. Under pressure, the Ugandan government decided not to prosecute these cases (Happold 2006), but this decision did not establish a national policy. Recently, the Ugandan government again charged a child soldier with treason. According to Human Rights Watch, the child was abducted at age nine by the rebel forces of the Allied Democratic Front and was arrested when he was 15 (Human Rights Watch 2009). The Democratic Republic of the Congo executed a 14-year-old child soldier in 2000 (Amnesty International 2000). In another instance in the Democratic Republic of the Congo, four children who were 14 to 16 years old when they were arrested were sentenced to death by Congo's Court of Military Order. After government officials met with Human Rights Watch representatives, the lives of these children were spared (Human Rights Watch 2001).

The actual number of children tried and convicted in national courts seems relatively low given the reported number of child soldiers and the widespread claims that children have been frequently involved in war crimes. As in the case of Sierra Leone, this may be a result of popular reluctance in national jurisdictions to put anyone on trial, adults or children, in favor of a "forgive and forget" attitude that dominates postwar reconstruction efforts (Shaw 2005). But this attitude itself may arise from war weariness, and a general sense that local justice systems are too broken by conflict leading to the belief that children should not be put on trial (Wilson 2001).

The cases that have come to trial, however, suggest that there is a chasm between local and international notions of justice. It may not be effective for international law to adopt the extreme position that all persons under 18 should stand outside the system of law and justice; chronological age should not be an absolute bar to accountability (Morris 2004). But it is important to find a middle ground for dealing with children's culpability, such as the one created in the Special Court in Sierra Leone.

A step in the right direction would be to develop an international standard of culpability for child soldiers, modeled on existing juvenile justice systems that takes into account local ideas of justice and with levels of culpability for children that are less than that of adults (Dore 2008). The problem of child soldiers is not going away. Current ethnographic research in Sierra Leone shows that children are once again being recruited into the structures of political violence, the very same structures that brought them into armed forces and groups during the Sierra Leone civil war (Christiansen and Utas 2008). The failure to develop a system of juvenile justice that actually deals with child soldiers who commit war crimes will only continue the conflict between domestic law and international law and the ad hoc solutions that characterize the current situation.

DDR: Disarming, Demobilizing, and Reintegrating Child Soldiers

When wars end, soldiers return to civilian life. Demobilization is always fraught with difficulties, but the problems for children who are returning to civilian life are particularly complicated. There have been intense national and international efforts to demobilize child soldiers both during and after the war. The process of demobilization is usually referred to by the acronym DDR, which stands for disarmament, demobilization, and reintegration. Disarmament means the collection, documentation, control, and disposal of weapons, ammunition, and explosives from both combatants and civilians. Demobilization is the formal separation and removal of active combatants from armed forces and armed groups, and reintegration refers to the process by which ex-combatants return to full civilian status and obtain regular employment and income. Reintegration is ordinarily seen to be an open-ended social and economic process that takes place within communities at a local level.

The United Nations regards the reintegration of children as a complex, long-term process that requires major resources. The immediate practical focus is tracing the families of the children in order to return them to their families and communities. While this may sound simple, it is frequently fraught with challenges. In many instances, the families and communities may have been badly affected by war, are in dire economic straits, and cannot provide for returning soldiers. Although it is sometimes said that child soldiers should be able to recover their "lost childhood," this ideal is really an impossible task. Child soldiers who return home have often held positions of power and authority in the military and are unwilling or unable to resume the role of a child. Although they may technically be children, they may inspire fear in their families and community members. For girls, participation in the military may carry a great stigma that effectively bars their return to full family life, especially if they were raped or sexually abused or had children during their time with the armed forces or groups. Additionally, families or communities may be unreceptive and unwelcoming to children who have committed war crimes or other atrocities during the war. Communities may include people who were members of warring factions with unabated animosities, and returning child soldiers may be subject to threats and retaliation.

In some instances, child soldiers are the object of hatred and resentment because of benefits they receive after they are demobilized. Most humanitarian agencies regard child soldiers as the victims of war regardless of whether they committed war crimes. For this reason, as well as to discourage their reenlistment, child soldiers often receive economic, educational, and social benefits for their reintegration that are denied to the civilian victims of war. It is not surprising, therefore, that local peoples sometimes see child soldiers as having benefited from their crimes while innocent civilians continue to suffer. In Sierra Leone, many child soldiers who are known to have committed war crimes have never been held accountable for those crimes. As we have seen, at the end of the civil war, the Special Court for Sierra Leone tried only the persons "most responsible" for war crimes, so while a number of the most important leaders of the warring factions were put on trial and convicted, none of the individuals who actually carried out the countless murders, rapes, and mutilations that marked this war were tried. Most perpetrators, both children and adult, remain free.

Some commentators have suggested that many Sierra Leoneans are far less interested in expanded judicial or quasi-judicial proceedings designed to expose and punish perpetrators than they are in getting on with their lives (Shaw 2005). But it is also true that reintegrating child soldiers into their families and communities means placing them in a complex social landscape laden with tension and contradictions.

Child soldiers are often quick to understand this reality when they return home. Shepler (2005) reports that former child soldiers in Sierra Leone swiftly learn to adapt to the complexity of this situation. Many have adopted what Shepler terms the discourse of "abdicated responsibility" in which they present themselves as blameless victims of the war. But those same children wear old uniforms, sunglasses, and brag about their military exploits, presenting themselves as "victims" only when they are seeking support from humanitarian agencies (Shepler 2005).

The DDR process can sometime be extremely difficult to implement. Some child soldiers are reunited with families, but in other instances that is impossible, so those children are placed in demobilization centers or foster care. For example, during the conflict in Darfur in western Sudan, the 2006 Darfur Peace Agreement between the Sudan Liberation Army (a rebel group in Sudan) and the Sudanese government laid the groundwork for the demobilization of child soldiers ("Darfur Peace Agreement" 2006). The Sudan Liberation Army was one of several rebel movements in western Sudan that were defending their villages against the Janjaweed militia, a Sudan government–backed Arab force that was carrying out a campaign of murder, ethnic cleansing, and genocide in western Sudan. The treaty provided that the parties release all children under 18 associated with armed forces and groups. UNICEF, the United Nations Commission on Refugees, and the International Committee of the Red Cross were designated to assist in the identification, removal, family unification, and reintegration of children (Darfur Peace Agreement 2010, para. 275). The DDR plan developed by the African Union–United Nations Mission in Darfur (2010) provided that (1) all children under the age of 18 were to be demobilized and removed from all armed movements and groups, (2) demobilized child soldiers were to be returned to families as part of family tracing and reunification for separated children, (3) community-based reintegration for vulnerable children were to be implemented, and (4) there be monitoring and prevention of recruitment of child soldiers. Unfortunately, the peace agreement did not fully end the conflict, and only a paltry number of child soldier were demobilized. Over 2,000 children were identified as possible participants in the DDR program, but in 2009 only 36 child soldiers who had been part of the rebel force were voluntarily demobilized and given material assistance to return to their schools and their communities.

The main problem in trying to reintegrate these children is the lack of money and opportunities in very poor, war-ravaged countries and communities. Indeed, poverty is one of the most intractable issues facing all demobilized soldiers, including children. Many of the countries where child soldiers are recruited are extremely poor. The Democratic Republic of the Congo, Liberia, and Sierra Leone, for example, have gross domestic products that are among the lowest in the world. Demobilized child soldiers face terrible problems in trying to make a living, return to school, receive any kind of employment training, or find a job in an economy where jobs are scarce or nonexistent. While unemployment throughout the world rose from 11.9 percent in 2007 to 13 percent in 2009, in Sierra Leone youth unemployment has been cited as over 60 percent and in Liberia over 88 percent, although no doubt many youth work in the informal economy and are outside those official statistics (African Development Institute 2010; Munive 2010).

Southern Sudan, where despite a signed treaty the demobilization of child soldiers has been incredibly slow, is a typical example (Brethfeld 2010). Here the United Nations reported that that 33 former child soldiers had been demobilized in 2010, only to be rerecruited by the south's army. Children awaiting demobilization were understandably skeptical about the ability of anyone to have the resources to implement demobilization. They asked, " 'Why are you removing us from the army and taking us to the village where we do not get clean water, where we are not getting schooling, we're not getting medication, and we're not getting enough food?' " (Baddorf 2010).

These examples show that the most pressing needs of returning child soldiers are practical ones. Chris Blattman (2007) has pointed out that that despite the often wild, exaggerated, and extravagant claims that children who become soldiers suffer long-term psychological disabilities and are callous and violent, the evidence shows that most children who are demobilized have not engaged in extreme forms of violence and are ultimately able to reintegrate quite well. The real problems for most youth are practical: accelerated education, secondary school support, and livelihood assistance. Similarly, Robert Wessells interviewed more than 400 former child soldiers in Afghanistan, Angola, Kosovo, Sierra Leone, South Africa, and Uganda. His research points out that most children who are recruited as child soldiers are quite resilient and that their identities as soldiers should not be the key way of defining them as persons (Wessells 2006).

Moreover, just as wars are different, so are the ways in which children are incorporated into them. Wessells (2006) warns that the experiences of girl soldiers are frequently sensationalized and portray the girls as the victims of mass rape or sexual exploitation when, in fact, girls and boys experience a diversity of roles as soldiers. Indeed, even when girls are exploited, many of the tasks they perform may not be very different from the peacetime roles they would assume in their own societies. Clearly, there are some situations in which children are brutally exploited, but the picture is more nuanced than the sensationalized reporting in the media would suggest.

Nonetheless, the difficulties of helping children make the transition from soldiers to civilians can be quite daunting when families are broken by war, communities are overwhelmed by poverty, and job opportunities are absent. Sometimes family reintegration is a component of the solution, but sometimes it is not, especially where children have long assumed adult roles and are no longer regarded as children by their families and communities or even by themselves. Insisting that they be treated as children is a pointless exercise in Western hubris. Wessells (2006) advocates a much more fact-based approach based on local knowledge of the kinds of solutions that will work. He also argues that a great deal of advance preparation is needed, as is extensive follow-up with families that are trying to adapt to the return of child soldiers.

In light of this, Wessells (2006) is critical of approaches to reintegration that focus primarily on psychological counseling, especially in situations where people are struggling to meet basic needs. In his view, counseling should be less about "healing wounds" or mental illness than about helping young people socially integrate into the practical rhythms of civil life. Various forms of counseling and help, whether psychological counseling, traditional healing, or exercises in nonviolent conflict resolution, need to be harnessed in support of the key goal, which is to enable former child soldiers to make decent lives for themselves in situations plagued by chronic poverty. Finally, there is a real need for agencies to help former child soldiers acknowledge the abilities of children to take charge of their own lives.

Psychological studies of former child soldiers tend to support these views, although there are only a few major scientific studies of the effects of serving as a child soldier on children's mental health. Bayer, Klasen, and Adam (2007) surveyed 169 former child soldiers most of whom had been forcibly recruited by the LRA, widely regarded as one of the most ruthless and cultlike organizations that have recruited child soldiers. At the time of the survey, the former soldiers were residing in a rehabilitation center and were at least 18 years of age. The average age of the participants in the study was 15.3, and their average age of recruitment was 12.1 years. The average time served was 38 months, and the participants had been demobilized, on average, for 2.3 months. The former child soldiers reported having been exposed to a number of traumatic events: 92.9 percent had witnessed shooting, 89.9 percent had witnessed someone wounded, and 84 percent had been seriously beaten; 54.4 percent claimed to have killed someone. They were evaluated for symptoms of posttraumatic stress disorder (PTSD) as well as for their feelings about revenge and reconciliation. The results of the study were mixed. Slightly more than a third (34.9%) met the symptom criteria for PTSD, but there was no significant positive association between the traumatic experiences and the presence of PTSD symptoms. The study showed that those with positive symptoms of PTSD were less open to reconciliation with former enemies and had greater feelings of revenge. Likewise, children who had been threatened with death and serious harm were less open to reconciliation and had more feelings of revenge than those who did not. These former child soldiers had been demobilized for only a short period of time.

Kohrt et al. (2008) studied 141 former child soldiers as well as 141 children who were matched by age, sex, education, and ethnicity but who were not conscripted. The conscripted children were part of the Maoist rebels in Nepal who started a civil war in Nepal that lasted from 1996 to 2006. All subjects came from active conflict zones. All children had been exposed to bombings, beatings, and torture. Former child soldiers reported more symptoms for depression (53%) than nonsoldiers (24.1%), anxiety (46.1 vs. 37.6%), and PTSD (55.3 vs. 20%) Overall, the mental health burden of former child soldiers ranged from 39 to 62 percent compared to the mental health burden of those who were never conscripted, which was 18 to 45 percent. The findings suggest that the difference between former child soldiers and civilians is concentrated among the soldiers with greater trauma exposure. Girls especially were found to have elevated symptoms of depression and PTSD.

The study found that child soldiers who were still associated with an armed group had better mental health outcomes than those that were not. It would be surprising if some child soldiers, especially among those who have experienced combat, did not experience the psychological traumas of war; in this, they have much in common with adult combatants. But these studies show the importance of not exaggerating and pathologizing child soldiers as a whole. Psychological support, where it is needed, should be focused on the specific needs of individuals.

The problems of reintegration may be more difficult than those of actually being in the military, especially where children are maltreated when they return to their families and communities. In the documentary film *Returned* (cowritten by Brandon Kohrt, the leading author of the previously mentioned study), the filmmakers focused heavily on the problems of returning children. In many instances, the processes of return were far more difficult and traumatic than their actual service in armed groups. The filmmakers report, for example, that Asha, a 13-year-old girl from a poor low-caste family in Nepal, joined a Maoist women's battalion in order to escape from domestic servitude. She loved school, but her family thought it was a waste of money to educate a girl. In contrast, the Maoist battalion had an ideology of gender egalitarianism and gave her the opportunity to use her art skills in painting propaganda posters. After being gone for a year, she returned home. Her mother locked her in the house and within a day arranged for the 14-year-old Asha to marry a 22-year-old man from a distant village. The marriage was characterized by violence and domestic abuse. Indeed, after her in-laws found out she had been a Maoist, they treated her like an animal. After a failed suicide attempt, Asha was kicked out of the house and sent back to her mother (Koenig 2008).

This example makes it clear that simply returning child soldiers to their families and communities may offer little to children who joined armed forces and groups in the first place to escape deep inequalities in their families and communities. The key is listening to the needs of child soldiers rather than deciding, in advance, what these needs are.

It is an enormous challenge for veterans of war to reenter civilian life, even in the richest of societies. Veterans of the Continental Army of the American Revolution suffered from widespread deprivation and alienation from society (Resch 1999). In 1932, the poverty-stricken protestors of the Bonus Army of more than 17,000 World War I veterans, whose lives were ravaged by the Great Depression, were forcibly driven from their protest site in Washington, D.C., by combined force of police, infantry, and tanks, and their dwellings were burned to the ground. To prevent this from happening again, after World War II, the U.S. Congress passed the GI Bill to provide funding that enabled returning U.S. servicemen to participate in the growing middle class in American society. Throughout the world, returned veterans have often played a role in political instability in postwar eras. Solutions to potential dangers of political instability posed by veterans have sometimes been incorporated into peace treaties between contending parties (Schafer 2007), but in poor countries, real solutions are often elusive. Thus, the special problems of child soldiers take place within circumstances that have historically have not augered well for veterans of war. Today, child soldiers in the poorest places in the world return to civilian life, only to find themselves eking out extremely marginal postconflict existences (Denov 2010, 170–76).

This chapter examined the situation of child soldiers in conflicts raging across the globe. In the next chapter, we examine the child soldier situation in the United States. The United States does not generally recruit child soldiers, although it has done so in the past. Instead, the United States faces the problem of child soldiers in two broad areas: managing its relationship with countries that do recruit child soldiers and, perhaps most challenging, its unhappy treatment of children captured in the wars in Afghanistan and Iraq.

References

"African Charter on the Rights and Welfare of the Child." 1990. Organization of African Unity Doc. CAB/LEG/24.9/49. http://www.africa-union.org/root/au/Documents/Treaties/Text/A.%20C. %20ON%20THE%20RIGHT%20AND%20WELF%20OF%20CHILD.pdf. Accessed February 6, 2011.

African Development Institute. 2010. "Sierra Leone Youth Unemployment." http://www.africaecon.org/index.php/africa _business_reports/read/53. Accessed February 6, 2011.

African Union–United Nations Mission in Darfur (UNAMID) 2010. "Disarmament, Demobilisation and Reintegration." *(DDR): Information Sheet.* http://unamid.unmissions.org/Default.aspx?tabid=2484. Accessed February 6, 2011.

Amnesty International. 2000 "Democratic Republic of Congo: Massive Violations Kill Human Decency." http://www.amnesty.org/en/library/

asset/AFR62/011/2000/en/f9c8bebf-748a-4c0c-9a37-3ca3a3dad950/
afr620112000en.pdf. Accessed February 6, 2011.

Baddorf, Zack. 2010. "Sudanese Rebels Reluctant to Demobilize Child
Soldiers." *Deutsche Welle.* July 5. http://www.dw-world.de/dw/article/
0,,5749199,00.html. Accessed February 6, 2011.

Banks, Angela M. 2003. "The Growing Impact of Non State Actors on the
International and European Legal System." *International Law Forum du
Droit International* 5:293–99.

Bayer, Christophe Pierre, Fionna Klasen, and Hubertus Adam. 2007.
"Association of Trauma and PTSD Symptoms with Openness to
Reconciliation and Feelings of Revenge among Former Ugandan and
Congolese Child Soldiers." *Journal of the American Medical Association*
298:555–59.

Bellinger, John B., III, and William J. Haynes II. 2007. "A US Government
Response to the International Committee of the Red Cross Study
Customary International Humanitarian Law." *International Review of the
Red Cross* 89, no. 866 (June). http://www.icrc.org/Web/eng/siteeng0
.nsf/htmlall/review-866-p443/$File/irrc_866_Bellinger.pdf. Accessed
February 6, 2011.

Blattman, Christopher. 2007. *Making Reintegration Work for Youth in
Northern Uganda.* Survey of War Affected Youth. Accessed February 6,
2011. http://chrisblattman.com/documents/policy/sway/SWAY
.ResearchBrief.Reintegration.pdf. Accessed February 6, 2011.

Blattman, Christopher, and Jeannie Annan. 2006. *The State of Youth and
Youth Protection in Northern Uganda.* Survey of War Affected Youth.
http://chrisblattman.com/documents/policy/sway/SWAY.Phase1.
FinalReport.pdf. Accessed February 5, 2011.

Brethfeld, Julie. 2010. "Unrealistic Expectations: Current Challenges to
Reintegration in Southern Sudan. Small Arms Survey." Graduate
Institute of International and Development Studies, Geneva,
Switzerland.

"Cape Town Principles and Best Practice on the Prevention of
Recruitment of Children into the Armed Forces and on Demobilization
and Socialization Reintegration of Child Soldiers in Africa." 1987. http://
www.unicef.org/emerg/files/Cape_Town_Principles%281%29.pdf.
Accessed February 6, 2011.

Carpenter, Mary. 1856. *Juvenile Delinquents, Their Condition and Treatment.*
London: W. & F. G. Cash.

Christiansen, Maya M., and Mats Utas. 2008. "Mercenaries of
Democracy: The 'Politricks' of Remobilized Combatants in the 2007
General Election of Sierra Leone." *African Affairs* 107:515–39.

Cohn, Ilene. 2001. "The Protection of Children and the Quest for Truth and Justice in Sierra Leone." *Journal of International Affairs* 55 (1):1–34.

"Confronting the Lord's Resistance Army." 2010. Voice of America. June 1. http://www.voanews.com/policy/editorials/Confronting-The -Lords-Resistance-Army-95319329.html. Accessed February 5, 2011.

"Convention on the Rights of the Child, Nov. 20, 1989." N.d. *United Nations Treaty Series* 1157: 3. http://www.icrc.org/ihl.nsf/FULL/540 ?OpenDocument. Accessed February 6, 2011.

Cox, Caroline. 2009. "Boy Soldiers of the American Revolution: The Effects of War on Society." In *Children and Youth in a New Nation*, edited by James Marten. New York: New York University Press.

Darfur Peace Agreement. 2006. http://allafrica.com/peaceafrica/ resources/view/00010926.pdf. Accessed February 6, 2011.

Deng, Francis. 1972. *The Dinka of the Sudan*. Prospect Heights, IL: Waveland Press

Denov, Miriam. 2010. *Child Soldiers: Sierra Leone's United Revolutionary Front*. Cambridge: Cambridge University Press.

Dore, Christopher. 2008. "What to Do with Omar Khadr? Putting a Child Soldiers on Trial: Questions of International Law, Juvenile Justice and Moral Culpability." *John Marshall Law Review* 41:1281–320.

Edgerton, Robert. 1989. *MauMau: An African Crucible* New York: Free Press.

Elkins, Caroline. 2005. *Imperial Reckoning: The Untold Story of Britain's Gulag in Kenya*. New York: Holt.

Fanthorp, Richard. 2007. "Sierra Leone: The Influence of Secret Societies, with Special Reference to Female Genital Mutilation." United Nations High Commission for Refugees 2, 2007

Farley, Suzanne. 2007. "Juvenile Enemy Combatants and the Juvenile Death Penalty in U.S. Military Commission." *Santa Clara Law Review* 47:829–53.

Ferme, Mariane C. 2001. *The Underneath of Things: Violence, History and the Everyday in Sierra Leone*. Berkeley: University of California Press.

Ferme, Mariane C., and Danny Hoffman. 2004. "Hunter Militias and the International Human Rights Discourse in Sierra Leone and Beyond." *Africa Today* 50:73–95.

Gettleman, Jeffrey. 2010a. "Children Carry Guns for a U.S. Ally, Somalia." *New York Times*, June 14. http://www.nytimes.com/2010/06/14/world/ africa/14somalia.html?_r=1&ref=africa. Accessed February 6, 2011.

Gettleman, Jeffrey. 2010b. "UN Voices Concern on Child Soldiers in Somalia." *New York Times*, June 16.

Happold, Matthew. 2006. "The Age of Criminal Responsibility for International Crimes under International Criminal Law." In *International Criminal Accountability and the Rights of Children*, edited by Karin Arts and Vesselin Popovski. The Hague: Hague Academic Press.

Happold, Matthew. 2008. "Child Soldiers: Victims or Perpetrators?" *University of La Verne Law Review* 29:56–87.

Hass, Jonathan. 1990. *The Anthropology of War*. Cambridge: Cambridge University Press.

Hirsch, John L. 2001. *Sierra Leone: Diamonds and the Struggle for Democracy*. New York: International Peace Academy.

Hoebel, E. Adamson. 1978. *The Cheyennes*. New York: Holt, Rinehart and Winston.

Human Rights Watch. 2001. "Congo: Don't Execute Child Soldiers: Four Children to Be Put to Death." May 2. http://www.hrw.org/en/news/2001/05/02/congo-dont-execute-child-soldiers. Accessed February 6, 2011.

Human Rights Watch. 2007. "The Omar Khadr Case: A Teenager Imprisoned at Guantanamo." http://www.hrw.org/en/reports/2007/06/01/omar-khadr-case. Accessed February 6, 2011.

Human Rights Watch. 2009. "Letter to Ugandan Minister of Justice Regarding Abducted Child." January 6. http://www.hrw.org/en/news/2009/01/06/letter-ugandan-minister-justice-regarding-abducted-child.

"ILO Convention (No. 182) concerning the Prohibition and Immediate Action for the Elimination of the Worst Forms of Child Labor, June 17, 1999." 1999. S. Treaty Doc. No. 106-5, 2133 *United Nations Treaty Series* 161.

Koenig, Robert. 2008. "Returned: Child Soldiers of Nepal's Maoist Army." http://nepaldocumentary.com/TheFilm.aspx. Accessed February 6, 2011.

Kohler, Martin. 1998. "From the National to the Cosmopolitan Public Sphere." In *Re-Imagining Political Community: Studies in Cosmopolitan Democracy*, edited by Daniele Archibugi, David Held, and Martin Kohler. Stanford, CA: Stanford University Press.

Kohrt, Brandon A., Mark J. D. Jordans, Wietse A. Tol, Rebecca A. Speckman, Sujen M. Maharjan, Carol M. Worthman, and Ivan H. Komproe. 2008. "Comparison of Mental Health between Former Child Soldiers and Children Never Conscripted by Armed Groups in Nepal." *Journal of the American Medical Association* 6:691–702.

Lancy, David F. 2008. *The Anthropology of Childhood: Cherubs, Chattel, Changelings*. Cambridge: Cambridge University Press.

Little, Kenneth. 1949. "The Role of the Secret Society in Cultural Specialization." *American Anthropologist* 51:199–212.

Little, Kenneth. 1951. *The Mende of Sierra Leone: A West African People in Transition.* London: Routledge.

Little, Kenneth. 1965. "The Political Function of the Poro, Part I." *Journal of the International African Institute* 35:349–65.

Malanczuk, Peter. 1997. *Akherst's Modern Introduction to International Law.* 7th ed. London: Routledge.

Military Commissions Act. 2006. Public Law No. 109-366. *United States Statutes at Large* 120: 2600.

Montgomery, Heather. 2009. *An Introduction to Childhood: Anthropological Perspectives on Children's Lives.* London: Wiley-Blackwell.

Morris, John R. 2004. "The Status of Child Offenders under International Criminal Justice: Lessons from Sierra Leone." *Deakin Law Review* 9: 213–25. http://www.austlii.edu.au/au/journals/DeakinLRev/2004/9.html. Accessed February 6, 2011.

Munive, Jairo. 2010. "The Army of 'Unemployed' Young People." *Young: Nordic Journal of Youth Research* 18: 321–38.

"Naxal Problem Not an Armed Conflict, India Tells UN." 2010. *The Times of India.* June 18. http://timesofindia.indiatimes.com/india/Naxal -problem-not-an-armed-conflict-India-tells-UN/articleshow/6063604. cms. Accessed February 6, 2011.

"Optional Protocol to the Convention on the Rights of the Child on the Involvement of Children in Armed Conflict." 2000. *United Nations Treaty Series* 2173: 222. http://www2.ohchr.org/english/law/crc-conflict.htm. Accessed February 5, 2011.

Platt, Anthony M. 2009. *The Child Savers: The Invention of Delinquency.* New Brunswick, NJ: Rutgers University Press.

Principles and Guidelines on Children Associated with Armed Forces and Armed Groups.1987. http://www.un.org/children/conflict/ _documents/parisprinciples/ParisPrinciples_EN.pdf. Accessed February 5, 2011.

Prosecutor v. Bosco Ntaganda. 2006. Case No. ICC-01/04-02/06. *Warrant of Arrest* (August 22).

Prosecutor v. Brima. 2007. Case No. SCSL 04-16-T. *Trial Court Judgment,* para. 1276 (June 20).

Prosecutor v. Fofana. 2004. Special Court for Sierra Leone. Case No. SCSL-04-14-T.

Prosecutor v. Fofana. 2007a. Case No. SCSL-04-14-T, Special Court for Sierra Leone. *Judgment.* Trial Chamber I. August 2, 290–92.

Prosecutor v. Fofana. 2007b. Case No. SCSL 04-14-T. *Sentencing Judgment,* para.55 (October 9).

Prosecutor v. Fofana. 2008. Case No. SCSL-04-14-T. Special Court for Sierra Leone. *Appeal Judgment.* Appeals Chamber 28 (May).

Prosecutor v. Germain Katanga and Mathieu Ngudjolo Chui. 2007. Case No. ICC-01/04-01/07.

Prosecutor v. Joseph Kony, Vincent Otti, Okot Odhiambo and Dominic Ongwen. 2005. Case No. ICC-02/04-01/05. *Warrants of Arrest* (July 8).

Prosecutor v. Norman. 2004. *Decision on Preliminary Motion Based on Lack of Jurisdiction (Child Soldiers).* Special Court for Sierra Leone. Case No SCSL -04-14-AR72E (May 31). http://www.sc-sl.org/LinkClick.aspx ?fileticket=XSdlFGVsuTI%3d&tabid=193. Accessed February 5, 2010.

Prosecutor v. Omar al Bashir. 2009. *Warrant of Arrest.* International Criminal Court. Case No. ICC-02/05-01/09 (March 4). http://www.icc-cpi.int/iccdocs/doc/doc639078.pdf.

Prosecutor v. Sesay. 2009. Case No. SCSL 04-15-T, *Trial Court Judgment,* para 186 (March 2).

Prosecutor of the Special Court v. Charles Taylor. 2008. Case No. SCSL 2003-01 (January 8).

Prosecutor v. Thomas Lubanga Dyilo. 2006. Case No. ICC-01/04-01/06. International Criminal Court.

"Protocol Additional to the Geneva Conventions of 12 August 1949, and Relating to the Protection of Victims of International Armed Conflicts (Protocol I), June 8, 1977." 1125 *United Nations Treaty Series.* 3.

"Protocol Additional to the Geneva Conventions of 12 August 1949, and Relating to the Victims of Non-International Armed Conflicts (Protocol II), June 8, 1977." 1125 *United Nations Treaty Series* 609.

Quaifem, M. 1930. "A Boy Soldier under Washington: The Memoir of Daniel Granger." *Mississippi Valley Historical Review* 16 (4): 538–60.

Rapp, Steven. 2008. "The Compact Model in International Criminal Justice: The Special Court for Sierra Leone." *Drake Law Review* 57:11–49.

"Report of the Secretary General on the Establishment of a Special Court for Sierra Leone." 2004. United Nations Doc. S/2000/915 (October 4, 2000).

Resch, John. 1999. *Suffering Soldiers: Revolutionary War Veterans. Moral Sentiment and Political Culture in the Early Republic.* Amherst: University of Massachusetts Press.

Rice, Xan 2009. "Life with Joseph Kony, Leader of Uganda's Lord's Resistance Army." *The Guardian.* September 4. http://www.guardian.co.uk/world/2009/sep/14/uganda-lords-resistance-army. Accessed February 5, 2011.

"Rome Statute of the International Criminal Court." 1998. *United Nations Treaty Series* 2187:3. http://untreaty.un.org/cod/icc/statute/romefra. htm. Accessed February 1, 2010.

Rosen, David. 2005. *Armies of the Young: Child Soldiers in War and Terrorism.* New Brunswick, NJ: Rutgers University Press.

Salamon, Lester. 2002. *The Tools of Government: A Guide to the New Governance.* Oxford: Oxford University Press.

Sandoz, Yves, Christopher Swinarski, and Bruzo Zimmerman, eds. 1987. *Commentary on the Additional Protocols of 8 June 1977 to the Geneva Conventions of 12 August 1949.* Geneva: International Committee of the Red Cross. http://www.icrc.org/ihl.nsf/WebList? ReadForm&id=470&t=com. Accessed February 6, 2011.

"Security Council Resolution 1315." 2000. United Nations Doc. S/RES/ 1315 (August 14).

Shaw, Rosalind 2005. "Rethinking Truth and Reconciliation Commissions: Lessons from Sierra Leone." Special Report 130. Washington, DC: United States Institute of Peace.

Shepler, Susan. 2005. "The Rites of the Child: Global Discourses of Youth and Reintegrating Child Soldiers in Sierra Leone." *Journal of Human Rights* 4:197–211.

Spencer, Paul. 2004. *The Samburu: A Study of a Gerontocracy in a Nomadic Tribe.* London: Routledge.

"Statute of the Special Court for Sierra." 2002. Special Court for Sierra Leone. http://www.sc-sl.org/LinkClick.aspx?fileticket=uClnd1MJeEw %3D&.

"UN Says Sierra Leone War Crimes Court Should Be Able to Try Children." 2000. Agence France Presse. October 5. http://www .globalpolicy.org/security/issues/sierra/court/001005af.htm.

UNICEF. 2002. *Adult Wars, Child Soldiers.* New York: United Nations.

United Nations Transitional Administration in East Timor. 2000. *Transitional Rules of Criminal Procedure,* 45 (1). United Nations Doc. UNTAET/REG/2000/30 (September 25).

U.S. Department of State. 2004. *Trafficking in Persons Report.* http://www .state.gov/g/tip/rls/tiprpt/2004/34021.htm.

Voice of America. 2009 "AU Ignores Bashir ICC Arrest Warrants, Human Rights Groups Outraged." July 5. *Voice of America News.* http://www .voanews.com/english/news/a-13-2009-07-06-voa1-68819002.html. Accessed February 2, 2011.

Webster, Timothy. 2007. "Babes with Arms: International Law and Child Soldiers." *George Washington International Law Review* 39:227–53.

Wessels, Michael. 2006. *Child Soldiers: From Violence to Protection.* Cambridge, MA: Harvard University Press.

Wilson, Richard. 2001. "Children and War in Sierra Leone: A West African Diary." *Anthropology Today* 17:20–22.

www.otherindia.org/dev/images/stories/feda_child.pdf. Accessed February 5, 2011.

Zimring, Franklin E. 2005. *American Juvenile Justice.* New York: Oxford University Press.

3

Special U.S. Issues

Grappling with the Child Soldier Problem: U.S. Achievements and Failures

The United States is active in efforts to ban the recruitment and use of child soldiers, introducing domestic legislation, lobbying in international forums, and covering the issue in the press. But its record is not entirely positive, and the history of the United States on the use and treatment of child soldiers reflects how complex this issue has become. On the international level, it has ratified the Optional Protocol to the Convention to the Rights of the Child on the Involvement of Children in Armed Conflict (United States 2000), which was designed to strengthen restrictions on child recruitment and to protect children who have been unlawfully recruited. The United States has also enacted important domestic legislation targeting the recruiters of child soldiers, and the U.S. military itself does not recruit child soldiers. But faced with the reality of dealing with child soldiers in contemporary conflicts, U.S. actions fall well short of its aspirations. In this chapter, we explore the sometimes disturbing and controversial gap between U.S. aspirations and the way the United States has dealt with other nations that recruit child soldiers and, perhaps more important, how it has dealt with the many child soldiers it has captured during the long conflicts in Afghanistan and Iraq. It is a complex story with many difficult challenges.

The Recruitment of Child Soldiers

The United States and the Optional Protocol

Although the United States is a party to the Optional Protocol and publicly decries the use of child soldiers, it is not a party to all the treaties that address the issue of recruitment and protection of children under arms. The United States is not a party to the Convention of the Rights of the Child, the Rome Treaty of the International Criminal Court (ICC), or the Additional Protocols to the Geneva Convention. Moreover, while it is a party to the Optional Protocol, it has also made a number of important official declarations and understandings that outline its interpretation of its treaty obligations. These reflect the reasons for the reluctance of the United States in recent years to become party to international treaties.

When any nation-state ratifies a treaty, it is entitled at the time of ratification to add certain reservations, understandings, and declarations that clarify and thereby limit precisely what the state is agreeing to. When a state makes a "reservation" to a treaty, it declares that it accepts most of its obligations under the treaty but specifically excludes or modifies the legal effect of one or more provisions. An "understanding" is a declaration by a state that a particular provision of a treaty has a generally accepted meaning and that in this statement it explicitly articulates its understanding of that generally accepted meaning and therefore precisely what it is agreeing to by signing the treaty. A "declaration" is a statement that a specific provision of a treaty has a particular meaning for that state. In making a declaration at the signing of a treaty, a state provides its interpretation of any terms of the treaty that it believes require clarification (Doebbler 2004, 279).

The U.S. declarations and understanding regarding the Optional Protocol affect primarily Articles 1, 2, and 3 of the treaty. These relevant sections of these articles are the following:

Article 1: Parties shall take all feasible measures to ensure that members of their armed forces who have not attained the age of 18 years do not take a direct part in hostilities.

Article 2: Parties shall ensure that persons who have not attained the age of 18 years are not compulsorily recruited into their armed forces.

Article 3.1: Parties shall raise the minimum age for the voluntary recruitment of persons into their national armed forces from that set out in article 38, paragraph 3, of the Convention on the Rights of the Child, taking account of the principles contained in that article and recognizing that under the Convention persons under the age of 18 years are entitled to special protection.

In its declaration, the United States made plain that it has set age 17 as the minimum age of voluntary recruitment into the armed forces of the United States. With respect to Article 2's ban on compulsory recruitment, it made clear that recruitment of 17-year-olds was voluntary and that it required both the written consent of the enlistee's parent or guardian and reliable proof of age for any 17-year-old to enlist.

In its understandings, the United States added that in signing the Optional Protocol to the Convention of the Rights of the Child, it did not assume any obligations under the original Convention on the Rights of the Child, which it has not ratified. In addition, the United States offered its interpretation of two terms in Article 1: "feasible measures" and "direct part in hostilities." The position of the United States is that the term "feasible measures" means only those measures that are practical or practically possible, taking into account all the circumstances at the time, including humanitarian and military considerations. This means that under some circumstances, it might not be possible to exclude 18-year-olds from direct hostilities in a combat zone. For example, if U.S. forces were attacked, the military might need all soldiers, including 17-year-olds, to repulse the attack. The United States also interprets the phrase "direct part in hostilities" to mean immediate and actual action on the battlefield likely to cause harm to the enemy, with a direct causal relationship between the activity engaged in and the harm done to the enemy. It specifically stated that it does not mean other, more indirect activities, such as gathering and transmitting military information; transporting weapons, munitions, or other supplies; or forward deployment. This means that children under 18 years old can be very active in military activities in conflict zones as long as they are not specifically part of designated combat troops. The United States also wants to be sure that its interpretation of the Optional Protocol cannot be nullified or second-guessed by any international court, so it stated clearly that in ratifying the treaty, it was not accepting the jurisdiction of any international tribunal, including the ICC on any issue covered by the treaty (United States 2002).

Thus, as a general principle, the United States accepts the basic terms of the Optional Protocol, and, consistent with its terms, the United States does not recruit child soldiers. However, the U.S. interpretation of the Optional Protocol does depart from the goals of many humanitarian and human rights groups that have targeted 18 as the minimum age of recruitment in all armed forces and groups. Such groups continue to insist that in accepting the voluntary enlistment of 17-year-olds, the United States is recruiting child soldiers.

Several human rights organizations monitor U.S. compliance with the Optional Protocol. The Coalition to Stop the Use of Child Soldiers (2008) reported that as of 2003, all the U.S. armed services—the U.S. Army, Navy, Marines and Air Force—had adopted plans to comply with the Optional Protocol. Despite this, the U.S. Army acknowledged that approximately 60 17-year-old U.S. soldiers were deployed to Iraq and Afghanistan in 2003 and 2004. The Department of Defense has taken action to prevent any recurrence (Coalition to Stop the Use of Child Soldiers 2008). Between 2004 and 2007, the United States recruited 94,005 17-year-olds into all the armed services, representing 7.6 percent of all recruits (United Nations Committee on the Rights of the Child 2008). Human Rights Watch (2009) reported that compliance with the recruitment provisions of the Optional Protocol was complete, none of the services allow 17-year-olds into conflict areas, and the army does not deploy 17-year-olds outside the United States.

U.S. Domestic Legislation

In additional to its international commitments, the U.S. Congress has passed several significant pieces of legislation to curb the use of child soldiers. These include (1) the Child Soldier Accountability Act (CSAA 2008), making the recruitment and use of child soldiers a federal crime; (2) the Child Soldier Prevention Act (CSPA 2008), banning military assistance to countries designated by the State Department as recruiting child soldiers; and (3) the Human Rights Enforcement Act (2009), creating a criminal division within the Department of Justice that is responsible for enforcing the laws against suspected participants in serious human rights offenses, including the recruitment of child soldiers.

The CSAA was signed into law by President George W. Bush in 2008. The CSAA makes it a criminal offense to recruit, enlist, or conscript any person under 15 years of age into an armed force or group or to use that person to participate actively in hostilities. Violators can be fined or imprisoned for up to 20 years and can be subject to life imprisonment if a child dies as a consequence of being recruited. The law applies to citizens, nationals, or permanent residents of the United States. Even visitors to the country who are involved in the recruitment of child soldiers anywhere in the world, including in the United States, can be arrested and tried under this law. The law also allows the United States to refuse admission to the United States or to deport offenders who are noncitizens. With the CSAA, the United States now has very clear domestic legislation that is similar to the Rome Statute of the ICC.

The CSPA, which was incorporated as a component of the Wilberforce Trafficking Victims Protection Reauthorization Act of 2008, prohibits the United States from providing a range of military assistance to countries that are designated by the Department of State as having governmental armed forces or government-supported armed groups, including paramilitaries, militias, or civil defense forces, that recruit or use child soldiers. The State Department publishes this designation in its annual country reports on human rights. The CSPA is directed against states rather than against individuals. The kind of military assistance it covers includes arms sales, training, payment of salaries to troops, and a wide variety of indirect assistance as well. Unlike a criminal law, this law allows the president to waive the prohibition if the president deems it to be in the national interest of the United States.

Compliance with Domestic Legislation

Although its record is good on recruitment of its own soldiers, the United States has been criticized for its support of nations whose armed forces *do* recruit child soldiers. For example, in 2009, in compliance with the CSPA, the State Department listed six countries as subject the sanction under the act: Burma, Chad, the Democratic Republic of the Congo (DRC), Somalia, Sudan, and Yemen (U.S. Department of State 2010c). Nonetheless, on

October 25, 2010, President Obama issued a waiver of the CSPA to four of the six countries: Chad, the DRC, Sudan, and Yemen (President 2010). In justifying this waiver, President Obama cited the importance of these countries in cooperating with key foreign policy objectives of the United States and the negative impact that sanctions would have on U.S. interests. In two countries, the presidential waivers were given in recognition of the role these countries played in cooperating with the United States in antiterrorism activities. President Obama stated that Chad was involved in combating trans-Saharan terrorism and in aiding in the humanitarian crisis in Darfur. Yemen was cited for its role in counterterrorism operations against al-Qaeda in the Arabian Peninsula. Broader foreign policy considerations played a role in the other two states. With respect to the DRC, the president cited a need to continue defense reform services and to influence the negative behavior patterns of the military as well as to transform the military into a nonpolitical professional force respectful of human rights. In the case of Sudan, the United States cited the need to implement the peace agreement in southern Sudan and to bring about a democratic transformation in country. All four of the countries were cited by the president as making progress in the elimination of child soldiers (President 2010). But it is by no means clear that the memorandum of justification actually squares with the facts, especially in the case of the DRC, where the recruitment of child soldiers may, in fact, be increasing.

The Transitional Federal Government (TFG) of Somalia also has been designated by the State Department as a recruiter of child soldiers. It continues to receive funds even though sanctions were not waived by the president. Senator Richard J. Durbin of Illinois expressed concern that continued U.S. military assistance was in violation of the CSPA, the CSAA, and the Human Rights Enforcement Act (Durbin 2010). The State Department has said that it has pressured the TFG not to use child soldiers and has taken steps to verify that it does not pay soldiers under 18 years of age (Gettleman 2010; U.S. Department of State 2010b).

The United States does not directly provide funds to Somalia, but it continues to receive indirect aid. In 1992, the United Nations established an arms embargo on Somalia and created a Sanctions Committee to supervise the embargo. However, a number of countries, including the United States, France, and the Russian Federation, have received exemptions from the embargo and continue to supply arms or training to the Somali TFG. This is not direct military assistance; assistance is provided via the

African Union peacekeeping Mission on Somalia (AMISON), with much if it channeled through Uganda, whose forces are directly involved in the peacekeeping mission (U.S. Department of State 2010b). The United States has thereby provided millions of dollars for arms, training, and soldiers salaries to the armed forces of the TFG that are not subject to the sanctions of the CSPA (Amnesty International 2010). In sum, with the exception of Burma, the United States continues to militarily support virtually all the countries that recruit child soldiers that, in theory, are subject to sanctions under U.S. law. Because of this, Human Rights Watch has accused President Obama of essentially nullifying the law (Becker 2010).

To date, no prosecutions and trials have taken place under the CSAA. Like some other laws, the CSAA criminalizes actions that take place outside the United States. It tries to prevent the United States from becoming a refuge for recruiters. A law with similar provisions, the Federal Torture Statute (1994), was used to convict Charles McArther Emmanuel, better known as Chuckie Taylor, a U.S. citizen and son of former Liberian president Charles Taylor. In 2008, a federal jury convicted Chuckie Taylor of torture and conspiracy for his role as commander of the so-called Demon Forces, an antiterrorist unit in Liberia that engaged in terrible acts of torture and widespread human rights abuses. It is likely that at some point, a recruiter of child soldiers will be prosecuted under the CSAA, but the fact that Taylor's 2008 conviction was the first conviction under the 1994 law suggests that prosecutions under the CSAA may not be frequent (U.S. Department of Justice 2008a).

The United States is now is a major participant and shaper of both international and domestic legal structures that target recruiters of child soldiers. But it also true that foreign policy considerations and U.S. national interests have trumped human rights concerns in the enforcement of laws against child recruiters and the states that harbor them. At this point, U.S. law is more a symbol of U.S. attitudes toward the use of child soldiers than it is a serious tool of law enforcement.

The Protection of Child Soldiers: The United States and the Treatment of Child Captives

For the first time in many years, the wars in Iraq and Afghanistan have brought American soldiers face-to-face with child soldiers.

No doubt, many child soldiers have been killed in combat, but a large number have been captured, and this has raised the issue of how captive children should be treated under U.S. law. In 2008, the United States reported that since 2002, it held approximately 2,500 juvenile combatants who were under 18 years of age at the time of their capture. About 2,400 were held in Iraq. Ninety were held in Afghanistan. Eight juveniles between ages 13 and 17 were held at Guantanamo Bay in Cuba. As of April 2008, about 500 juveniles were still being held by the United States in Iraq, although an unknown number had been transferred to Iraqi custody. As of April 2008, approximately 10 juveniles were being held at the Bagram Theater Internment Facility in Afghanistan. Of the Guantanamo Bay detainees, three juveniles under age 16 were transferred back to Afghanistan in January 2004, and three others were sent to their home countries between 2004 and 2006. Two were held for trial under the Military Commissions Act of 2006 (United Nations Committee on the Rights of the Child 2008). In January 2010, the United States reported that it had vastly reduced the number of juveniles held in detention and that it had released or turned over virtually all the juveniles it held in Iraq to the government of Iraq for prosecution. As of December 31, 2009, the United States reported that it held in detention fewer than five individuals under the age of 18 in Iraq and Afghanistan. At Guantanamo Bay, only one former child soldier, Omar Khadr, remains in detention following his sentencing by a U.S. military commission. Khadr was captured at age 15 (U.S. Department of State 2010a).

Rules for the Treatment of Detainees

Recall that the Optional Protocol sets forth clear restrictions on the recruitment and use of child soldiers by both the armed forces of state parties and the armed group of nonstate actors. But it also provides for the protection of child soldiers as victims of war. Article 4 of the Optional Protocol, which applies to nonstate parties, absolutely bans recruiting or using children under 18 years old in hostilities. Under the Optional Protocol, state parties are required to regard the recruitment or use of child soldiers by nonstate actors as a violation of those children's human rights. Article 7 defines such unlawfully recruited child soldiers as victims of war who require rehabilitation and social reintegration.

Here it is important to recall the distinction between human rights law and the laws of war. Remember that while the United

States is a party to the Geneva Conventions of 1949, it is not a party to Additional Protocols I and II of 1977 and is not legally bound by these latter agreements. The Geneva Convention did not consider the issue of child soldiers as a special category. With some exceptions, children who were combatants had the same legal status as adult combatants. Like adults, they can fall into one of two categories: lawful combatants who received the protected status of prisoners of war or unlawful combatants whose actions can be deemed criminal. Lawful combatants are especially privileged. They are entitled to kill other soldiers without being subject to any criminal penalties, although they could be treated as criminals if they committed war crimes, such as killing civilians. Unlawful combatants have no special privileges. They are not legally entitled to take up arms, and if they harm or kill anyone, soldier or civilian, it is a criminal offense.

Children who are unlawful combatants have some minimal but very important protections under Common Article 3 of the 1949 Geneva Conventions. They are protected against "outrages upon personal dignity, in particular humiliating and degrading treatment" and against the "passing of sentences and the carrying out of executions without previous judgment pronounced by a regularly constituted court, affording all the judicial guarantees which are recognized as indispensable by civilized peoples." The Fourth Geneva Convention (Article 68) also protects children who are unlawful combatants from receiving the death penalty. This is the international legal framework for treating child soldiers who are captured. What is the reality in actual combat situations in the real world? How did the U.S. obligation under the Optional Protocol to treat child soldiers as victims of war square with the actual treatment of child soldiers?

Unlawful Combatants and the War against Terror

On September 11, 2001, 19 terrorists belonging to the international terrorist network al-Qaeda, hijacked four commercial airplanes in the United States. Two were crashed into the twin towers of the World Trade Center in New York, one was crashed into the Pentagon, and a fourth, headed toward the U.S. Capitol, was diverted by the bravery of its passengers and crashed into a field in Pennsylvania. In all, about 3,000 people were killed. Fifty-five military personnel died at the Pentagon, but the rest of the victims were civilians. Even if they imagined themselves as being at war with the United States, none of the terrorists were lawful combatants. They were part of no state armed force, and the very nature or their heinous act required that they remain hidden within a civilian population. It would not matter if they had attacked only military personnel. These were individuals who had no right under law to take up arms. All their actions were criminal.

There were a number of ways in which the United States could have responded to this attack, and these were hotly debated in the immediate aftermath of the attack. It could simply have treated the 9/11 hijackers and their coconspirators and terrorist supporters as criminals to be tried within the criminal justice system of the United States. There is strong precedent for this. There have been a significant number of terrorist trials in the United States for acts of terrorism, both before and after 9/11, and the conviction rates have been very high: nearly 91 percent. These cases include the Kenya and Tanzania embassy bombings, the attack on the USS *Cole* in Yemen, and the trial of the so-called twentieth hijacker, Zacharias Moussaoui. The U.S. courts have proven to be powerful tools in dealing with terrorists, which at the same time provide time-tested protections for the rights of defendants (Zabel and Benjamin 2009, 27).

The primary U.S. response, however, was not to use the criminal courts. Instead, on October 7, 2001, the United States launched Operation Enduring Freedom: the war against Afghanistan. Although none of the hijackers came from Afghanistan (most were from Saudi Arabia), the attack was organized by al-Qaeda, whose leader, Osama bin Laden, had found a safe haven in Afghanistan under the protection of the Taliban-led government of the country. In Afghanistan, with the support of the Taliban, al-Qaeda was able to operate training bases and organize a wide variety of military and terrorist activities.

Detaining Child Soldiers

During the course of the war in Afghanistan, a large of people, including children, were detained in a number of places, including the Bagram Detention Center in Afghanistan and the Guantanamo Bay Detention Camp in Cuba. Virtually all detainees were labeled "enemy combatants" by the Bush administration (President 2001). This was a very confusing term. As we have already learned, the laws of war distinguish between lawful combatants (privileged belligerents) and unlawful combatants (unprivileged belligerents), both of whom are deemed enemies. What the Bush administration meant by "enemy combatant" was an unlawful combatant (unprivileged belligerent). But the Bush administration also made two strikingly unusual claims about unlawful combatants. First, the Bush administration lumped together al-Qaeda and the Taliban fighting forces of the government of Afghanistan. Al-Qaeda is a terrorist network, and the members of al-Qaeda were unlawful combatants. But the fighting forces of the Taliban were the military force of a sovereign state, even if that state was aiding and harboring a significant terrorist group.

Like the United States, the country of Afghanistan was and is a signatory to the 1949 Geneva Conventions. By definition, a war between two state parties to the Geneva Conventions in an international armed conflict required the parties to obey all the rules and afford all the protections of the Geneva Conventions. Under the laws of war, captured Taliban fighting under the standards set by the Geneva Convention should ordinarily have been presumptively regarded as lawful combatants and accorded prisoner-of-war status. Unlike al-Qaeda fighters, their actions on the battlefield were not criminal per se.

Instead, the Bush administration characterized Afghanistan as a "failed state" and asserted that the laws of international armed conflict did not apply to the U.S. invasion of Afghanistan and that none of the Taliban fighters would be regarded as true soldiers, that is, lawful combatants entitled to the major protections of the Geneva Conventions. Second, the Bush administration announced that such unlawful combatants would not have even the minimal protections of Common Article 3, the only provision of the Geneva Conventions that was specifically created to provide humane standards for captured unlawful combatants. This was a complete reversal of the usual applications of the laws of the laws of war that captive prisoners are presumed to be lawful combatants unless otherwise shown not to be entitled to prisoner-of-war status. Following Bush's decision, virtually all armed opposition to the U.S. invasion of Afghanistan was regarded as presumptively criminal. Hundreds if not thousands of detainees were held with little or no distinction made as to whether they were lawful combatants, unlawful combatants, or even combatants at all.

The Treatment of Child Soldiers: The Legal Context

A long and complex legal controversy followed President Bush's decision, much of which is outside the scope of this volume. But to understand the situation of child soldiers in the war against terror, we must examine at least a few of the key presidential and executive branch decisions and the legal challenges that were brought to counter them.

Presidential Orders

On November 13, 2001, a few weeks after the invasion of Afghanistan, President Bush issued a presidential order stating that in the light of the al-Qaeda attacks, it would be necessary to take a military approach and use the U.S. armed forces to identify terrorists and their supporters, disrupt their activities, and eliminate their ability to conduct or support further attacks. This response, the president stated, would require individuals to be detained and, if tried, "to be tried for violations of the laws of war and other applicable laws by military tribunals." The order also stated that it would not be practical to "apply the principles of law and the rules of evidence generally recognized in the trial of criminal cases in the United States district courts" (President 2001).

Three months later, on February 2, 2002, the president issued another order declaring that Common Article 3 of the Geneva Convention applied to neither al-Qaeda nor Taliban detainees. These detainees, the president asserted, were not legally entitled to humane treatment. The order further stated that as a matter of policy—but not because of any requirements of international law—the U.S. armed forces would treat detainees humanely but only to the extent humane treatment was appropriate and consistent with military necessity (President 2002). With these presidential orders, the United States set aside and abrogated both the Geneva Conventions and the Optional Protocol from the very beginning of the war against terror. The United States rejected being obligated to meet the most minimal standards of the humane treatment of detainees, stating that it was not bound by the laws of war, nor was it required to provide any of the protections afforded to child soldiers contained in the Optional Protocol. The implication of this position was that the United States did not believe it was required to provide the protections outlined in the Optional Protocol to any child combatant. The president's order thereby opened the door for the widespread commission of war crimes by the United States and its allies in Iraq and Afghanistan.

On March 31, 2002, the Department of Defense issued an order providing for trials before military commissions for persons charged as enemy combatants (U.S. Department of Defense 2002). The military would decide whether an individual was an enemy combatant, and it would be a military tribunal that would put such a person on trial. By fiat, President Bush created a new system of detention and trial that was not bound by the traditional principles of American criminal or military law and in which the humane treatment of prisoners was optional.

Legal Challenges

The new system of detention was soon put to the test by a number of legal challenges. These focused on (1) the procedures by which individuals were classified as unlawful combatants, (2) the constitutionality of setting aside the Geneva Conventions, and (3) the legality of the military commissions established by the president. In the cases of *Hamdi v. Rumsfeld* (542 U.S. 507 [2004]) and *Rasul v. Bush* (542 U.S. 466 [2004]), the U.S. Supreme Court determined that detained individuals had the right to bring a habeas corpus proceeding in U.S. federal court to challenge their detention and classification by the military as enemy combatants (unlawful combatants). The court determined that detainees had the right to due process in challenging their detention and that, if due process was not available to a detainee in the military court, the detainee could turn to the civil courts for help. But the Supreme Court also held that the constitutional standards could be met by a properly constituted military tribunal that gave detainees an appropriate means to challenge their detention.

Shortly after the decisions in *Hamdi* and *Rasul*, the Department of Defense issued an order creating the Combatant Status Review Tribunals (CSRT), which were to be made of three officers of the U.S. armed forces but were not bound by the rules of evidence of ordinary U.S. courts. The tribunals' sole purpose was to make a determination as to whether a person was an enemy combatant, meaning "an individual who was part of or supporting Taliban or al-Qaeda forces, or associated forces that are engaged in hostilities against the United States" (U.S. Department of Defense 2004).

In another key case, *Hamdan v. Rumsfeld* (548 U.S. 557 [2006]), the Supreme Court held that military commissions set up by the Bush administration in 2002 to try detainees could not go forward because their "structures and procedures violate both the Uniform Code of Military Justice and the four Geneva Conventions signed in 1949." Specifically, the ruling asserted that these commissions violated Common Article 3 of the Geneva Conventions. The Court made clear that the government could not walk away from its obligations under the Geneva Conventions. To meet the concerns raised by the Supreme Court, Congress passed the Military Commissions Act of 2006. Despite this act, the Supreme Court ruled in *Boumediene v. Bush* (553 U.S. 723 [2008]) that detainees would still have the right to challenge their detentions in civil court. The Court focused on the probability of errors that might still exist in the initial CSRT's determination as to who was an enemy combatant. The Court stated that "although we make no judgment as to whether the CSRTs, as currently constituted, satisfy due process standards . . . even when all the parties involved in this process act with diligence and in good faith, there is considerable risk of error in the tribunal's findings of fact" (*Boumediene v. Bush* 2008, 56). The Supreme Court's decision allowed the CSRTs to determine who was an unlawful combatant and allowed the military commissions to try enemy combatants for alleged criminal activities, but given the demonstrated history of error in the new system of military justice, the Court upheld the detainees' right to challenge their detention in U.S. federal courts.

In 2009, more than eight years after the invasion of Afghanistan, not a single detainee had yet been tried before a military commission. That year, however, in an attempt to remedy the defects of previous presidential orders and congressional legislation, Congress passed the Military Commissions Act of 2009 to bring the military commissions up to the standards of constitutional law. The new act "establishes procedures governing the use of military commissions to try alien unprivileged enemy belligerents for violations of the law of war and other offenses triable by military commission" (Military Commissions Act, sec. 948b). The law specifically notes the U.S. obligations under the Geneva Conventions and distinguishes between lawful combatants (privileged belligerents) and unlawful combatants (unprivileged belligerents). While it places members of al-Qaeda in the category of unlawful combatants, it does not prejudge the status of other detainees and thereby allows for a factual determination as to whether an individual is a lawful combatant, an unlawful combatant, or a mere civilian. The new law essentially reverses President Bush's order of February 8, 2007, and makes it plain that detainees have the legal right to humane treatment and that subjecting detainees to cruel and inhumane treatment in breach of Common Article 3 of the Geneva Convention is a war crime. The first person to be tried under this act, indeed the first person to be tried by any military court in the war against terror, was Omar Khadr, a child soldier. In 2010, he became the first child soldier to be put on trial in any Western country since World War II.

Putting Child Soldiers on Trial: U.S. Military Commissions

The implications of these decisions can be seen in the cases of two child soldiers who came before U.S. military commissions: Mohammed Jawad and Omar Khadr. Both teenaged boys were captured in Afghanistan. After many years at Guantanamo Bay, Jawad was released from custody and repatriated to Afghanistan. In contrast, Khadr recently pled guilty before the U.S. Military Commission and in a plea bargain was sentenced to eight years in prison with no credit for the time he had been held at Guantanamo Bay.

The Case of Mohammed Jawad: Tortured for Sport

Mohammed Jawad was detained as a child soldier and charged with attempted murder. It was alleged that he threw a hand grenade at a passing American convoy on December 17, 2002. If Jawad were a lawful combatant, he would have been perfectly entitled to throw a hand grenade at a military convoy without criminal penalty. Of course, soldiers in the convoy would also be entitled to kill him as well. It is only because he was regarded as an unlawful combatant that he could be criminally charged.

There was considerable disagreement over Jawad's age, as there are no written records of his birth. His family claims that he was 12 years old when he was detained. A bone scan done almost a year after his detention indicated that he was 18 at the time of the scan, and this would have made him approximately 17 at the time of detention. The evidence of a bone scan is often unreliable, so the best that can be said is that he was somewhere between 12 and 17 when he was detained. Jawad was first arrested by the Afghan police and taken to an Afghan police station to be interrogated. At his interrogation, armed Afghan police officers and officials threatened to kill him and his family if he did not confess to throwing the hand grenade. He allegedly confessed and was turned over to U.S. authorities. Shortly thereafter, he was interrogated at a U.S. military base where he allegedly confirmed his confession. Jawad was transferred to the Bagram Theater Internment Facility in Afghanistan and later transported to Guantanamo Bay, where it is undisputed that he was systematically abused.

The abuse of Jawad took place in the context of the widespread abuse of detainees by the U.S. military in Iraq and Afghanistan and at Guantanamo Bay. The abuses began early in the war against terror and are directly linked to presidential orders rejecting the legal right of detainees to humane treatment. Among the most extreme examples of abuse were the killings of two Afghan detainees, Mullah Habibullah and Dilawar of Yakubi, who were chained and suspended from the ceiling and beaten to death over a five-day period in December 2002 (Jehl 2005). Both the U.S. Army and the U.S. Senate Armed Services Committee confirmed that these two detainee deaths were homicides (Committee on Armed Services 2009).

Reports on the torture and abuse of Dilawar show that he was tormented even as he was dying. He was hauled from his cell at the detention center at Bagram in Afghanistan at around 2:00 A.M. to answer questions about a rocket attack on an American base. An interpreter who was present reported that Dilawar's legs were bouncing uncontrollably in the plastic chair and that his hands were numb because he had been chained by his wrists to the top of his cell for much of the previous four days. When Dilawar asked for a drink of water, one of the two interrogators, Specialist Joshua R. Claus, picked up a large plastic bottle. But Clause first punched a hole in the bottom so that as Dilawar fumbled weakly with the cap, the water poured out over his orange prison scrubs. Clause then grabbed the bottle and began squirting the water forcefully into Dilawar's face. Following that, Claus made the guards try to force Dilawar to his knees, but his legs—which had been beaten by guards for several days—could no longer bend. Dilawar was sent back to his cell and chained to the ceiling. Within a few hours, he was dead (Golden 2005).

Because of widespread public reports of abuse of detainees, the Department of Defense initiated an investigation of the allegations. In 2005, Vice Admiral Albert Church, the navy inspector general, issued a report that investigated cases of substantiated abuse of detainees by military personnel (U.S. Department of Defense 2005). According to the Church Report, the abuses were perpetuated by members of all armed services, including active-duty, reserve, and National Guard personnel. Most abuses took place in Afghanistan and Iraq, with a smaller number taking place at Guantanamo Bay. The report focused on serious abuse, meaning abuse that had the potential to lead to death or grievous bodily harm. These included actions that fractured or dislocated bones, created deep cuts, tore bodily members, or seriously damaged internal organs as well as sexual assaults and threats of death or grievous bodily harm. The report did not cover lesser injuries to detainees, such as black eyes and bloody noses (U.S. Department of Defense 2005, 88–89).

In 2008, the U.S. Department of Justice issued a report of its investigation of FBI involvement in the interrogations of detainees in Afghanistan and Iraq and at Guantanamo Bay. At Guantanamo Bay, FBI agents saw or became aware of a variety of abusive techniques used against detainees, including depriving detainees of food, water, and clothing; exposure to cold and heat; death threats; short shackling to the floor to induce pain and stress; choking; and strangling. One FBI agent observed a female interrogator bending back the thumb of a detainee and grabbing his genitals while the detainee grimaced in pain (U.S. Department of Justice 2008b, 175). The FBI also reported that its agents observed a so-called pep rally where Guantanamo Bay interrogators were told to get as close to the legal limits of torture as possible (U.S. Department of Justice 2008b, 174).

This pattern of abuse was applied to juveniles like Jawad. When he was first transferred to American custody, he was subjected to inhumane and degrading treatment. He was required to remove all his clothing, strip-searched, and forced to pose naked for photographs in front of witnesses. He was blindfolded and hooded and subjected to interrogation techniques designed to "shock" him into the extremely fearful state associated with his initial arrest. For example, while he was blindfolded, interrogators told him to hold on to a water bottle that he believed was actually a bomb that could explode at any moment. Again, he was told that if he ever wanted to see his family, he should cooperate and confess.

When he was transferred to Bagram, the pattern of abuse continued. He arrived at Bagram only a few days after Mullah Habibullah and Dilawar of Yakubi were beaten to death by U.S. forces. At Bagram, he was forced into so-called stress positions, and his interrogators forcibly hooded him, placed him in physical and linguistic isolation, pushed him down stairs, chained him to a wall for prolonged periods, and subjected him to death threats. He was also subjected to sleep deprivation and was so disoriented that he could not tell night from day, and was psychologically pressured by the sounds of screams from other prisoners and rumors of other prisoners being beaten to death.

When Jawad was finally transferred to Guantanamo Bay, he was treated as an adult and housed with adults in violation of the U.S. treaty obligation under the Optional Protocols. Moreover, he never received rehabilitation treatment, special education, or other rights due to him as a juvenile. Instead, military records show that Jawad repeatedly cried and asked for his mother during interrogation and that he fainted and complained of dizziness and stomach pain but was given an IV and forced to go through interrogation. Moreover, a psychological assessment by the Behavioral Science Consultation Team at Guantanamo Bay was undertaken—not for the purpose of treatment, but to learn about and exploit his vulnerabilities for further interrogation.

Among the abuses of detainees cited by both the Church Report and the FBI was the sleep deprivation program dubbed the "Frequent Flyer Program" by interrogators and guards. At Guantanamo Bay, the FBI was briefed on the use of this technique, which was designed to disorient detainees and make them cooperative. The Detainee Incident Management System records at Guantanamo Bay revealed that Mohammed Jawad was subject to this program. According to the records, Jawad was shackled and moved 112 times from cell to cell over a period of two weeks—an average of eight moves a day for two weeks. His abuse had no purpose, and his former military prosecutor described it as "gratuitous mistreatment." As his defense counsel, Major David Frakt, stated, there was no special effort to collect intelligence from Jawad and no belief that he actually had any special intelligence, and no interrogations were undertaken around the times he was being tortured. "The most likely scenario," according to Major Frakt, "is that they simply decided to torture Mr. Jawad for sport" (Frakt 2009, 417). The records also revealed that Jawad tried to kill himself by banging his head repeatedly against his cell wall.

The government's case against Jawad received a major setback on October 28, 2008, when Colonel Stephen Henley, the judge of the military commission set to try Jawad, ruled that the admission of guilt that Jawad allegedly had made to the Afghan police at the time of his detention was obtained by torture. According to the Military Commissions Rules of Evidence, statements obtained by torture cannot be admitted into evidence. As a result, any oral or written statements made by Jawad were suppressed by the court (*United States v. Mohammed Jawad* 2008a). In addition, on November 19, 2008, Henley ruled that statements made later by Jawad to U.S. authorities were inadmissible as evidence as well, as they were also the result of the preceding death threats (*United States v. Mohammed Jawad* 2008b).

Without Jawad's confession, the government would now have to produce witnesses to the events. But the government could not locate such witnesses. Even Jawad's military prosecutor came to doubt whether there actually had ever been a confession in the first place. The prosecutor failed to locate any eyewitnesses who supposedly told U.S. investigators that they saw Jawad threw the grenade. There were also both media accounts and intelligence reports that other Afghans had been arrested for the crime and had confessed. The prosecutor became convinced that the statements attributed to Jawad in his original interrogation had simply been made up by one of the Afghan policemen.

Major Frakt petitioned the U.S. courts for a writ of habeas corpus, asking for an order that Jawed be released from custody. As stated in the petition to the court, Jawad was an Afghan citizen who had been taken into U.S. custody as a teenager in December 2002 on the basis of a false "confession" that officials had obtained from him through torture and illegally removed from his homeland to the U.S. Naval Base at Guantanamo Bay to face an illegal military tribunal for a nonexistent "war crime." At the initial hearing, an exasperated Judge Ellen Segal Huvelle described the government case as "unbelievable." Referring to Jawad's continued detention without any evidence, she stated, "This guy has been there seven years, seven years. He might have been taken there at the age of maybe 12, 13, 14, 15 years old.

I don't know what he is doing there . . . I don't understand your case." She demanded that the government produce any witness to testify that Jawad had thrown a grenade at anyone (*Baca v. Obama* 2009a). No witnesses were ever produced. No one was able to show that Jawad was ever a combatant for any military or terrorist group. On July 30, 2009, Judge Huvell ordered that Jawad be released from detention, that he be treated humanely, and that he be returned to Afghanistan, where he now resides (*Baca v. Obama* 2009b).

Omar Khadr: The First Child Soldier Tried since World War II

Omar Khadr was charged with the "intentional murder by an unlawful combatant" of U.S. Army Sergeant Christopher Speer by throwing a hand grenade at U.S. forces. According to the charges, Khadr was trained by a member of al-Qaeda in the use of small arms and explosives, and he and other al-Qaeda operatives planted improvised explosive devices where U.S. troops were expected to travel. On July 27, 2002, U.S. troops surrounded Khadr and other al-Qaeda members in their compound. In the ensuing firefight, Khadr threw a grenade, killing Sergeant First Class Christopher Speer. In addition to Sergeant Speer, two Afghan Militia Force members accompanying U.S. forces were shot and killed in the firefight, and several other U.S. service members were wounded. Khadr was very badly wounded during the firefight but was treated, hospitalized, and detained as an enemy combatant. Like Mohammed Jawad, Khadr was charged with a number of criminal offenses, including murder, because he was regarded as an unlawful combatant and lacked the combatant's privilege. He was age 15 when he was detained.

According to reports, Khadr's family, particularly his father, Ahmed Said Khadr, was deeply connected with al-Qaeda. An al-Qaeda website praises him as a fighter for the poor. An al-Qaeda news service also featured him in its "Book of 120 Martyrs in Afghanistan." The elder Khadr was born in Egypt, married a Palestinian woman, and came to Canada, where Omar was born. He later returned with Omar to Pakistan, where he became an al-Qaeda commander. He was killed by Pakistani troops in a 2003 firefight. The al-Qaeda website praises him for "tossing his little child [Omar] in the furnace of the battle ("Khadr Patriarch" 2008).

There were no eyewitness who could identify Khadr as having thrown the grenade that killed Sergeant Speer, so much of the case depended on his alleged confession. As in the Jawad case, a key element in Khadr's defense was that his confession was involuntary. It is clear that he was often handled harshly as a detainee, so the key question was whether his confession could be used as evidence against him despite this harsh treatment.

Could Khadr's confession have been used against him if he were an ordinary criminal charged with murder in a U.S. criminal court? Should the same standards used in such courts be applied to criminal cases before a U.S. military commission? The Supreme Court has frequently heard cases dealing with confessions by children and youth. On the whole, the Court has been skeptical of confessions obtained from young people where circumstances suggest the possibility that the child has been psychologically coerced.

The Supreme Court has set aside, as a violation of their due process rights under the U.S. Constitution, confessions by young people who were not allowed access to counsel or parents while being questioned by the police. For example, in *Haley v. Ohio* (332 U.S. 596 [1948]), a 15-year-old boy, convicted of murder on the basis of a signed confession, was detained at midnight and questioned alone for five hours without the support of an attorney or his parents. The Court held the confession inadmissible. The court stated that "when, as here, a mere child—an easy victim of the law—is before us, special care in scrutinizing the record must be used. Age 15 is a tender and difficult age . . . we cannot believe that a lad of tender years is a match for the police in such a contest. He needs counsel and support if he is not to become the victim first of fear, then of panic. He needs someone on whom to lean lest the overpowering presence of the law, as he knows it, crush him."

Likewise, in *Reck v. Pate* (367 U.S. 433 [1961]), a mentally retarded 19-year-old youth with no criminal record was arrested on suspicion of stealing bicycles. After being held virtually incommunicado and interrogated by groups of police officers for nearly four days, sick and faint, inadequately fed, without a hearing, and without the advice of counsel, family, or friends, he confessed to participating in a murder. The Supreme Court held that his confession was involuntary and reversed his conviction.

In *Gallegos v. Colorado* (370 U.S. 49 [1962]), a 14-year-old defendant and another boy assaulted and robbed an elderly man in his hotel room. Gallegos was picked up 12 days later by police and admitted the assault and robbery, but after the victim died, Gallegos was charged with first-degree murder. He was later found guilty of murder on the basis of the formal confession he signed before the victim died. At the time he signed the confession, he had been held for five days without seeing a lawyer, parent, or other friendly adult, even though his mother had attempted to see him. The Supreme Court reversed his conviction. These and numerous other cases make clear that the Supreme Court holds that special care must be taken when it comes to children and youth to ensure that confessions are not psychologically coerced.

Clearly, these constitutional standards were not applied to Khadr. Khadr made numerous allegations that he was tortured and subjected to cruel, inhumane, and degrading treatment throughout the course of his capture and ultimate detention at Guantanamo Bay. Among the most serious of his charges were that he was threatened with rape and sexual violence and that he was told that uncooperative detainees are sent to Afghanistan to be raped and that "they like small boys in Afghanistan." In a different interrogation, Khadr also alleged that he was told that someone identified as "Soldier Number 9" would be sent to interrogate and rape him or that he would be sent to Egypt, Syria, Jordan, or Israel to be raped (*United States v. Omar Ahmed Khadr* 2010a).

During his detention at Bagram, Khadr was alleged to have confessed to throwing the hand grenade that killed Sergeant Speer as well as to helping build and plant improvised explosive devices (IEDs). The principal issue prior to trial was whether Khadr's admissions were obtained through torture or other forms of abuse. Some of Khadr's claims of having been tortured or abused were corroborated at his pretrial hearing in May 2010. Particularly important was the testimony of Interrogator No. 1, who was later identified as John Claus, the same interrogator who was involved in the beating death of Dilawar. Claus's interrogation of Khadr took place in the summer of 2002 after Khadr had been released from a military hospital. Claus admitted that he had interrogated the badly wounded Khadr, who was 15 years old at the time, and that he had told Khadr a fictitious tale of an Afghan kid who was sent to an American prison where he was gang-raped and died. Claus testified, "We'd tell him about this Afghan who gets sent to an American prison and there's a bunch of big black guys and big Nazis." He said that he described the Afghan kid as "a poor little kid . . . away from home, kind of isolated." Claus went on to tell Khadr that he had sent the kid to an American prison because he was disappointed in his truthfulness and that when the American prisoners discovered that the Afghan kid was a Muslim, they raped him in their rage over the September 11, 2001, attacks (Rosenberg 2010a).

Another of Khadr's allegations was corroborated by a former army combat medic, identified as M, who treated Khadr. M testified that he found Khadr chained by the arms to the door of a five-square-foot cage at a U.S. lockup in Afghanistan, hooded and weeping. He also testified that Khadr's wrists were chained just above eye level although with enough slack to allow his feet to touch the floor. He did not remember whether Khadr's feet were shackled. When he pulled the hood from Khadr's head, the teenager was in tears (Rosenberg 2010b).

Despite evidence of abuse, the military judge ruled that statements made by Khadr during his detention admitting his involvement were not the product of torture and/or abuse and were therefore voluntary (*United States v. Omar Ahmed Khadr* 2010b). The judge's ruling did not specifically reject the truthfulness of the witnesses' testimony but rather ruled that whatever abuse Khadr may have suffered was unrelated to his admissions of involvement in Sergeant Speer's death. Following this ruling, both the government and the defense began to speak about a plea bargain, something that Khadr had always previously rejected.

The U.S. government had some incentive to engage in a plea bargain. First of all, it did not want to be the first Western country in modern history to put a former child soldier on trial. There had been considerable international pressure for the United States to live up to its treaty obligations under the Optional Protocol, including the requirement that persons under the age of 18 be given special protection. Neither Jawad nor Khadr had ever received these required protections and instead had been subject to the same systematic abuses as adult detainees.

The United Nations tried to remind the United States of its treaty obligations. In a letter to the military commissions, Radhika Coomaraswamy, the special representative of the secretary-general for children in armed conflict, argued that the Khadr case is a "classic child soldier narrative" in which a child is recruited by the adults of unscrupulous groups to fight in battles that the child barely understands. She argued that Khadr's father was instrumental in the abuse and harm done to him. Coomaraswamy also pointed out that no child could be tried before the ICC and that prosecutors of the Special Court for Sierra Leone had also declined to try children under 18 years old. She insisted that the United States, as a party to the Optional Protocol, was required to support child soldiers in their reintegration into their families and communities (United Nations 2010).

There were other pressures on the U.S. government as well. Khadr's family had intermittently lived in Canada, and Khadr was a Canadian citizen. Although Canada was given notice of Khadr's citizenship after his detainment, it refused originally to intervene in the matter. As a result, Khadr was interrogated; denied access to Canadian consular officials, to counsel, or to his family; and faced a possible sentence of death. Under pressure from Canada, however, Khadr's case was not designated a capital case. Canadian Department of Foreign Affairs and International Trade officials also reported that Khadr had been subject to systematic sleep deprivation under the frequent-flyer program. Ultimately, on April 23, 2009, the Canadian Supreme Court ruled that Khadr had being illegally detained at Guantanamo Bay, that he had been tortured and deprived of legal counsel, and that the government of Canada should seek his repatriation to Canada (*Khadr v. The Prime Minister of Canada* 2009).

On October 13, 2010, Khadr entered into a plea bargain with military prosecutors (*United States v. Omar Ahmed Khadr* 2010c). As part of his guilty plea, Khadr admitted to all the crimes he was charged with as an unlawful combatant (*United States v. Omar Ahmed Khadr* 2010d). He stipulated that he was an unprivileged enemy belligerent and that at no time did he have any legal basis to commit any warlike acts. He stated that he was sent by his father at age 15 to serve as a translator for known members of al-Qaeda and the Libyan Islamic Fighting Group associated with al-Qaeda in Afghanistan. There he had been trained in the use of rocket-propelled grenades, various assault rifles, pistols, grenades, and explosives and received personal terrorist training from a member of al-Qaeda. Khadr indicated that his father made statements that the training was to be used in attacks against the Jews. Khadr admitted that he shared the goal of targeting and killing all Americans, whether civilian or military, anywhere they can be found.

Khadr agreed that he had joined a terrorist cell that constructed and planted IEDs to be used in an effort to kill U.S. and coalition forces, personally transformed a dozen land mines into IEDs, and planted IEDs on a road traveled by a U.S. military convoy. While working with the al-Qaeda explosives cell, one of his duties was to collect information on U.S. forces in order to determine where to plant IEDs to maximize the likelihood of death and destruction. On at least one occasion, he spied on U.S. troop movements near the airport in Khowst, Afghanistan. Khadr admitted that he did not wear a uniform and attempted to blend in with the civilian population in order to gain as much actionable intelligence as possible.

Khadr admitted that on July 27, 2002, he was at a compound with the al-Qaeda cell when they learned that the Americans were coming and that he stayed to fight the Americans. When U.S. forces arrived at the compound and asked the occupants, including Khadr, to come outside the compound to talk, they refused to do so or to speak to the U.S. forces. When two members of the accompanying Afghan Military Forces entered the compound to ask the occupants to come out and speak, individuals in the house opened fire, instantly killing both Afghan soldiers. A four-hour firefight ensued between U.S. soldiers and the al-Qaeda cell.

Khadr agreed that U.S. forces gave the occupants inside the compound multiple chances to surrender and that at one point the women and children in the compound exited the compound and U.S. forces escorted them to safety. Khadr and the others made a pact that they would rather die fighting than be captured, and he was given an AK-47 Kalashnikov and a pistol and took up a fighting position within the compound. Close air support was called in by the U.S. forces. A-10s and Apache attack helicopters dropped bombs (including two 500-pound bombs) and fired thousands of rounds of ammunition into the compound. During the bombing, Khadr was injured in the eyes and leg by shrapnel. After the U.S. forces believed that the firefight was over, they began clearing the compound under the belief that everyone inside the compound had been killed. After entering the compound, the unit was fired on by someone in the compound whom they killed. At that point, Khadr admitted that he had thrown a Russian F-1 grenade in the vicinity of the talking soldiers with the intent of killing or injuring as many Americans as he could. The grenade killed Sergeant Speer, and a U.S. Special Forces soldier then shot Khadr twice in the torso.

It is worth noting that in his stipulation, which is part of his plea bargain, Khadr admitted knowledge of military strategy and details of the attack on the compound, something that it is unlikely that he would have personally known. These details include who called in reinforcements, the number and weight of the bombs dropped, and what the U.S. forces "believed" about the firefight being over.

Khadr agreed to a prison sentence of eight years with no credit given for his detention since 2002. The agreement provided that the first of these years would be spent in U.S. custody but that, if so requested by the Canadian government, the remaining seven years could be spent in Canada. Under the procedural rules of the Military Commission, even after Khadr's guilty plea was entered, the military jury deliberated his sentence without knowledge of the plea bargain. The jury had no knowledge that Khadr would be entitled to the lesser of two sentences: the eight years agreed to or the one handed down by the jury. Before beginning their deliberations, the jurors were informed that Khadr had pled guilty to five war crimes, including throwing the hand grenade that killed Sergeant Speer. The prosecution asked for a sentence of 25 years, and the defense asked that he be repatriated to Canada. On October 31, 2010, the military jury sentenced him to 40 years in prison. In the humanitarian and human rights community, the sentence has been derided as "stunningly punitive" (Rosenberg 2010c). Khadr began serving the first year of his eight-year sentence at Guantanamo Bay in January 2010. Under an agreement with Canada after serving the first year of his sentence in United States custody he may be able to serve the remainder in Canada.

Conclusion

The United States has a reputation as a supporter of human rights and a proponent of abolishing the use of child soldiers. It has a long history of using its power as a member of the world community to promote the goals of ending the use of child soldiers and advocating the humane treatment of children. But this broad idealism has been sorely tested in practice. It is not reflected in the record of the hard facts of its foreign policy or in its treatment of child soldiers during the war on terror. When the United States has had to actually come to grips with the reality of child soldiers, thus far it has set aside its ideals and treaty commitments.

References

Amnesty International. 2010. *Somalia International Military and Policing Assistance Should Be Renewed.* London: Amnesty International.

Baca v. Obama. 2009a. Transcript of Hearing before the Honorable Ellen Segal Huvelle, United States District Court Judge, Civil Case No. 05-2385, July 16. http://www.aclu.org/pdfs/safefree/jawad _transcriptofhearing.pdf.

Baca v. Obama. 2009b. Order Granting Petition of Habeas Corpus., Civil Case No. 05-2385. July 30. http://documents.nytimes.com/ jawad-s-hearing-in-federal-district-court#p=1.

Becker, Jo. 2010. "The US Blinks and Children Will Suffer," *Huffington Post*, November 9. http://www.hrw.org/en/news/2010/11/10/ us-blinks-and-children-will-suffer. Accessed January 8, 2010.

Child Soldier Accountability Act. 2008. Public Law No. 110-340. U.S. Statutes at Large 122:3733

Child Soldier Prevention Act. 2008. Title IV of the *William Wilberforce Trafficking Victims Protection Act*. Public Law 110-457. U.S. Statutes at Large 122:5044.

Coalition to Stop the Use of Child Soldiers. 2008. *Global Report*. http:// www.childsoldiersglobalreport.org/content/united-states-america.

Committee on Armed Services. 2009. *Inquiry into the Treatment of Detainees in US Custody*. Washington, DC: U.S. Senate. http://armed-services.senate .gov/Publications/Detainee%20Report%20Final_April%2022%202009.pdf.

Doebbler, Curtis F. J. 2004. *International Human Rights Law*. Vol. 1. Washington, DC: CD Publishing.

Durbin, Dick. 2010. "Letter to Secretary of State Hilary Clinton." July 16. http://durbin.senate.gov/showRelease.cfm?releaseId=325712. Accessed December 1, 2010.

Federal Torture Statute. 1994. Public Law 103-236. U.S. Statutes at Large 108: 463. 994, 108.

Frakt, David R. 2009. "Closing Argument at Guantanamo: The Torture of Mohammed Jawad." *Harvard Human Rights Journal* 22: 401–23.

Gettleman, Jeffrey. 2010. "U.N. Voices Concern on Child Soldiers in Somalia," *New York Times*, June 1.

Golden, Tim. 2005. "In U.S. Report, Brutal Details of 2 Afghan Inmates' Deaths." *New York Times*, May 20. http://www.nytimes.com/2005/05/ 20/international/asia/20abuse.html?pagewanted=1&_r=1.

Human Rights Enforcement Act. 2009. Public Law 111-122. U.S. Statutes as Large 123: 3480.

Human Rights Watch. 2009. *Congressional Testimony on the Law of the Land: U.S. Implementation of Human Rights Treaties*. http://www.hrw.org/en/ news/2009/12/15/congressional-testimony-law-land-us-implementation -human-rights-treaties.

Jehl, Douglas. 2005. "Army Details Scale of Abuse of Prisoners in an Afghan Jail." *New York Times*, March 12. http://www.nytimes.com/2005/03/12/politics/12detain.html.

"Khadr Patriarch Disliked Canada, Says al-Qaeda Biography." 2008. CBC News. February 7. http://www.cbc.ca/world/story/2008/02/07/khadr-bio.html.

Khadr v. The Prime Minister of Canada. 2009. (2009 FC 405). Reasons for Judgment and Judgment. http://www.bccla.org/othercontent/09Khadrdecision.pdf.

Military Commissions Act of 2006. Public Law No. 109-366. U.S. Statutes at Large 120 (2006): 2600.

National Defense Authorization Act Title XVII. Public Law 111-84, U.S. Statutes at Large 123 (2009): 2190.

President. 2001. "Detention, Treatment, and Trial of Certain Non-Citizens in the War against Terrorism." Military Order of November 13, 2001. *Federal Register* 66 (November 16): 57833–36. http://federalregister.gov/a/01-28904.

President. 2002. "Human Treatment of al Qaeda and Taliban Detainees." Memorandum. February 7. http://www.dod.mil/pubs/foi/detainees/dia_previous_releases/fourth_release/DIAfourth_release.pdf.

President. 2010. "Presidential Determination with Respect to Section 4040 (c) of the Child Soldier Prevention Act of 2008, No. 2011-4." Determination. *Federal Register* 75 (October 25): 75855–63. http://www.gpo.gov/fdsys/pkg/FR-2010-12-07/pdf/2010-30828.pdf.

Rosenberg, Carol. 2010a. "Medic: I Saw Omar Khadr Shackled as Punishment." *Miami Herald*, May 3. http://www.miamiherald.com/2010/05/03/1610812/medic-i-saw-omar-khadr-shackled.html #ixzz1ClEDDkLk.

Rosenberg, Carol. 2010b. "Interrogator Says Khadr Was Told He'd Likely Be Raped in U.S." *Miami Herald*, May 6. http://www.miamiherald.com/2010/05/06/1616825/interrogator-says-he-told-detainee.html.

Rosenberg, Carol. 2010c. "Despite 40-Year Sentence, Khadr Likely to Go Home in a Year." *Miami Herald*, October 31. http://www.miamiherald.com/2010/10/31/v-fullstory/1931820/despite-40-year-sentence-khadr.html#storyBody.

United Nations. 2010. "Letter from Radhika Coomaraswamy, the Special Representative of the Secretary General for Children in Armed Conflict to the Members of the Military Commissions, October 27. 2010." http://www.cbc.ca/news/pdf/omar-khadr-letter.pdf.

United Nations Committee on the Rights of the Child. 2008. *Written Replies by the Government of the United States of America concerning the List of Issues re the Optional Protocol.* CRC.C.OPAC.USA.Q.1.Add.1.Rev.1, 2008. http://www2.ohchr.org/english/bodies/crc/docs/ AdvanceVersions/CRC.C.OPAC.USA.Q.1.Add.1.Rev.1.pdf.

United States. 2000. Optional Protocol to the Convention on the Rights of the Child on the Involvement of Children in Armed Conflict. May 25. Treaties and Other International Acts Series. 13094. http://www.state .gov/s/l/treaty/tias/2000/126277.htm.

United States. 2002. U.S. Declarations and Understandings, Optional Protocol to the Convention on the Rights of the Child on the Involvement of Children in Armed Conflict. http://www.icrc.org/ihl.nsf/a/ cbd3f057edc894954125693d0047efe6?opendocument. Accessed February 7, 2011.

United States v. Mohammed Jawad. 2008a. Ruling on Defense Motion to Suppress Out of Court Statements of the Accused to Afghan Authorities. October 28. .http://www.defenselink.mil/news/d20081104JawadD 022Suppress.pdf.

United States v. Mohammed Jawad. 2008b. Ruling on Defense Motion to Suppress Out of Court Statements Made by the Accused while in U.S. Custody. November 19. http://www.defenselink.mil/news/d20081223 Jawadexhibitsa-h.pdf.

United States v. Omar Ahmed Khadr. 2007. "Charge Sheet" *United States v. Omar Ahmed Khadr.* April 5. http://www.defense.gov/news/Apr2007/ Khadrreferral.pdf.

United States v. Omar Ahmed Khadr. 2010a.Supplemental Defense Motion. March 8. http://www.defense.gov/news/Khadr_D-094.pdf.

United States v. Omar Ahmed Khadr. 2010b. Ruling on Defense Suppression Motion. August 17.

http://www.defense.gov/news/D94-D111.pdf.

United States v. Omar Ahmed Khadr. 2010c. "Offer for Pretrial Agreement." October 13. http://www.defense.gov/news/Khadr%20Convening% 20Authority%20Pretrial%20Agreement%20AE%20341%2013%20Oct% 202010%20%28redacted%29.pdf.

United States v. Omar Ahmed Khadr. 2010d. "Stipulation of Fact." October 13. http://media.miamiherald.com/smedia/2010/10/26/19/ stip2.source.prod_affiliate.56.pdf.

U.S. Department of Defense. 2002. *Military Commission Order No. 1.* March 31. http://www.defense.gov/news/Mar2002/d20020321ord.pdf.

U.S. Department of Defense. 2004. *Order Establishing Combat Status Review Panel.* July 7. http://www.globalsecurity.org/security/library/policy/ dod/d20040707review.pdf.

U.S. Department of Defense. 2005. *Review of Department of Defense Detention Operations and Detainee Interrogation Techniques (Church Report).* March 3. http://www.cfr.org/publication/11092/church_report.html.

U.S. Department of Justice. 2008a. "Roy Belfast Jr. A/K/A Chuckie Taylor Convicted on Torture Charges Conviction Is First under Torture Statute." October 30. http://www.justice.gov/opa/pr/2008/October/08-crm-971.html.

U.S. Department of Justice. 2008b. *A Review of the FBI's Involvement in and Observations of Detainee Interrogations in Guantanamo Bay, Afghanistan, and Iraq.* http://www.justice.gov/oig/special/s0805/final.pdf.

U.S. Department of State. 2010a. *Periodic Report of the United States.* January 22. http://www.state.gov/documents/organization/135988.pdf.

U.S. Department of State. 2010b. *2009 Human Rights Reports: Somalia.* March 11. http://www.state.gov/g/drl/rls/hrrpt/2009/af/135976.htm.

U.S. Department of State. 2010c. "U.S. Policy in Somalia—No Direct Support for Somali Government Military Operations." http://www.hoa.africom.mil/getArticle.asp?art=4154.

Zabel, Richard B., and James J. Benjamin. 2009. *In Pursuit of Justice: Prosecuting Terrorism Cases in the Federal Courts.* New York: Human Rights First.

4

Chronology

1429   Joan of Arc, age 17, leads French armies to victory over the English in Orleans.

1775–1783   American Revolution. Many youngsters who would today be considered child soldiers are involved in the American Revolution on both sides of the conflict. Most were volunteers. One of the most highly regarded descriptions of army life during the American Revolution was written by Joseph Martin Plumb, who enlisted at age 15.

1776–1783   More than 11,000 American rebel prisoners, men and boys, some as young as age 12, die in British prison ships in Wallabout Bay, Brooklyn.

1777   George Washington's troops, including many boy soldiers, spend the terrible winter in Valley Forge, Pennsylvania.

1780   Andrew Jackson, the seventh president of the United States, joins the armed forces of the American Revolution at age 13. Both of Jackson's brothers, one only slightly older than he, died during the war, as did his mother. By the end of the war, Jackson was an orphan. Jackson's service and bravery as a young soldier in the revolution was a central part of his presidential campaigns.

1798   Giacomo Casabianca, age 12, is killed during the Battle of the Nile on the French flagship *Orient*. His death was immortalized in the nineteenth-century poem *Casabianca* by British poet Felicia Dorothea Hemans. The poem's first lines, "The Boy Stood on the Burning Deck...,": was recited and later satirized by generations of American and British schoolchildren.

1812   The War of 1812 continues the tradition of large numbers of youngsters serving in the local militia forces that made up the bulk of American armed forces.

1857   Thomas Flynn, age 15, displays conspicuous gallantry in battle during the Indian Rebellion (also known as India's First War of Independence), for which he was later awarded the Victoria Cross, Great Britain's highest military decoration for valor.

1860   Andrew Fitzgibbon, age 15, demonstrates bravery in battle during the Second Opium War, for which he was later awarded the Victoria Cross.

1861   Luther Ladd, age 17, is killed in the secessionist riots in Baltimore on April 19, 1861, and said to be the first Union soldier killed in the Civil War. Thousands of mourners attend his funeral in Lowell, Massachusetts, where he is hailed as the "martyr that fell as a sacrifice for his country."

           Clarence Mackenzie from Brooklyn, New York, known as the "The Little Drummer Boy," is killed at age 12 in Annapolis. As with Luther Ladd, his funeral attracts thousands of mourners devoted to the cause of abolition. On his tomb is engraved "This young life was the first offering from Kings County in the War of the Rebellion."

1861–1865   U.S. Civil War. In the war, thousands of youngsters between ages 9 and 17 join the ranks of both the

Union and the Confederate forces despite the official enlistment age of 18.

1862 John Cook, age 15, is awarded the Congressional Medal of Honor for service as a cannoneer under enemy fire in the Civil War.

Julius Langbein is awarded the Congressional Medal of Honor for heroic action under fire at Camden, North Carolina, at age 15.

George Hollat is awarded the Congressional Medal of Honor at age 16 for heroic action aboard the USS *Varuna* in 1862.

Oscar Peck is awarded the Congressional Medal of Honor for heroic action aboard the USS *Varuna* at age 14.

1863 John Lincoln Clem, the 12-year-old "Drummer Boy of Chickamauga," becomes the youngest noncommissioned officer in the U.S. Army.

The Lieber Code, also known as *Instructions for the Government of Armies of the United States in the Field*, provides an early codification of the laws of war.

William "Willie" Johnston, age 13, a drummer boy of the 3rd Vermont Infantry, is awarded the Congressional Medal of Honor for bravery in battle when he was 11.

Orion P. Howe is awarded the Congressional Medal of Honor for heroic action at age 14 at the siege of Vicksburg, Mississippi.

John Kountz enlists at age 14 and is awarded the Congressional Medal of Honor for heroic action at age 16 in the battle of Missionary Ridge.

1864 James Machon, aged 16, is awarded the Congressional Medal of Honor for service on the USS *Brooklyn* during successful attacks against Fort

1864 (*cont.*)	Morgan, rebel gunboats, and the warship *Tennessee* in Mobile Bay, Alabama, on August 5, 1864.

Robinson Barr Murphy enlisted at age 13 as an orderly. He is awarded the Congressional Medal of Honor for heroic action under fire at age 15, when he led two regiments into battle near Atlanta.

James Snedden, age 15, is awarded the Congressional Medal of Honor for heroic action under fire at Piedmont, Virginia.

Duncan Gordon Boyes, age 17, is awarded Great Britain's Victoria Cross for gallantry in the face of the enemy during the British Shimonoseki Expedition in Japan in 1864.

John Angling, age 15, cabin boy aboard the USS *Pontoosuc*, is awarded the Congressional Medal of Honor for gallantry, skill, and courage while under fire.

1865   Julian Scott is awarded the Congressional Medal of Honor for heroic action under fire when he was age 15 at the Battle at Lee's Mill, Virginia, in 1862. His younger brother also enlisted at age 13.

William Horsfall is awarded the Congressional Medal of Honor for heroic action under fire at age 15 during the siege of Corinth, Mississippi.

1866   William Magee is awarded Congressional Medal of Honor for heroic action under fire at Murfreesboro, Tennessee, in 1864 at age 15.

1899   Hague Convention of 1899 concerning the Laws of War. The 1899 Convention is an early codification of the laws of war by Western powers.

1907   Hague Convention of 1907 concerning the Laws of War furthers the work of the 1899 Convention in establishing international laws of war.

1914–1918 World War I. In the British army, some 250,000 soldiers were underage, and about 55 percent of these were killed or wounded during the war. Underage enlistment was at its highest in the beginning of the war, when Britain relied on a volunteer army in which about 10 to 15 percent of the army was underage.

1916 Abraham (Aby) Bevistein, age 16, is executed for desertion by the British army. Like many others, he probably suffered from shell shock but was executed to set an example.

John Travers Cornwall of the Royal Navy is killed at age 16 the Battle of Jutland and awarded the Victoria Cross. Cornwall's funeral in London drew thousands of mourners, including schoolchildren and Boy Scouts. He was honored as an example of devotion to duty and widely acclaimed throughout the British Empire.

1919–1920 Mexican Revolution. A great number of women and girls associated with the Mexican revolutionary armies serve as *soldaderas*, who sometimes fought as combatants but were usually in support roles as cooks, nurses, and other service providers. Many of the women and girls, however, served as actual female combatants.

1922 Hitler Youth founded as a Nazi paramilitary organization for boys ages 14 to 18 in Germany. By 1944, the Hitler Youth is supplying the German Volkssturm, or "People's Army," with boys as young as 16. By 1945, 12-year-olds are being conscripted.

1926 The Slavery Convention is passed as an international treaty under the League of Nations, which resolves to eliminate slavery "in all its forms." This language is later applied to the forced use of children as soldiers.

1927 Moshe Dayan, age 14, joins the Jewish militia known as the Haganah in Mandatory Palestine. Dayan became one of the most important military leaders in modern Israel.

1939–1945   World War II. With some exceptions, most national armed forces during the war do not routinely recruit many child soldiers. Nevertheless, children are a regular part of the partisan armed groups across Europe that fight the Nazi occupation and German-backed regimes in eastern and western Europe.

1942   Jack Lucas, age 14, enlists in the U.S. Marine Corps by forging his mother's signature to an enlistment waiver. At age 17, he becomes the youngest marine ever to win the Congressional Medal of Honor.

Audie Murphy, age 17, enlists in the U.S. Army by altering his birth certificate. He became the most highly decorated soldier in the history of the United States.

1943   R. V. Steed, galley boy on the SS *Empire Morn*. At age 14, he becomes the youngest British sailor killed in World War II.

12th SS Panzer Division Hitlerjugend, an armor infantry unit drawn from the Hitler Youth, is deployed against British and Canadian forces in the Battle of Normandy in World War II.

The Warsaw Ghetto Uprising against the Germans is led by Jewish socialist and Zionist youth movements. Jewish youth are the driving force behind Jewish resistance to the Germans in eastern Europe.

1944   Yasser Arafat, age 15, begins to organize the paramilitary force "Storm Troops of Arab Liberation" in Gaza. Arafat went on to lead the Palestine Liberation Organization and became president of the Palestinian National Authority.

The Warsaw Ghetto Uprising, the Polish uprising against the Germans, includes many Boy Scouts and other children. After the war, a monument, the *Little Partisan*, was erected in Warsaw to honor the children who fought and were killed in the uprising.

1945   United Nations established. Founded at the end of World War II as a replacement for the League of Nations, one of its major missions is to prevent the outbreak of war and achieve world peace.

Insurgencies in Burma (Myanmar) break out, beginning the world's longest civil war.

1948   Formation of the Myanmar Armed Forces, the national armed forces of Burma, officially known as Tatmadaw-Kyi.

1949   The Geneva Conventions. These Conventions, codifying the laws of war, do not mention child soldiers, but they put into effect many legal protections for children during wartime.

In Burma, the Karen National Liberation Army, the military arm of the Karen National Union, is formed. It has been at war against the Burmese government to achieve the self-determination of the Karen people of Burma.

1950   United Nations High Commissioner for Refugees is established to deal with the refugee issues arising out of World War II. Its mission soon expands, and it has responsibility for many refugees, including former child soldiers.

1951   In 1951, the United Karenni States Independence Army (UKSIA) begins fighting to secede from Burma. (In 1974, the UKSIA became the Karenni Army.)

Convention Relating to the Status of Refugees.

1952–1960 Many children serve in the Mau Mau Rebellion, the attempt to forcibly end British colonial rule in Kenya.

1960   The Armed Forces of the Democratic Republic of Congo (Forces Armées de la République Démocratique du Congo) is founded as the state military force of the Democratic Republic of the Congo.

1960 (*cont.*)	Chadian opposition groups emerge in neighboring Darfur, Sudan.
1961	The Kachin Independence Army of Burma, the military wing of the Kachin Independence Organization, is formed. It has been fighting for the independence or ethnic autonomy of the Kachin.
	The Republic of Sierra Leone Armed Forces (Sierra Leone army) is formed after Sierra Leone gains independence from the British.
1961–1991	Eritrean War of Independence. Involves many child soldiers.
1964	National Liberation Army (Ejército de Liberación Nacional) is founded as a rebel group in Colombia.
	The Revolutionary Armed Forces of Colombia–People's Army (Fuerzas Armadas Revolucionarias de Colombia), also known as FARC, is formed as a revolutionary guerrilla organization involved in Colombia.
	The Shan State Army is formed to resist the military government of Burma. It later split into the Shan State Army North and the Shan State Army South. The latter remains an opposition rebel group.
1964–1975	Mozambique War of Independence. Involves many child soldiers.
1964– present	Armed conflict in Colombia.
1967–1970	War in Biafra, or the Nigerian Civil War.
	Popular Front for the Liberation of Palestine is formed as a terrorist organization.
1967– present	Naxalite-Maoist Insurgency in India.

1969   Convention Governing the Specific Aspects of the Refugee Problem in Africa.

New People's Army, the armed wing of the Communist Party of the Philippines, forms and brings a "People's War" against the government of the Philippines.

1969– present   Philippine Insurgency.

1973   International Labour Organization Convention 138 concerning Minimum Age for Admission to Employment sets the minimum age for admission to any type of employment or work that is likely to jeopardize the health, safety, or morals of young persons at age 18.

1974   Kareni Army formed in Burma, seeking to establish an independent Kareni state.

1975   Hezb-i-Islami, an Islamist armed group in Afghanistan, is formed out of the Muslim Youth organization in Kabul.

1976   The Liberation Tigers of Tamil Eelam, known as the LTTE or the Tamil Tigers, is formed as a armed separatist militant organization in northern Sri Lanka. It fights an unsuccessful war for an independent state in Sri Lanka for the Tamil people, which develops into the Sri Lankan Civil War (1983–2009). The Tamil Tigers were defeated by the Sri Lankan military in 2009.

1977   Geneva Protocol I Additional to the Geneva Conventions of 12 August 1949, and Relating to the Protection of Victims of International Armed Conflicts.

Geneva Protocol II Additional to the Geneva Conventions of 12 August 1949, and Relating to the Protection of Victims of Non-International Armed Conflicts.

The Moro Islamic Liberation Front fighting against the government of the Philippines is founded.

1978	Human Rights Watch is founded.
	Kareni National People's Liberation Front is formed in Burma.
1979	Convention on the Elimination of All Forms of Discrimination against Women.
	The Islamic Jihad Movement in Palestine, or Palestinian Islamic Jihad, is formed as a terrorist group.
1980	Indigenous Miskito Indians, with many child recruits, begin guerilla war against the Sandinista regime in Nicaragua.
1981	The Moro Islamic Liberation Front, an Islamic insurgent group fighting against the government of the Philippines, is formed.
1983	The Sudan People's Liberation Army is formed as the armed wing of the Sudan People's Liberation Movement in southern Sudan, fighting in the Second Sudanese Civil War against the Sudanese government.
1983–2005	Second Sudanese Civil War and the Lost Boys of Sudan. The Lost Boys of Sudan include more than 20,000 Dinka and Nuer boys in southern Sudan who have been displaced by the war. Many become child soldiers.
1983–2009	Sri Lanka Civil War.
1987	Hamas ("Islamic Resistance Movement") terrorist organization is formed in the Gaza Strip, along with its military wing, the Izz ad-Din al-Qassam Brigades.
1987– present	Lord's Resistance Army insurgency in Uganda, the Central African Republic, Sudan, and Congo. The Lord's Resistance Army is an armed religious and military group. It was engaged in armed conflict with Uganda until 2007 and is also active as an armed group in southern Sudan, the Central African

Republic, and the Democratic Republic of the Congo. It is notorious for the abduction of children and their use as child soldiers.

1988   Al-Qaeda, the Sunni Islamist militant and terrorist group, is founded by Osama bin Laden.

1989   Convention of the Rights of the Child.

The National Patriotic Front of Liberia, a rebel group, initiates and participates in the First Liberian Civil War (1989–1996).

The Myanmar National Democratic Alliance Army, a rebel army in northeastern Burma, is formed.

The United Wa State Army, the largest ethnic rebel army in Burma, is formed.

1989–1996   First Liberian Civil War.

1991   The Civil Defense Forces of Sierra Leone, a paramilitary force supporting the government of Sierra Leone during the Sierra Leone Civil War, is formed. Some of its key leaders are convicted of recruiting child soldiers by the Sierra Leone Special Court.

The Revolutionary United Front, the rebel army defeated in the Sierra Leone Civil War, is formed. Some of its key leaders are later convicted of recruiting child soldiers by the Sierra Leone Special Court.

Abu Sayyaf, also known as al-Harakat al-Islamiyya, an Islamic separatist organization, begins insurgency in southern Philippines.

Ishmael Beah is recruited into the Sierra Leone army at age 13. His book *A Long Way Gone* is an important first-hand account of the experience of being a child soldier.

1991–2002   Sierra Leone Civil War. All parties in the civil war recruit child soldiers.

1991–present	Somalia Civil War.
1993	Statute of the International Criminal Tribunal for the former Yugoslavia.

The Liberians United for Reconciliation and Democracy emerges as a rebel group and seeks the overthrow of President Charles Taylor during the Second Liberian Civil War.

1994	Emergence of the Haqqani network, an independent insurgent group in Afghanistan and Pakistan closely allied with the Taliban.

Statute of the International Criminal Tribunal for Rwanda.

Democratic Karen Buddhist Army forms in Burma, breaking away from the Karen National Liberation Army.

Rwandan Genocide. The mass murder of an estimated 800,000 people (mostly Tutsi) leads to further armed conflict in the neighboring Democratic Republic of the Congo.

The Democratic Karen Buddhist Army forms as a separate armed group of Buddhist soldiers and officers from the of the Karen National Liberation Army.

1994–1996	The Unified Communist Party of Nepal (Maoist) organizes an insurgency against the Nepalese monarchy.
1995	Tanzim, a terrorist faction of the Palestinian Fatah movement, is formed and recruits children and youth.

World Conference on Human Rights adopts the Beijing Platform for Action, which states that the human rights of women and of the girl child are an inalienable, integral, and indivisible part of universal human rights.

1996   The Taliban, an Islamist militia and terrorist group, comes to power in Afghanistan.

Report by Graca Machel, *The Impact of Armed Conflict on Children*, submitted to the UN General Assembly. The report has a major impact on international policy regarding child soldiers.

Amended Protocol II on prohibitions or restrictions on the Use of Mines, Booby-Traps and Other Devices to the Convention on Prohibitions or Restrictions on the Use of Certain Conventional Weapons Which May Be Deemed to Be Excessively Injurious or to Have Indiscriminate Effects 1980.

1996–2006   Nepal Civil War. The civil war between the Nepalese government and the Maoist rebels is started by armed groups of the Communist Party of Nepal, a major recruiter of child soldiers. (The Communist Party of Nepal became the ruling party in 2008.)

1997   UN secretary-general appoints special a representative to study the impact of armed conflict on children.

Cape Town Principles and Best Practices on the Recruitment of Children into the Armed Forces and on Demobilization and Social Reintegration of Child Soldiers in Africa

Convention on the Prohibition of the Use, Stockpiling, Production and the Transfer of Anti-Personnel Land-mines and on Their Destruction (Ottawa Treaty).

Armed Forces of Liberia come under control of President Charles Taylor and engage in recruiting child soldiers.

The Armed Forces Revolutionary Council, a group of Sierra Leone soldiers allied with the rebel Revolutionary United Front, is formed. The Sierra Leone Special Court later convicts some of its key leaders of recruiting child soldiers.

1998   Rome Statute of the International Criminal Court. The statute of the International Criminal Court makes the recruitment of children under age 15 years a war crime under international law.

The Mai-Mai, a variety of local community-based militia group involved in the Second Congo War, form to resist the invasion of Rwandan forces.

Coalition to Stop the Use of Child Soldiers formed.

Guiding Principles on Internal Displacement.

1998–
present   Second Congo War.

1999   African Charter in the Rights and Welfare of the Child.

International Labor Organization Convention (No. 182) concerning the Prohibition and

Immediate Action for the Elimination of the Worst Forms of Child Labor.

International Labour Organization's Recommendation 190 concerning the Prohibition and Immediate Action for the Elimination of the Worst Forms of Child Labor.

Lomé Peace Accord (ending the Sierra Leone Civil War).

UN Security Council Resolution 1261 concerning children in armed conflict calls for states to take action on issues such as the proliferation of small arms, the recruitment and use of children, and humanitarian access to children.

1999–2003   Second Liberian Civil War.

2000   Optional Protocol to the Convention on the Rights of the Child on the involvement of children in armed conflict.

Resolution 1709 of the Organization of American States on Children and Armed Conflict

Truth and Reconciliation Commission Sierra Leone is established, as provided for in the Lomé Peace Accord 1999, Article XXVI.

Arusha Peace and Reconciliation Agreement (Burundi).

UN Security Council Resolution 1306 imposes sanctions on rough diamonds from Sierra Leone. The Sierra Leone diamond fields in eastern Sierra Leone are under the control of the Revolutionary United Front, which uses children as both child soldiers and slave labor in diamond production during the Sierra Leone Civil War.

UN Security Council Resolution 1314 concerning children and armed conflict and recognizing the problems facing internally displaced persons calls for the protection and assistance to internally displaced children and refugee children and reaffirms the need for unhindered access for humanitarian purposes to children affected by armed conflict.

UN Security Council Resolution 1325 concerning women and peace and security and calling for the adoption of a gender perspective that includes the special needs of women and girls during repatriation and resettlement, rehabilitation, reintegration, and postconflict reconstruction.

Optional Protocol to the UN Convention on the Rights of the Child on the Sale of Children, Child Prostitution, and Child Pornography.

Formation of the Democratic Forces for the Liberation of Rwanda (Forces démocratiques de libération du

2000 (*cont.*)	Rwanda), the main Rwandan Hutu rebel group located in the Democratic Republic of the Congo. Many of its original members were involved in the Hutu massacre of Tutsi during the Rwandan Genocide.

Justice and Equality Movement, a rebel group with an Islamist ideology, formed in the Darfur conflict of Sudan.

Al-Aqsa Martyrs' Brigades, a Palestinian terrorist organization, formed. It organized many suicide terrorist attacks, some of which involved the use of child suicide terrorists.

2001–
present

War in Afghanistan begins on October 7, 2001, with the start of Operation Enduring Freedom.

The first American soldier killed in the war, Sergeant First Class Nathan Ross Chapman, was killed by a child soldier.

Protocol against the Illicit Manufacturing of and Trafficking in Firearms, Their Parts and Components and Ammunition, supplementing the United Nations Convention on Transnational Organized Crime.

UN Conference on the Illicit Trade in Small Arms and Light Weapons in All Its Aspects.

UN Security Council Resolution 1379 concerning children and armed conflict and asking the secretary-general to add to his annual report a list of parties that recruit or use children in violation of international law, the so-called list of shame.

2002

Statute of the Special Court for Sierra Leone. The Sierra Leone Special Court was the first court in history to place recruiters of child soldiers under the age of 15 on trial for war crimes.

The Guantanamo Bay detention camp at the Guantanamo Bay Naval Base, Cuba, is opened. Detained child soldiers are routinely abused by U.S. military personnel in violation of international law.

The Front for Patriotic Resistance of Ituri (Forces de Résistance Patriotique d'Ituri) is an armed militia and political party in eastern Congo. Founded in 2002, its early leader, Germain Katanga, is on trial at the International Criminal Court on the grounds of using children under the age of 15 to take active part in hostilities.

Nationalist and Integrationist Front (Front des Nationalistes et Intégrationnistes) is formed as an armed group involved in the Ituri conflict in the Democratic Republic of the Congo

Issa Bdeir, 16, blows himself up and kills two Israelis in suicide terrorist attack sponsored by the Al Aqsa Martyrs' Brigades.

The Sudan Liberation Movement Army founded as the Darfur Liberation Front.

Inter-Agency Standing Committee Task Force on Protection from Sexual Exploitation and Abuse in Humanitarian Crises.

President Bush issues order declaring that Common Article 3 of the Geneva Convention applies neither to al-Qaeda nor to Taliban detainees. These detainees, including captured children, are deemed not legally entitled to humane treatment.

The Al-Aqsa Martyrs' Brigades sends teenager Ayat al-Akhrasas on a suicide terrorist mission in an Israeli supermarket.

2002–2007 First Côte d'Ivoire Civil War.

2003– present The Iraq War begins with the U.S. invasion of Iraq.

2003   Al-Qaeda in Iraq emerges as Iraqi division of al-Qaeda and as part of the Iraqi insurgency.

Rebel groups, including the Union of Democratic Forces for Unity (Union des forces démocratiques pour le rassemblement) and the People's Army for the Restoration of Democracy APRD (L'Armée Populaire pour la restauration de la république et la démocratie) initiate the Central African Republic Bush War.

Emergence of the Movement for Democracy in Liberia, a rebel group in Liberia, allies with Côte d'Ivoire and seeks the ouster of President Charles Taylor.

UN Security Council Resolution 1460 on Children in Armed Conflict endorsing the secretary-general's call for "an era of application" of international norms and standards for the protection of children affected by armed conflict. The resolution requests that the secretary-general include a proposal for enhancing monitoring and reporting on violations committed against children in the next report on children and armed conflict.

Protocol V Explosive Remnants of War to the Convention on Prohibitions or Restrictions on the Use of Certain Conventional Weapons Which May Be Deemed to Be Excessively Injurious or to Have Indiscriminate Effects.

European Union Guidelines on Children and Armed Conflict.

Report of the special representative of the secretary-general for children and armed conflict to the Security Council .

Sam Hinga Norman, Moinian Fofana, and Allieu Kondewa, leaders of the Civilian Defense Forces during the Civil War in Sierra Leone, are indicted for numerous war crimes, including conscripting or enlisting children under the age of 15 years into armed forces or groups or using them to participate actively in hostilities.

Issa Hassan Sesay, Morris Kallon, and Augustine Gbao, former leaders of the former Revolutionary United Front, the main rebel faction during the civil war in Sierra Leone, are indicted for numerous war crimes, including conscripting or enlisting children under the age of 15 years into armed forces or groups or using them to participate actively in hostilities. Alex Tamba Brima, Brima Bazzy Kamara, and Santigie Borbor Kanu of the Armed Forces Revolutionary Council during the Sierra Leone Civil War are indicted for numerous war crimes, including conscripting or enlisting children under the age of 15 years into armed forces or groups or using them to participate actively in hostilities.

Charles Taylor, president of Liberia, is indicted by the Sierra Leone Special Court for war crimes, including the recruitment of child soldiers. Taylor was arrested in 2006, and his trial, in The Hague, concluded in 2011.

2003–2010   Darfur Conflict.

2006   Thomas Lubanga Dyilo becomes the first person ever arrested by the International Criminal Court and charged with the recruitment of child soldiers under the age of 15. He was an important military commander during the Second Congo War. He was the founder of the Union des Patriotes Congolais and its armed wing, the Forces patriotiques pour la libération du Congo. Final arguments for this trial were held in August 2011, and a verdict is expected in 2012.

2007   Tora Bora Front, a Taliban group named after Tora Bora, established from former members of Hezb-i-Islami.

| 2007 (*cont.*) | Paris Commitments to protect children from unlawful recruitment or use by armed forces or armed groups.

Paris Principles and guidelines on children associated with armed forces or armed groups.

Alex Tamba Brima, Brima Bazzy Kamara, and Santigie Borbor Kanu of the Armed Forces Revolutionary Council during the Sierra Leone Civil War are convicted by the Special Court for Sierra Leone for numerous war crimes, including conscripting or enlisting children under the age of 15 years and sentenced to lengthy prison terms.

Moinian Fofana and Allieu Kondewa, leaders of the Civilian Defense Forces during the Sierra Leone Civil War, are convicted by the Special Court for Sierra Leone for numerous war crimes, including conscripting or enlisting children under the age of 15 years into armed forces or groups or using them to participate actively in hostilities and sentenced to prison. Codefendant Sam Hinga died while in custody. |

| 2007–2008 | Germain Katanga, also known as "Simba," alleged commander of the Force de résistance patriotique en Ituri, and Mathieu Ngudjolo Chui, alleged former leader of the Front des nationalistes et intégrationnistes in the Democratic Republic of the Congo, surrender to the International Criminal Court and are transferred to The Hague for trial on the grounds of using children under the age of 15 to take active part in the hostilities. |

| 2008 | U.S. Child Soldier Prevention Act.

U.S. Child Soldier Accountability Act.

United States reports holding captive, since 2002, approximately 2,500 juvenile combatants who were under 18 years of age at the time of their capture. |

UN Security Council Resolution 1820 concerning Women and Peace and Security.

Convention on Cluster Munitions.

Convention of Patriots for Justice and Peace forms as a rebel splinter group from the Union des forces démocratiques pour le rassemblement in the Central African Republic.

2009   UN Security Council Resolution 1882 condemning the use of and asking member states to respect resolutions against the use of children in armed conflict.

UN Security Council Resolution 1888 mandates peacekeeping missions to protect women and girls from sexual violence in armed conflict.

UN Security Council Resolution 1889 reaffirms Resolution 1325 (2000) on "women and peace and security" and condemns continuing sexual violence against women in conflict and postconflict situations.

Issa Hassan Sesay, Morris Kallon, and Augustine Gbao, former leaders of the former Revolutionary United Front, the main rebel faction during the Sierra Leone Civil War, are convicted by the Special Court for Sierra Leone for numerous war crimes, including conscripting or enlisting children under the age of 15 years, and are sentenced to lengthy prison terms.

Hizbul Islam ("Islamic Party"), a Somali Islamist insurgent group, formed to fight the government of Somalia. It has since merged with al-Shebaab.

Mohammed Jawad, child captive, is repatriated after having being released from Guantanamo Bay detention camp on a habeas corpus petition.

2010–2011 Second Côte d'Ivoire Civil War.

2010 President Obama waives application of the Child Soldiers Prevention Act of 2008 for four countries using child soldiers: Chad, the Democratic Republic of the Congo, Sudan, and Yemen.

Sudanese government Central Reserve Police, combat-trained forces known in Darfur as "police soldiers," are increasingly involved in Darfur in violent attacks on civilians.

Omar Khadr, the youngest child soldier held in the Guantanamo Bay detention camp by the United States, is the first minor since World War II to be convicted by a military commission for war crimes committed while still a minor.

2011 UN Security Council Resolution 2002 tightening sanctions against Eritrea and Somalia.

Indian Supreme Court declares as illegal the Salwa Judum, an armed youth militia allied with the government in Chhattisgarh, India, and an opponent of the Naxalites.

War crimes trial of Charles Taylor, former president of Liberia, before the Special Court for Sierra Leone concludes. A verdict is expected in 2012.

War crimes trial of Thomas Lubanga Dyilo, former military leader in the Democratic Republic of the Congo, before the International Criminal Court concludes. A verdict is expected in 2012.

5

Biographical Sketches

Child Soldiers

al-Akhras, Ayat (1984?–March 29, 2002)

On March 29, 2002, Ayat al-Akhras walked into a grocery store in Jerusalem and detonated the explosives that were belted to her body, killing herself and two Israeli citizens. With this act, she became the third female Palestinian suicide bomber—and the youngest. She was between 16 and 18 (reports vary). In great measure because of her youth and the fact that one of her victims was also a teenage girl, the incident received widespread international attention. A documentary film was made about al-Akhras and her Israeli victim, Rachel Levy, called *To Die in Jerusalem: Two Daughters Lost in Conflict*.

Ayat al-Akhras, one of 10 children, grew up in the Deheishe Refugee camp outside Bethlehem. An excellent student, she planned to become a journalist after college and was engaged to be married in the summer of 2002. Her plans took a different turn when she joined the Al-Aqsa Martyrs' Brigade and was sent on a suicide mission into Jerusalem.

Al-Akhras's recruitment by a terrorist organization engendered huge international debate about the social forces that could induce a young girl, a successful student with a bright future, to take her own life for a political cause. President George W. Bush said, at the time, "When an 18-year-old Palestinian girl is induced to blow herself up and in the process kills a 17-year-old Israeli girl, the future itself is dying; the future of the Palestinian people and the future of the Israeli people."

Arafat, Yasser (August 1929– November 11, 2004)

Yasser Arafat was born in Cairo to Palestinian parents, the second youngest of seven children and a distant cousin of the mufti of Jerusalem. His father was active in the Egyptian-based Muslim Brotherhood, the ideological precursor of Hamas and Islamic Jihad. It was a time of intense political activism, with many youth movements encouraging youngsters to participate. In the early 1940s, Arafat's father organized a fighting force in Gaza to support the exiled Mufti and recruited many youth, including his 12-year-old son, Yasser, and his two older brothers.

Over the next decade, Arafat took on greater leadership responsibilities in the resistance. By age 16, at the end of World War II, he was the leader of about 300 boys known as the "Storm Troops of Arab Liberation" and engineered many terrorist and resistance activities, including smuggling guns and ammunition from Egypt into Palestine. In 1944, Arafat enrolled in the university and graduated in 1950 with a degree in civil engineering.

As an adult, Arafat became the key Palestinian leader and a Nobel Peace Prize winner. He was chairman of the Palestine Liberation Organization, president of the Palestinian National Authority, and leader of the Fatah political party, which he founded in 1959. Moving from armed conflict to diplomacy, Arafat spent much of his life fighting against Israel for Palestinian self-determination and later engaged in serious negotiations with Israel to try to end the decades-long conflict. Arafat, Yitzhak Rabin, and Shimon Peres received the 1994 Nobel Peace Prize for their negotiations at Oslo. He died November 11, 2004, at the age of 75.

Beah, Ishmael (born November 23, 1980)

Ishmael Beah may be the most well known contemporary child soldier because of his best-selling memoir *A Long Way Gone: Memoirs of a Boy Soldier.* Born in Mattru Jong, Bonthe District, Sierra Leone, he was 11 years old when civil war erupted in Sierra Leone, and his parents and brother were killed. The Sierra Leone army recruited him to be a soldier when he was 13. He fought for nearly three years until UNICEF rescued him and helped him reenter civilian life. He fled to Freetown and made his way to New York, where he was adopted by Laura Simms, whom he had met in Sierra Leone.

He attended high school in New York, earned a degree in political science from Oberlin College, and has become a public spokesperson for children in war situations. He worked on children's advocacy issues in college and with Human Rights Watch. His riveting accounts of his life as a child soldier, his difficulty in returning to civilian life, and his articulate advocacy for children continue to bring attention to this subject.

Some critics have disputed the accuracy of Beah's accounts, suggesting that he had conflated his own experiences with those of other children. Whatever inaccuracies there may be of specific dates and events in Beah's book, there is little argument that he was a child soldier in Sierra Leone, that the events that he recounts did happen to children who fought in that war, and that his book has been instrumental in raising awareness of these issues.

Bevistein, Abraham (Aby) (1900–1916)

Abraham (Aby) Bevistein was a Polish Jewish immigrant from London's East End who enlisted in the 11th Battalion of the Middlesex Regiment. He was executed by firing squad for desertion at Labourse near Calais, France. He enlisted in the British army in September 1914 at age 16, lying about his age and giving his name as Abraham Harris. He had been in France for at least eight months when, on December 29, 1915, he was wounded in a mine explosion. Suffering from his wounds and from shock, he was sent to a field hospital. He was released on January 19, 1916, and sent back to his unit, still suffering from shock. He appears to have wandered off on the evening of February 12, 1916, after being deafened by three grenades that exploded near him in a German attack on his lines. He was arrested and charged with desertion on February 13, 1916, and was court-martialed and sentenced to death on March 4, 1916.

Bevistein was one of 306 men and boys who were executed by the British in World War I. After his execution, his case was taken up by Sylvia Pankhurst, a noted women's and workers' rights activist. The case was also taken up by several members of Parliament who hostilely questioned Harold Tennant, the undersecretary of war, as to whether it was "customary" for the military to execute boys who had only recently suffered nervous breakdowns from their wounds. His life is the subject of a 2005 book by David Lister titled *Die Hard, Aby!*

Casabianca, Giancomo (Giocanta) (1786–1798)

Giancomo Casabianca was the son of Louis de Casabianca, the flag captain on the French flagship *Orient*, which was fired on and blown up by Admiral Nelson in Abukir Bay during the Battle of the Nile in August 1798. The boy refused to relinquish his post on the burning ship until he received orders to do so from his father and died when the powder magazine exploded and the ship sank. His bravery was immortalized in British poet Felicia Dorothea Hemans's poem:

> The boy stood on the burning deck
> Whence all but he had fled;
> The flame that lit the battle's wreck
> Shone round him o'er the dead.

Generations of American schoolchildren memorized the poem as an example of youthful bravery, patriotism, and devotion to duty. The poem, like many that schoolchildren memorize, was parodied widely (e.g., "The boy stood on the burning deck/The flames 'round him did roar/He found a bar of Ivory Soap/And washed himself ashore.")

Clem, John Lincoln (August 13, 1851–May 13, 1937)

Born John Joseph Klem in Newark, Ohio, Johnny Clem started his career as a drummer boy with the Union army during the Civil War. Famous for his battlefield bravery—and his youthful determination—he became the youngest noncommissioned officer in army history. He retired from the army in 1915 as a brigadier general and the last veteran of the Civil War still on duty in the armed forces. Congress promoted him to major general when he retired.

At 10 years old, Clem ran away from home to become a Union army drummer boy. He tried to enlist in the 3rd Ohio Infantry but was rejected because he was so young and small. Then he tried to join the 22nd Michigan; when they refused him, he simply tagged along. Eventually, the 22nd adopted him as mascot and drummer boy, and officers chipped in to pay him a regular soldier's wage. He officially enlisted two years later.

He was promoted to sergeant because of his bravery at the Battle of Chickamauga, where he carried a musket trimmed to his small size and rode an artillery caisson to the front. He became known as the "Drummer Boy of Chickamauga." After the war, he finished high school and then reenlisted in the army, where he trained in artillery, then transferred to the quartermaster department. By the time he retired in 1915, he had reached the rank of brigadier general. He died in San Antonio, Texas, in 1937, and is buried in Arlington National Cemetery. A statue of young John Clem stands near the Buckingham Meeting House in Newark, Ohio, and a feature-length film was made about him called *Johnny: The True Story of a Civil War Legend.*

Cornwall, John Travers (January 8, 1900–June 2, 1916)

Known as Jack, or the Boy Cornwall, John Cornwall was posthumously awarded a Victoria Cross for his bravery at the Battle of Jutland. The third child of a working-class family in Essex, he was a Boy Scout who left school at age 14 to worked as a delivery boy. When World War I began, his father, a former soldier, volunteered to fight and was sent to France. Jack's older brother was also an infantryman in Flanders. Without asking his father, Jack Cornwell enlisted in the Royal Navy in October 1915. After being trained as a sight setter for heavy naval guns, he joined the crew of the HMS *Chester* in early 1916. His ship came under intense fire during the Battle of Jutland, and Jack stayed at his post after everyone around him had been killed. His recommendation for the Victoria Cross includes this description of his exemplary bravery:

> The instance of devotion to duty by Boy (1st Class) John Travers Cornwell who was mortally wounded early in the action, but nevertheless remained standing alone at

a most exposed post, quietly awaiting orders till the end of the action, with the gun's crew dead and wounded around him. He was under 16½ years old … but I recommend his case for special recognition in justice to his memory and as an acknowledgement of the high example set by him.

The epitaph on Jack's grave monument reads,

It is not wealth or ancestry
but honourable conduct and a noble disposition
that maketh men great.

Dayan, Moshe (May 20, 1915–October 16, 1981)

Most famous as the rakish Israeli military leader and politician with the dramatic eye patch and a symbol of the military prowess of the state of Israel, Moshe Dayan's career began at age 14, when he joined the Jewish resistance militia known as the Haganah. His parents were Zionist pioneers who moved from Ukraine to Kibbutz Degania Alef near the shores of the Sea of Galilee. He was the second child born on the kibbutz and was named Moshe after Moshe Barsky, the first member of the kibbutz to be killed in an Arab attack.

After his family moved to Nahalal, the first moshav (communal farm) in Israel, he attended agricultural school. It was at Nahalal that he joined the Haganah and his qualities as a leader began to emerge. He details his long and complicated military career in his autobiography *Moshe Dayan: The Story of My Life*. At age 23, he became a motorized police commander, and in June 1941, at age 26, he was assigned to a small reconnaissance task force that was helping the Allied forces prepare for their invasion of Syria and Lebanon. His binoculars were struck by a French rifle shot, and the impact destroyed his eye socket, so he was forced to wear his signature eye patch the rest of his life.

After a long military career, where he became chief of staff of the Israel Defense Forces, Dayan later served the Israeli government as both defense minister and foreign minister.

Jackson, Andrew (March 15, 1767–June 8, 1845)

As a boy of 13, Andrew Jackson joined a local militia as a courier and fought in the American Revolution. Both he and his brother were captured by the British. While held as prisoners, the two nearly starved to death, and both contracted smallpox. Andrew survived, but his brother died of the disease. His eldest brother also died of heat exhaustion at the Battle of Stone Ferry. Jackson's father had been killed in an accident only a couple of weeks before he was born, and his mother died during the war of cholera, which she contracted while nursing prisoners of war. Thus, at age 14, Jackson was an orphan who had lost virtually his entire immediate family to the hardships of war.

Jackson was smart, but his education was spotty: he studied in a local primary school and apprenticed for a while as a saddler. He taught school and studied law in North Carolina and was admitted to the bar in 1787. He moved to Jonesborough, then in western North Carolina and now Tennessee. He rejoined the military, fought in several Indian wars, and led the Americans to victory in the Battle of New Orleans in the War of 1812. Over six feet tall and extremely lean, Jackson had a shock of red hair and bright blue eyes.

Jackson became the seventh president of the United States (1829–1837) and the last president who was directly involved in the American Revolution. His nickname "Old Hickory" reflected his toughness and aggressive personality. His long military career and particularly his bravery as a young soldier were an important part of the mythology built up by and about him. He published the story of his life as part of his strategy to establish himself as a credible candidate for president—the first "campaign biography." One story was of young Jackson's refusal, while being held prisoner by the British, to clean the boots of a British officer. The officer was infuriated and slashed Andrew with a sword, leaving him with scars on his head and left hand. For Jackson, being a "child soldier" was seen as an early indication of the bravery and leadership that would make him a good president.

Jackson's career spanned some of the most contentious issues faced by the young country of the United States, including the issue of slavery, questions of class and privilege, the status of Native American peoples, the growth of the nation in both land

and population, and the relationship between the federal and state governments. In many ways, he embodied the crosscurrents that were shaping the nation as it emerged from its revolutionary period. He was a military hero and a politician, a self-educated man from nonaristocratic roots, but also a rich slave owner. He promoted the idea of states' rights but fought fiercely to maintain the union. He cast himself as a protector of individual liberty but was ferocious in his actions to remove Native Americans from their lands. He advocated a limited federal government but greatly expanded the power of the president while he was in office.

Jal, Emmanuel (born 1980)

Emmanuel Jal uses music as a way to heal the traumas of war and spread his message of hope and peace. Having come a long way from his early life as a child soldier in Sudan, he is known for his rap/hip-hop/African beat music with a positive message and a call for social action. Born in southern Sudan, Emmanuel was seven years old when his mother was killed by government soldiers in the civil war. He, along with thousands of other children, left his home in southern Sudan for Ethiopia because they were told that they would be able to get an education there. The "school," however, turned out to be a recruiting front for the Sudanese People's Liberation Army (SPLA), and many of the children, Emmanuel included, were being trained as fighters. In Ethiopia, he fought with the SPLA for several years until war broke out there also, and the child soldiers returned to Sudan to fight. Along with several other children who were sick of fighting, he ran away from the SPLA and after about three months reached the town of Waat, the headquarters of a splinter group of the SPLA. There he met Emma McCune, who was an aid worker from Britain. She convinced Emmanuel, then 11 years old, that he should not be a soldier any longer. She adopted him and helped him escape to Kenya, where he attended school.

Seeing the hardships endured by many children in urban Kenya, he resolved to try to do something to help. Through his music and as a spokesperson for various causes, Emmanuel has dedicated his life to saving other kids from losing their childhoods to war as he had. His music, which combines hip-hop, rap, and soul layered with African rhythms, is all about overcoming ethnic divisions and hatred. He has become an outspoken advocate for children who are at risk from poverty, warfare, and hunger. He founded a charity called Gua Africa, which builds schools and provides scholarships for children in Sudan and Kenya. Reflecting the powerful effect of his early experiences as a child soldier, he has recorded an album, written an autobiography, and had his life recounted in a documentary film—all of them called *War Child*.

Jawad, Mohammed (born sometime between 1985 and 1992)

One of many children caught up in the conflict in Afghanistan, Mohammed Jawad was arrested in December 2002 and held first in Bagram prison and then at Guantanamo Bay, charged with having attempted to murder American soldiers by throwing a grenade at them. It is unclear how old he was when he was arrested. The American military claims that he was 17, but his family says that he was 12. In either case, he was under the age of 18. Over the next seven years of imprisonment, he appeared before many military tribunals that sought to establish whether he should be treated as an enemy combatant or simply as a criminal.

Jawad was born in an Afghan refugee camp in Miransha, Pakistan, and educated through sixth or seventh grade in a local school, described by U.S. military authorities as "Jihadi" but tat Jawad describes as a regular school. At his mosque in Miransha, some men approached him about a taking a job clearing land mines in Kabul, Afghanistan, and he left Pakistan to take on this dangerous work. According to Jawad, when he arrived in Kabul, the men gave him drugs and taught him how to throw grenades, but he said that he had not actually thrown the grenade at the American convoy.

While he was held at Guantanamo Bay, Jawad was subject to treatment known as the "frequent-flyer program," in which a prisoner is deprived of sleep and thereby disoriented by arbitrarily moving him from one location to another multiple times a day. His case became emblematic of the problems of U.S. policy in holding suspected terrorists, particularly child soldiers, at Guantanamo Bay. The charges against him were eventually thrown out when a judge in district court ruled that his original confession had been obtained through coercion by the Afghan authorities. He was finally sent back to Afghanistan in 2009.

Joan of Arc (Jeanne d'Arc) (1412–1431)

Joan of Arc, a young peasant girl, led the French army to "miraculous" victory in several battles in the Hundred Years' War between England and France. The daughter of a farmer who was also a minor public official in the small village of Domremy, Joan and her family lived in an area of northeastern France that remained loyal to the French crown though surrounded by the opposition. Like many modern child soldiers, she personally experienced the war. During her childhood, there were several raids, and on one occasion her village was burned.

At age 12 she began having visions that she should help drive the English out of France, and at 16 she made a prediction that the French would win a battle at Orleans. After her prediction proved true, Joan was able to convince Dauphin Charles VII that she would, with divine guidance, be able to lead the French to victory. Left with few other options, Charles armed her and sent her on a relief mission to Orleans, dressed in male military garb. She inspired the people and the army, and the English were defeated in several spectacular battles. However, she was captured and sold to the English, who found her guilty of heresy and burned her at the stake. She was 19. A quarter of a century later, Pope Callixtus III reversed the ecclesiastical court's decision and declared her a martyr. She was beatified (declared a saint) in 1920. She became known as Saint Joan of Arc, the Maid of Orleans, and is one of the patron saints of France.

Perhaps because she was so young—and a girl—the story of Joan of Arc has caught the imagination of generations of artists and writers. Writers as diverse as Shakespeare, Mark Twain, and George Bernard Shaw have portrayed her, and there are hundreds of statues of her, including one in the French Quarter in New Orleans, Louisiana.

Khadr, Omar (born September 19, 1986)

Omar Khadr is the youngest prisoner held at Guantanamo Bay and was the first child soldier to be prosecuted for war crimes since World War II. He was 15 years old when he was captured in a firefight in Afghanistan. His situation garnered international attention, as it became clearer that in the course of his incarceration he had been subjected to multiple forms of torture and psychological pressure and had not been treated in accordance with the protocols for underage detainees.

Omar was born in Toronto and is therefore a Canadian citizen. Through his early childhood, he moved back and forth between Canada and Pakistan. He attended first grade in Canada, and when he was in Pakistan he attended a private school. He was homeschooled for several years. In February 2002, Omar was involved in a firefight that broke out when American forces were searching a compound for hidden weapons. He was badly wounded during the firefight and evacuated to the Bagram military base. After repeated interrogations, he finally confessed to his participation in the action and to murdering one of the U.S. soldiers. Because he was a Canadian citizen, the government of Canada was informed of his arrest, and though the Canadians requested that he not be moved to Guantanamo Bay, he was in fact transferred there in October 2002.

In the years following his arrest, Omar appeared before numerous military tribunals, and his case became a central focus of the attention of child soldier activists. Khadr claims to have been subjected to multiple forms of torture and psychological pressure, including being splashed with cold water, being humiliated, being subjected to the "frequent-flyer program" of repeated relocations to deprive him of sleep, and other abuses. Although the Canadian courts found that his civil rights had been violated, they did not move to have him extradited to Canada. Finally, in October 2010, eight years after his arrest, a deal was struck between Khadr, the United States, and Canada that would allow him to complete his sentence in Canada after serving the first year in U.S. custody.

Ladd, Luther C. (December 22, 1843–April 19, 1861)

Luther Ladd was born in Alexandria, Massachusetts. Killed at age 17, he is widely regarded as the first Union soldier to die in the Civil War. He enlisted in the 6th Massachusetts Volunteer Militia and was killed in the secessionist riots in Baltimore on April 19, 1861, along with three other Union soldiers. Ladd and a fellow soldier, Addison Whitney, were given a joint funeral in May 1861 in Lowell, Massachusetts, but because of his youth, it was the death of Ladd that drew the most attention. An account of Ladd's life, death, and funeral, titled the *Life of Luther C. Ladd, Who Fell in Baltimore, April 19, 1861 Exclaiming All Hail to the Stars and Stripes,*. was published in 1862, describing him as "the first martyr that fell as sacrifice to his country." Ladd's death came shortly after the fall of Fort Sumter in Charleston, South Carolina. President Abraham Lincoln had called for troops to defend Washington, so Ladd's regiment was on its way to defend the capital but was required to transfer to another railroad station in Baltimore. While marching to Baltimore's President Street Station, the regiment was attacked by a secessionist and proslavery mob. The first deaths of the Civil War came as a shock to the nation. On the day of Ladd's funeral, the town of Lowell closed its markets, and church bells tolled all day. The newspapers declared the deaths to be "murders."

Lucas, Jack (February 14, 1928–June 5, 2008)

Jack Lucas was only 14 when he joined the U.S. Marines in August 1942. He was muscular and big for his age, and he told the recruiting officer that he was 17. He was sent to recruit training camp on Paris Island, South Carolina, where it became clear that he had talent as a soldier; he was certified as a sharpshooter and trained as a heavy machine gun crewman. He was very physically fit, having played baseball, softball, basketball, and he participated in wrestling and boxing and was captain of the football team in high school at Edwards Military Institute. But his skills did not stop there: he also rode horses, shot traps and skeet, and hunted.

When it came to his military career, he occasionally bent the rules to get what he wanted. In addition to lying about his age to the recruiting officer, he simply walked off the base in Hawaii, frustrated that he was not getting into the action. When he did not show up again, he was declared a deserter. But he had not left the base to avoid the war; rather, he left to get into the thick of the action. He stowed away on the USS *Deuel*, which was taking units of the 5th Marine Division into combat, and once the ship was at sea, he surrendered himself to the senior officer aboard. The Marines allowed him to stay and assigned him to the 5th Marine Division. He turned 17 while at sea, six days before his unit joined the battle at Iwo Jima.

Jack was awarded the Medal of Honor for his actions on his second day in the Iwo Jima campaign. He saved the lives of his comrades by pushing a hand grenade into volcanic ash to disable it and throwing his body onto a second thrown grenade. In the ensuing explosion, he was severely wounded and, though initially left for dead, was eventually evacuated and taken to the hospital ship *Samaritan*. While he was a patient in the naval hospital in Charleston, South Carolina, the desertion charge was dropped from his record, and the Marines restored his rank as private first class. In 1945, he was awarded the Medal of Honor by President Harry S. Truman. He was the youngest marine ever awarded this highest military decoration.

Classified as disabled because of his wounds, he was discharged from the Marines in 1945. He carried enough shrapnel in his body from the grenades that for the rest of his life he would set off metal detectors. But his military career did not entirely end with his discharge from the Marines: in the 1960s, after earning a business degree from High Point University, Jack joined the U.S. Army to train as a paratrooper, and he actually survived a training jump in which both of his parachutes failed to open. He died of leukemia in 2008 at the age of 80 in Hattiesburg, Mississippi.

Mackenzie, Clarence (1849–1861)

The "little drummer boy of Brooklyn" was only 12 when he joined Brooklyn's 13th Regiment and marched with them to fight in the Civil War. He became the first casualty of the war from Brooklyn, when he was killed by a stray bullet during a training exercise in Annapolis, Maryland. His body was packed in ice and sent back to Brooklyn, where he was buried in Green-Wood Cemetery. His funeral was a huge public event, with thousands gathering to mourn the loss of such a young and innocent boy and praising his patriotism and virtue. The Dutch Reformed Church, whose Fulton Street Meeting Sunday School Clarence had attended, published a pamphlet extolling his virtues, citing him as an example of Christian goodness and dedication and describing him as a martyr to the noble cause of the Union. Sometime after his death, his body was relocated to the Soldier's Lot, an area of Green-Wood Cemetery dedicated specifically to veterans of the Civil War, and a 10-foot-tall monument was erected above his grave, with a realistic statue of the boy and his drum, inscribed, "Our Drummer Boy."

Murphy, Audie (June 20, 1925–May 28, 1971)

Now well known as the soft-spoken sharpshooting cowboy of over 44 films, including 33 westerns, and America's most highly decorated soldier, Audie Murphy lied about his age to get into the army after the Japanese attack on Pearl Harbor. He was first turned away for being underage, then his sister Corinne allegedly altered his birth certificate to indicate that he was 18 years old, and he tried again. First the U.S. Marines and the U.S. Army Paratroopers turned him down for being too short (five feet, eight inches), and then the U.S. Navy rejected him for being underweight. Finally, the regular U.S. Army accepted him, about a month before his actual eighteenth birthday. He fought in nine major battles in Europe—in France, in Sicily, on the Italian mainland—and in the process his bravery, leadership, and battle prowess won him every U.S. medal available at the time—some of them several times. He was also awarded five medals from France and one from Belgium.

He was born into a sharecropper's family in Hunt County, Texas, the sixth of 12 children. Audie's father abandoned the family when Audie was very young, and he dropped out of school in fifth grade to help support the family. His mother died when he was 15, and since neither he nor his older siblings were able to support all the younger children, Audie took several of them to an orphanage to be fed and cared for. He retrieved them when he returned from the war.

After 29 months in the service, he returned to the United States and was featured on the cover of *Life* magazine. His face caught the attention of Jimmy Cagney, who invited him to come to Hollywood to begin a movie career. One of Audie Murphy's best-known films is a cinematic version of his biography, *To Hell and Back*. He also starred in another film about a young soldier in the Civil War, the 1951 adaptation of Steven Crane's *The Red Badge of Courage*. He spent nearly a quarter of a century in Hollywood. In addition to his acting career, he was a country music songwriter and penned the hit songs "Shutters and Boards" and "When the Wind Blows in Chicago."

Plagued by depression, anxiety, and insomnia after his return from the war, Murphy had tremendous sympathy for the struggles of young soldiers returning from Korea and Vietnam and became an outspoken advocate for the United States spending more money to provide help for soldiers with posttraumatic stress disorder and other psychological problems stemming from their war experiences.

Audie Murphy died in a private plane crash in 1971, a few miles from Roanoke, Virginia, in the Blue Ridge Mountains. He was buried in Arlington National Cemetery with full military honors. Unlike the traditional gold-leafed headstones of most Medal of Honor recipients, Murphy's grave—at his request—is marked with a small, plain government-issued stone. His grave is the second most frequently visited site in Arlington National Cemetery after that of President John F. Kennedy.

Okafor, Ben (born 1956)

Ben Okafor was born in Enuga, in the eastern part of Nigeria that was once part of the successionist Republic of Biafra. He became a Kalashnikov-carrying soldier in the Nigeria-Biafran Civil War when he was only 13 years old. After the war ended, having lived in a series of refugee camps, he made his way to the Midlands of England in 1979, where he now lives. He is well known as a reggae musician, political activist, and tireless crusader in the campaign to stop the use of child soldiers. His music combines the rhythms of reggae, African Hi-Life, Ibo, and European church music with the classic rock sounds of the Beatles and the Rolling Stones. Okafor adds the musical influences of Fela Kuti and Bob Marley and the Wailers to that rich musical stew, producing a unique sound that won him the Outstanding British Reggae Artist award. Ben Okafor's music is profoundly shaped by his experiences as a child soldier, and he uses his music to try to ensure that other children are spared the scars of war and violence. He has released more than 10 albums and has toured widely, performing all over the world. In 2006, he wrote the introductory song, "No Child Soldiers," for an album called *Bemamou (Enfants Soldats)*.

Soldaderas (Mexican Revolution, 1910–1920)

Among the mythic figures of the Mexican Revolution were the women and girls who fought alongside Pancho Villa and his revolutionary forces. Known as the Soldaderas, many of these women were, in fact, only girls—and therefore technically "child soldiers" when they took up the cause of the revolution. One of them was Josefina Borquez, a Oaxacan Indian who was 14 years old when she followed her father into the revolution. At 15, she was married to an officer who beat her mercilessly and was himself killed in the war only a few years later. Borquez's tragic, poverty-stricken, and violent life became the model for the fictional Jesusa Palancares in Elena Poniatowska's novel *Here's to You, Jesusa!* Little information is available on how many women became Soldaderas, how many of those were under age 18, and what roles they actually played in the war. The mythology surrounding the Soldaderas is interesting in that the stories tend to divide into two camps. In one version, the women were simply camp followers who were the concubines of the soldiers and who handled traditional domestic tasks like cooking and mending clothing. In the alternative version, the Soldaderas were fierce armed warriors who bravely took their places on the battlefield next to the men and showed courage and skill under fire. The truth is probably a combination that falls somewhere between.

Tsam, Herzl Yankl (1835–1915)

Herzl Yankl Tsam was drafted at age 17 as a cantonist into the army of the Russian Empire and seems to have been the only Jewish officer in the czar's army who was promoted above the rank of captain. He served in Tomsk, Siberia, and was an able commander who was able to turn around one of the worst companies of his regiment and shape it into one of the best. In his application for promotion, his fellow officers attested to his leadership qualities and skill, but it was 41 years before he actually received the rank of colonel. He was promoted and given the rank just before he retired so that he would be eligible for a colonel's pension, but no one would have to serve under him as colonel. He came under great pressure to convert from Judaism to the Russian Orthodox Church, but he did not do so.

Tungwar, Lam (born August 27, 1983)

East African musician Lam Tungwar was born in Kalja Village of Bentiu in southern Sudan in 1983, the year the war broke out in Sudan. When he was seven years old, the militia took him to join the rebellion, and he lived as a child soldier for three or four years. He finally saw his father again nearly 14 years later after Lam had fled life as a child soldier with the resistance army and trekked overland into Kenya in 1993. As a refugee in Kenya, he lived in a refugee camp and was finally able to begin his education.

Lam learned to read and write English in the local primary school, finished high school, and attended African Nazarene

University. He became a musician, and his experiences as a child soldier have profoundly shaped the messages of his music. Both his first single recording and his autobiography bear the title *War Child*. He travels and performs widely, singing in five languages, and has been named a UN HABITAT Messenger of Truth for his work on issues of poverty, drugs, and youth empowerment. Lam often performs with Emanuel Jal to spread their anti–child soldier message through music.

Yurlova, Marina (1900–?)

Born in a small village in the Caucusus Mountains, Marina Yurlova volunteered at age 14 to fight with the Cossack army. For the next five years, she was a uniformed soldier, fought on the front lines during World War I and in the Russian Revolution, was repeatedly wounded but returned to the battlefield, and won the St. George Cross for bravery several times. She finally walked across Siberia and boarded a ship to escape to Japan. In 1934, she published an account of her harrowing exploits and the people she encountered during her five-year soldiering career in a memoir called *Cossack Girl*, which has recently been republished.

Prominent Recruiters of Child Soldiers

Dyilo, Thomas Lubanga (born December 29, 1960)

Thomas Dyilo is the first person ever to be placed on trial before the International Criminal Court for the charge of enlisting and conscripting children under the age of 15 and using those children to participate actively in hostilities. Little is known about his early life. He was a rebel leader from the Democratic Republic of the Congo. He founded and led the Union of Congolese Patriots and the Patriotic Forces for the Liberation of Congo (FPLC), its armed wing of about 15,000 soldiers. The FPLC was a key player in the Ituri conflict, which was rooted in underlying tensions between the agriculturalist Lendu ethnic group and the pastoralist Hema ethnic group in northeastern Democratic Republic of Congo. The conflict intensified as local conflicts were inflamed by the Second Congo War (1998–2003). The Union of Congolese Patriots was the armed group associated with the

Hema. In 2006, the pretrial chamber of the International Criminal Court issued a warrant for Dyilo's arrest. He was arrested in the Congo and transferred for trial to The Hague, where his trial began in 2009. A verdict is expected in early 2012.

Farhat, Maryam Mohammad Yousif (aka Umm Nidal) (born 1950)

Maryam Farhat was elected to the Palestinian Legislative Council as a candidate for Hamas in 2006. She is widely known as Umm Nidal, "the mother of Nidal." She is also sometimes referred to as Khansaa Falastin (Khansaa of Palestine) after the legendary Islamic poet Al-Khansaa, who is considered to be "the mother of the martyrs," whose four sons died in the battle of Al-Qadasiyya (637) during the Islamic conquest of Persia. Al Khansaa is said not to have mourned but instead to have thanked Allah for having "honored her with their deaths." Two of Farhat's sons died in suicide terrorist missions against Israel. Her eldest son, Nidal, was killed while preparing for an attack. Her son Mohammad, age 17, managed to penetrate the Jewish settlement of Atmona in the Gaza Strip in 2002 and killed five students and wounded many others. He was killed during the attack. A third son was killed in an Israeli attack on a car that was transporting a Quassam rocket. Maryam Farthat became widely known when she was filmed helping her 17-year-old son prepare for his suicide mission. She also publicly celebrated his death and gave numerous interviews to the press explaining the importance of supporting jihad and martyrdom.

Kony, Joseph (born 1961)

Joseph Kony is the most notorious leader of an armed group in Africa, the Lord's Resistance Army (LRA). The LRA is widely regarded as a violent military religious cult. According to some, Kony regards himself as a Christian and wants Uganda to be a Christian nation. According to Kony, if the LRA wins, Uganda will become a theocracy, with laws based on the biblical Ten Commandments. Kony was born in northern Uganda. His father was Catholic, and his mother was an Anglican. He is reported both to have been an altar boy in church and to have been involved in traditional healing. The name of his group was originally the United Holy Salvation Army (UHSA) and was one of many rebel

Christian millenarian groups that emerged in Uganda in the 1980s.

In 2005, the International Criminal Court issued arrest warrants against Kony and other senior LRA leaders, but no arrests have been made to date. According to the warrant, under Kony's leadership, the LRA has been carrying out an insurgency against Uganda since 1987. The LRA is charged with directing attacks against civilian populations that include murder, abduction, sexual enslavement, mutilation, mass burnings of houses, and looting of camp settlements. It has also carried out the mass abduction of civilians, including children, who are said to have been forcibly "recruited" as fighters, porters, and sex slaves. The United States has specifically targeted Kony and his followers, who appear to have fled into the Democratic Republic of the Congo and the Central African Republic.

Taylor, Charles Ghankay (born January 28, 1948)

Charles Ghankay Taylor, former president of Liberia, was born in Liberia 1948. He came to the United States and studied in Waltham, Massachusetts, at Bentley College, where he graduated with a BA in economics in 1977. He returned to Liberia in 1980 after a violent coup in which Samuel Doe became president of Liberia after murdering Liberian President William R. Tolbert Jr. Taylor obtained a position in the Doe government as the director of the General Services Agency, a position that allowed him to oversee government purchases. He was later accused by Samuel Doe of embezzling large sums of money, and he fled back to the United States in 1983. In 1984, he was arrested in the United States on the basis of an extradition request from Liberia. He was jailed in the Plymouth County House of Correction in Massachusetts, where, represented by former U.S. attorney general Ramsey Clark, he fought extradition proceedings. In 1985, he broke out of jail with a number of other inmates. It is claimed that he fled to New York and from there made his way to Libya, where he was given safe haven and trained in guerilla warfare under the patronage of Libyan President Muammar Gaddafi.

In 1989, Taylor returned to Liberia and became the head of the National Patriotic Front of Liberia. He launched the Liberian Civil War and came to power by executing Samuel Doe. In 1997, he was elected president of Liberia. As head of the National

Patriotic Front and later as president of Liberia, Taylor allegedly supported, sponsored, and helped to train the Sierra Leone rebel group the Revolutionary United Front. The rebel group launched its invasion of Sierra Leone from across the Liberian border. It is alleged that Taylor supplied weapons to the Revolutionary United Front in exchange for diamonds from the Sierra Leone diamond fields, which came under rebel control. Following the Second Liberian Civil War, Taylor agreed to step down as president of Liberia and later found refuge in Nigeria.

In 2003, Taylor was indicted by the Special Court for Sierra Leone for war crimes, crimes against humanity, and other serious violations of the laws of war, including the recruitment of child soldiers. In 2006, he attempted to flee Nigeria and was arrested. He was tried before the Special Court for Sierra Leone in a special courtroom established in The Hague. His trial concluded in 2011, and a verdict is expected in 2012.

Key Figures in the Movement to End the Use of Child Soldiers

Becker, Jo

Jo Becker is the director of children's advocacy for Human Rights Watch. She was the founding chairperson of the Coalition to Stop the Use of Child Soldiers. She has carried out field investigations on the recruitment of child soldiers for Human Rights Watch in Burma, India, Nepal, Sri Lanka, and Uganda. Becker graduated from Goshen College, a private Mennonite College in Indiana. As a student, she was very active in peace and antimilitarism activities, including a petition drive against U.S. intervention in Central America and various antinuclear events.

Becker graduated from Goshen College in Indiana and earned a master's degree in political science from Syracuse University. After college, she joined the Fellowship for Reconciliation (FOR), the oldest Interfaith Peace organization in the United States, which promotes nonviolent conflict resolution. As executive secretary of FOR, in 1995 she led the organization's delegation to Japan with a message of repentance for the U.S. atomic bombing of Hiroshima and Nagasaki that helped challenge anew the official U.S. view of the necessity of those bombings. In 1997, as executive director of FOR, she opposed the continuance of

U.S. military bases in Panama. She has been very active in promoting treaties restricting the use of child soldiers and was invited to the White House to witness President Clinton's signing of the Optional Protocol to the Convention on the Rights of the Child on the Involvement of Children in Armed Conflict.

Coomaraswamy, Radhika (born 1953)

Radhika Coomaraswamy of Sri Lanka is an undersecretary-general of the United Nations and the UN special representative for children and armed conflict. As special representative, she has four main goals: to raise awareness of the impact of armed conflict on children, to promote and protect the rights of children affected by armed conflict, to propose new ideas about furthering the protection of children, and to engage in specific diplomatic and humanitarian missions on behalf of affected children.

Coomaraswamy is a lawyer and internationally known human rights advocate. Before being appointed special representative for children, she was the UN special rapporteur on violence against women, where she reported to the UN Commission on Human Rights on issues such as community and family violence, violence against women during armed conflict, and international trafficking. In 2008, the United Nations requested that she be allowed to observe the trial of child soldier Omar Khadr before the U.S. military tribunal, but the United States denied her access to the trial.

She is a graduate of Yale University and received her JD from Columbia University and an LLM from Harvard University. She has written widely on judicial and constitutional issues as well as on the situation of women and girls in armed conflict. In her 2011 press conference, given in connection with the release of the UN secretary-general's annual report on children and armed conflict, she described the preceding year as a "mixed year" with uneven success of international efforts to reduce the presence of children in armed forces and groups.

Dellaire, Romeo (born June 25, 1946)

Lieutenant General (Retired) Roméo A. Dallaire is a distinguished Canadian military officer who commanded the United Nations Assistance Mission for Rwanda (UNAMIR) at the time of the genocide in Rwanda. Because of a very weak UN mandate, UNAMIR forces collapsed during the genocide and were unable to aid in saving countless human lives. Nonetheless, with only about 270 soldiers under his command, General Dellaire refused UN orders to abandon his mission and was able to save thousands of local Tutsi people from certain death. His request for more troops and reinforcements was denied by the United Nations, and he became a witness to the mass genocide in Rwanda. On returning to Canada, he suffered from posttraumatic stress disorder but has gone on to become a major campaigner for human rights and for the elimination of child soldiers. His experiences in Rwanda are detailed in his book *Shake Hands with the Devil*.

Dallaire founded the Child Soldiers Initiative, a nongovernmental organization that promotes the enforcement of laws against the recruitment of child soldiers and that works to improve the ability of governments, militaries, and civil society to end the use of child soldiers.

Machel, Graca (born October 17, 1945)

Graca Machel is an internationally recognized advocate for both children's rights and women's rights. She is the author of the 1996 UN report *The Impact of Armed Conflict on Children*, which has had a profound impact on humanitarian and human rights perspectives on child soldiers. She is also the wife of former South African president Nelson Mandela.

Machel was born in Mozambique when it was a Portuguese colony and later joined the Front for the Liberation of Mozambique (FRELIMO), the armed resistance movement attempting to end Portuguese colonial rule. She received military training but also began working in FRELIMO schools set up in guerilla bases in both Tanzania and Mozambique. When Mozambique obtained independence, FRELIMO formed its first government. Machel became a member of FRELIMO's Central Committee and the Minister of Education and Culture in 1975. At that time, she also married Samora Machel, the former commander of chief of FRELIMO forces, who became the first president of Mozambique. As minister of education and culture until 1989, she endeavored to implement universal education for all Mozambicans. Under her leadership, enrollment in primary and secondary schools expanded to more than 90 percent for males and 75 percent for females. Samora Machel, however, was killed in a plane crash. Within a few years of her husband's death, Graca Machel began to focus her energy on children's issues worldwide and as a result was appointed by the UN secretary-general to chair the "Study on the Impact of Armed Conflict on Children."

Otunnu, Olara A. (born 1950)

Olara A. Otunnu was the UN undersecretary-general and special representative for children and armed conflict from 1997 to 2005. He was succeeded in that role by Radhika Coomaraswamy. Under his leadership, the office of children and armed conflict initiated its campaign of protection for children in armed conflict, including child soldiers. He is noted for having placed child protection on the agenda of the UN Security Council and for establishing a comprehensive, international monitoring and reporting system to document grave violations against children, attempting to identify and publicly name offending parties and hold them accountable to international legal standards.

Born in northern Uganda, he received his early education in Budo and then in Kampala at Makerere University, where he was elected president of the student union. He went on to study at Oxford University and at Harvard Law School, where he was selected as a Fulbright scholar. He is now the president of LBL Foundation for Children, an international organization that promotes protection, hope, healing, and education for children in war-ravaged communities. In 2011, Otunnu became the president of the Uganda People's Congress. He was a candidate for president of Uganda in the 2011 elections but was defeated. In April 2011, the Uganda government arrested numerous opposition leaders, including Otunnu, as protests over rising fuel and food prices began to break out.

6

Data and Documents

Data Overview

Table 1 (Number of Child Soldiers under the Age of 18 in Key Current and Recent Conflicts) provides a general estimate of the numbers of child soldiers participating in current and recent conflicts across the globe. All of the numbers are estimates, as there are no accurate and reliable counts of the actual number of children involved in combat or support roles. All numbers are based on the definition of child soldier as a person under age 18. If age 15 were used as the benchmark, as it is in international criminal law, the numbers would be significantly lower.

Table 2 (Armed Forces and Groups Recruiting Child Soldiers in Current and Recent Conflicts) is a list of the armed forces and armed groups identified as key recruiters of child soldiers in current and recent conflicts. The great majority of recruiters are the armed groups of non-state actors, such as insurgents, militants, rebels, and terrorists. Some governments, such as Myanmar (Burma), continue to recruit child soldiers directly or, more commonly, indirectly by using local allied militias and self-defense groups that recruit children.

Table 3 (Size and Weights of Small Arms Commonly Used by Child Soldiers in Comparison with Other Small Arms) shows small arms that have become common on the world market in recent decades. The most common weapon used by child soldiers is the AK-47 assault rifle, which was originally developed in the former Soviet Union after World War II but has been widely copied by many other countries. Some experts have speculated that because these modern weapons are especially lightweight and easy for children to carry, they have contributed to the recruitment of child soldiers. This table indicates, however, that the weight of light weapons has remained fairly stable for more than 100 years, which casts doubt on the explanation of the recruitment of child soldiers as a function of light weaponry.

Table 4 (Population and Age Distribution in Countries with Current and Recent Conflicts Involving Child Soldiers) shows that in many areas of the world where child soldiers are found, children constitute a much larger percentage of the population than they do elsewhere. For example, in Sweden and the United States, children up to age 14 make up between 15 and 20 percent of the population, while in Uganda and the Democratic Republic of Congo, they make up nearly half the population. This indicates that in many conflict zones, children make up a large pool of individuals from which to draw recruits.

Table 5 (Poverty and Unemployment in Major Child Soldier Conflict Zones in Comparison with the United States and Sweden) shows that poverty can be an important factor in understanding why some children are drawn into armed forces and groups. They may join government armed forces simply to be able to have a salary, or they may join a rebel force whose political ideology involves eliminating of poverty and want. In some conflict zones, such as the Democratic Republic of Congo or Chad, between 70 and 80 percent of the population lives under the poverty line; in the United States, by comparison, only about 12 percent of the population lives below the poverty line.

TABLE 1

Number of Child Soldiers under the Age of 18 in Key Current and Recent Conflicts

Country[1]	Population (millions)	Population under Age 18 (millions)	Government Armed Forces (thousands)	Age of Conscription	Age of Voluntary Recruitment	Number of Child Soldiers
Afghanistan	29.9	15.8	50,000	No lawful conscription	18	8,000 child soldiers in all fighting forces, including the Taliban, the Northern Alliance, and Afghan military forces[2]
Central African Republic	4.0	2.0	3,200	18	18	2,000 child soldiers in government sponsored self-defense militias and a lesser but unknown number in rebel groups[3]
Chad	9.7	5.3	25,400	20	18	7,000–10,000
Colombia	45.6	16.8	208,600	18	18	15,000 in government forces and 6000 rebel groups.
Côte D'Ivoire	18.2	8.8	17,050	18	18	800–1,000[4]
Democratic Republic of the Congo	57.5	31.0	51,000	18	18	7,000
India	1,103.4	420.7	1,316,000	No lawful conscription	17.5	80,000[5]
Iraq	28.8	13.8	227,000	No lawful conscription	18	Large numbers of child soldiers were recruited under the regime of Saddam Hussein; no reports of under 18s serving in the Iraqi armed forces formed in 2003 after the U.S.-led occupation; Opposition groups, such as al-Qaeda in Iraq, continue to recruit child soldiers, although the numbers are unknown
Liberia	3.3 million	1.8	2,400	No lawful conscription	18	5,000–15,000[6]

(continued)

TABLE 1 (CONTINUED)

Country[1]	Population (millions)	Population under Age 18 (millions)	Government Armed Forces (thousands)	Age of Conscription	Age of Voluntary Recruitment	Number of Child Soldiers
Myanmar (Burma)	50.5	18	375,000	No lawful conscription	18	70,000 in government army; 6,000–7,000 in nonstate actors[7]
Nepal	27.1	12.4	69,000	No lawful conscription	18	6,000–9,000[8]
Philippines	83.1	34.6	106,000	No lawful conscription	17 (training only)	2,550[9]
Sierra Leone	5.5	2.7	10,500	No lawful conscription	18	1,000–3,000[10]
Sri Lanka						6,248 by nonstate actors and 453 by progovernment militia[11]
Uganda	28.8	16.5	45,000	No lawful conscription	18	12,000[12]

1. Except as noted, figures are from the Child Soldiers Global Report 2008. All numbers are rough estimates. There few actual counts of the numbers of child soldiers.
2. Worst Forms of Child Labor 2005 Report. *Global March against Child Labour*, http://www.globalmarch.org/worstformsreport/world/afghanistan.html.
3. Kristina Kolesa, "Central African Republic Confronts Child Soldier Crisis." Media Global: Voice of the Global South. July 21, 2011, http://www.mediaglobal.org/article/2011-07-21/central_african_republic_confronts_child_soldier_crisis; *An Uncertain Future? Children and Armed Conflict in the Central African Republic.* New York: Watchlist, 2011, http://watchlist.org/wordpress/wp-content/uploads/Watchlist-CAR-report-EN.pdf.
4. UNICEF estimated that 5,000 children were "associated" with the various fighting forces for the duration of the conflict (2002–2005). Following the war, hundreds were demobilized. Bob Coen, "Former Child Soldiers Still at Risk as Instability Continues in Côte d'Ivoire," UNICEF, February 22, 2006, http://www.unicef.org/infobycountry/cotedivoire_31274.html.
5. The Indian nongovernmental organization Forum for Fact-Finding Documentation and Advocacy estimates that there are 80,000 persons under 18 years of age involved in the conflict with 68,000 with the Naxalite insurgent groups and 12,000 with government-supported militia. Ueli Zempi and Subash Mohapatra, *Child Soldiers in Chhattisgarh: Issues, Challenges and FFDA's Response*, http://www.otherindia.org/dev/images/stories/feda_child.pdf (accessed August 10, 2011).
6. A very speculative estimate by Human Rights Watch. Esther Pan, *Liberia: Child Soldier*, Council on Foreign Relations, August 9, 2003, http://www.cfr.org/liberia/liberia-child-soldiers/p7753#p8.
7. *"My Gun Was as Tall as Me": Child Soldiers in Burma* (New York: Human Rights Watch, 2002).
8. "Nepal: Maoists Should Release Child Soldiers Now." *Human Rights Watch,* May 8, 2007, http://www.hrw.org/en/news/2007/05/06/nepal-maoists-should-release-child-soldiers-now.

9. It is estimated that 15 percent (or 1,800) of the 12,000 soldiers in the Moro Islamic Liberation Front are under the age of 18. The New People's Army (NPA), an armed unit of the Communist Party of the Philippines, has an estimated 5,000 soldiers. The figure in the table assumes a similar percentage of under 18-year-olds for the NPA. "Philippines: Moves to End Use of Child Soldiers, but Problem Persists," Irin: *Humanitarian News and Analysis*, April 8, 2011, http://www.irinnews.org/report.aspx?reportid=92416.

10. It is estimated that some 7,000 persons below age 18 served on all sides of the conflict during the 10-year civil war in Sierra Leone. *Truth and Reconciliation Commission Report for the Children of Sierra Leone (Child Friendly Version)*. Freetown: Government of Sierra Leone. 2004, 8, http://www.unicef.org/infobycountry/files/TRCCF9SeptFINAL.pdf.

11. *No Safety No Escape: Children and the Escalating Armed Conflict in Sri Lanka* (New York: Watchlist, 2008), 2. Numbers are based on UNICEF's child recruitment database between April 2004 and December 2007. Watchlist argues that the actual number of children recruiter is higher.

12. Peter Singer, "Talk Is Cheap: Getting Serious about Preventing Child Soldiers," *Cornell International Law Journal* 37 (2004): 572. This is the estimated number of child soldiers in the force of the Lord's Resistance Army.

TABLE 2

Armed Forces and Groups Recruiting Child Soldiers in Current and Recent Conflicts

Country	Type of Government	Armed Group or Force	G = National Government Force or Government Allied Armed Group / N = Nonstate Party
Afghanistan	Islamic republic	Afghan National Police	G
		Haqqani network	N
		Hezb-i-Islami	N
		Jamat Sunat al-Dawa Salafia	N
		Taliban forces	N
		Tora Bora Front	N
Central African Republic	Republic	Armée populaire pour la restauration de la République et de la démocratie	N
		Convention des patriotes pour la justice et la paix	N
		Union des forces démocratiques pour le rassemblement	N
		Forces démocratiques populaires de Centrafrique	N
		Lord's Resistance Army	N
		Mouvement des libérateurs centrafricains pour la justice	N
		Self-defense militias supported by the government of the Central African Republic	G
Chad	Republic	Chadian National Army (Armée nationale tchadienne)	G
		Justice and Equality Movement (Sudanese-armed groups backed by the government of Chad	G
Colombia	Republic	National Liberation Army (Ejército de Liberación Nacional)	N
		Fuerzas Armadas Revolucionarias de Colombia-Ejército del Pueblo	N
Côte D'Ivoire	Republic	Forces armées des Forces nouvelles	N
		Progovernment militias	G

Democratic Republic of the Congo	Republic	Forces armées de la République démocratique du Congo, including fast-track integrated units of the Congrès national pour la défense du people, formerly led by Laurent Nkunda and currently led by Bosco Ntaganda	G
		Forces démocratiques de libération du Rwanda	N
		Forces de résistance patriotique en Ituri	N
		Front nationaliste et intégrationnaliste	N
		Lord's Resistance Army	N
		Mai-Mai groups in North and South Kivu, including Patriotes résistants congolais	N
India	Federal republic	People's Liberation Army Guerilla Army of the Communist Party of India "Naxalites"	N
		Salwa Judum (government-sponsored anti-Naxalite militia)	G
		Chhattisgarh state police special police officers	G
Iraq	Parliamentary democracy	al-Qaeda in Iraq	N
Liberia	Republic	Armed Forces of Liberia	G
		Liberians United for Reconciliation and Democracy	N
		Movement for Democracy in Liberia	G
Myanmar (Burma)	Military regime	Democratic Karen Buddhist Army	N
		Karen National Union-Karen National Liberation Army Peace Council	N
		Kachin Independence Army	N
		Karen National Liberation Army	N
		Karenni Army	N
		Karenni National People's Liberation Front	G
		Myanmar National Democratic Alliance Army	N
		Shan State Army-South	G
		Tatmadaw Kyi	G
		United Wa State Army	N

(continued)

167

TABLE 2 (CONTINUED)

Country	Type of Government	Armed Group or Force	G = National Government Force or Government Allied Armed Group; N = Nonstate Party
Nepal	Federal democratic republic	Unified Communist Party of Nepal-Maoist	N
Palestinian Territories		Hamas	G
		Palestinian Islamic Jihad	N
		Popular Front for the Liberation of Palestine	N
		Tanzim	N
		al-Aqsa Martyrs' Brigade	N
Philippines	Republic	Abu Sayyaf Group	N
		Moro Islamic Liberation Front	N
		New People's Army	N
Sierra Leone	Constitutional democracy	Civilian Defense Forces (Kamajors)	G
		Revolutionary United Front	N
		Armed Forces Revolutionary Council	N
		Sierra Leone Army	G
Somalia	No national government	Al-Shabaab	N
		Hizbul Islam	N
		Transitional Federal Government	G
Sri Lanka	Republic	Tamil Makkal Viduthalai Pulikal ((former element of Karuna faction, Iniya Barrathi)	N
		The Liberation Tigers of Tamil Eelam, known as the LTTE or the Tamil Tigers	N

Country	Type	Group	Code
Sudan	Republic	Southern Sudan	
		Sudan People's Liberation Army	N
		Lord's Resistance Army	N
		Darfur	
		Chadian opposition groups	G
		Police forces, including the Central Reserve Police and Border Intelligence Forces	G
		Progovernment militias	G
		Sudan Armed Forces	N
		Justice and Equality Movement (Peace Wing)	N
		Movement of Popular Force for Rights and Democracy	N
		Sudan Liberation Army/Abu Gasim/Mother Wing	N
		Sudan Liberation Army/Free Will	N
		Sudan Liberation Army/Minni Minnawi	N
		Sudan Liberation Army/Peace	N
		Justice and Equality Movement	N
		Sudan Liberation Army/Abdul Wahid	N
		Sudan Liberation Army/Unity	N
Uganda	Republic	Lord's Resistance Army	N

TABLE 3

Size and Weights of Small Arms Commonly Used by Child Soldiers in Comparison with Other Small Arms

Weapon	Length	Weight	Standard Magazine	Number Built	Countries of Origin
AK47 (Kalashnikov assault rifle)	34.21 in.	9 lb 7 oz. (4.30 kg)	30-round detachable box	75–100 million	Russia (Soviet Union)
AKM	34.49 in.	8 lb 7 oz.	30-round detachable box	10.3 million	Russia (Soviet Union), China
Gewehr 3 (G3)	40.35 in. 1,025 mm	9 lb 11 oz. (4.40 kg)	20-round detachable box	N/A	Germany
FN-FAL	41.50	9 lb 8 oz. (4.31 kg)	20-round detachable box	2 million	Belgium
M-16	39 in. (990 mm)	6 lb 5 oz. (2.86 kg)	30-round detachable box	8 million	United States
Springfield Model 1861 (Union army)	56 in.	9 lb (4.1 kg)	Muzzle loaded	1.0 million	United States
Pattern 1853 Enfield rifle-musket (Confederacy)	55 in.	9 lb 8 oz. (4.31 kg)	Muzzle loaded	1.5 million	United Kingdom
Lee-Enfield .303 (MLE) (UK)	30.2 in. (770 mm)	8.8 lb (4.0 kg)	10-round magazine	17 million (combined with SMLE)	United Kingdom
Springfield rifle model 1903 (USA)	43.9 in. (1,115 mm)	8.67 lb (3.9 kg)	5-round magazine	1.3 million (between 1903 and 1938)	United States
M1 carbine (USA)	35.6 in. (900 mm)	5.2 lb (2.4 kg)	15–30-round detachable box	6.5 million	United States
Lee-Enfield .303 (SMLE) (UK)	44 in. (1,100 mm)	8.8 lb (4.0 kg)	10-round magazine	17 million (combined with MLE)	United Kingdom
M14 rifle (USA)	46.5 in. (1,181 mm)	11.5 lb (5.2 kg)	20-round detachable magazine	1.5 million	United States

TABLE 4

Population and Age Distribution in Countries with Current and Recent Conflicts Involving Child Soldiers

Country	Total Population (millions)	Percent of Population Ages 0–14	Percent of Population Ages 15–64	Percent of Population Ages 65 and Over	Median Age, Male	Median Age, Female
United States	313.3	20.1	66.8	13.1	36.9	35.6
Sweden	9.1	15.4	64.8	19.7	40.8	43.1
Afghanistan	29.8	42.3	55.3	2.4	18.2	18.2
Central African Republic	4.9	41.0	55.3	3.7	18.8	19.6
Chad	10.7	46.0	51	2.9	15.6	17.9
Colombia	44.7	26.7	67.2	6.1	27.0	28.9
Côte D'Ivoire	21.5	38.9	57.2	3.0	19.7	19.5
Democratic Republic of the Congo	71.7	44.4	53	2.6	17.2	17.6
India	1,189.0	29.7	64.9	5.5	25.6	26.9
Iraq	30.4	38.0	58.9	3.1	20.9	20.8
Nepal	29.3	34.6	61.1	4.4	20.7	22.5
Philippines	101.8	34.6	61.1	4.3	22.4	23.4
Sierra Leone	5.36	41.8	54.5	3.7	18.6	19.5
Somalia	9.9	44.7	52.9	2.4	17.8	17.7
Sri Lanka	21.3	24.9	67.2	7.9	29.7	31.8
Sudan (including southern Sudan)	45.0	42.1	55.2	2.7	18.1	18.9
Uganda	34.6	49.9	48.1	2.1	15.0	15.1

Source: All data from U.S. Central Intelligence Agency, *World Factbook*, https://www.cia.gov/library/publications/the-world-factbook.

TABLE 5
Poverty and Unemployment in Major Child Soldier Conflict Zones in Comparison with the United States and Sweden

Country	Percentage of Population Below Poverty Line	Unemployment Rate	Percentage of Labor Force in Agriculture	Percentage of Labor Force in Industry	Percentage of Labor Force in Services	Per Capita Gross Domestic Product in U.S. Dollars (purchasing power)
United States	12.0	9.7	0.7	20.3	79.0	47,000.00
Sweden	N/A	8.3	1.1	28.0	70.9	39,000.00
Afghanistan	36.0	35.0	78.6	26	15.7	900.00
Central African Republic	N/A	8.0	N/A	N/A	N/A	700.00
Chad	80.0	N/A	80	0	20	1,600.00
Colombia	45.5	11.8	18	14	68	9,800.00
Côte D'Ivoire	42.0	N/A	68	N/A	N/A	1,800.00
Democratic Republic of the Congo	71%	N/A	N/A	N/A	N/A	300.00
India	25.0	10.8	52	14	34	3,500.00
Iraq	25.0	15.3	21.6	18.7	59.8	3,800.00
Nepal	24.7	46.0	75	7	18	1,200.00
Philippines	32.9	7.3	33	15	52	3,500.00
Sierra Leone	70.2	N/A	N/A	N/A	N/A	900.00
Somalia	N/A	N/A	71	29	29	600.00
Sri Lanka	23	5.4	32.7	26.3	41	5,000.00
Sudan (including southern Sudan)	40	18.7	80.0	7.0	13	2,300.00
Uganda	35	N/A	82	5	13	1,200.00

Source: All data from U.S. Central Intelligence Agency, World Factbook, https://www.cia.gov/library/publications/the-world-factbook.

International Treaties

Articles Relating to the Protection of Children from the Fourth Geneva Convention Relative to the Protection of Civilian Persons in Time of War, 12 August 1949

Although the Geneva Conventions of 1949 do not address the issue of child soldiers, many of the articles in the Fourth Convention show the growing concern with the protection of children.

Article 14. In time of peace, the High Contracting Parties and, after the outbreak of hostilities, the Parties thereto, may establish in their own territory and, if the need arises, in occupied areas, hospital and safety zones and localities so organized as to protect from the effects of war, wounded, sick and aged persons, *children under fifteen*, expectant mothers and mothers of children under seven.

Upon the outbreak and during the course of hostilities, the Parties concerned may conclude agreements on mutual recognition of the zones and localities they have created. They may for this purpose implement the provisions of the Draft Agreement annexed to the present Convention, with such amendments as they may consider necessary.

The Protecting Powers and the International Committee of the Red Cross are invited to lend their good offices in order to facilitate the institution and recognition of these hospital and safety zones and localities.

Article 17. The Parties to the conflict shall endeavour to conclude local agreements for the removal from besieged or encircled areas, of wounded, sick, infirm, and aged persons, *children* and maternity cases, and for the passage of ministers of all religions, medical personnel and medical equipment on their way to such areas.

Article 23. Each High Contracting Party shall allow the free passage of all consignments of medical and hospital stores and objects necessary for religious worship intended only for civilians of another High Contracting Party, even if the latter is its adversary. It shall likewise permit the free passage of all consignments of essential foodstuffs, clothing and tonics intended for *children* under fifteen, expectant mothers and maternity cases.

Article 24. The Parties to the conflict shall take the necessary measures to ensure that children under fifteen, who are orphaned or are separated from their families as a result of the war, are not left to their own resources, and that their maintenance, the exercise of their religion and their education are facilitated in all circumstances. Their education shall, as far as possible, be entrusted to persons of a similar cultural tradition.

The Parties to the conflict shall facilitate the reception of such children in a neutral country for the duration of the conflict with the consent of the Protecting Power, if any, and under due safeguards for the observance of the principles stated in the first paragraph.

They shall, furthermore, endeavour to arrange for all *children* under twelve to be identified by the wearing of identity discs, or by some other means.

Article 50. The Occupying Power shall, with the cooperation of the national and local authorities, facilitate the proper working of all institutions devoted to the care and education of children.

Should the local institutions be inadequate for the purpose, the Occupying Power shall make arrangements for the maintenance and education, if possible by persons of their own nationality, language and religion, of children who are orphaned or separated from their parents as a result of the war and who cannot be adequately cared for by a near relative or friend.

A special section of the Bureau set up in accordance with Article 136 shall be responsible for taking all necessary steps to identify children whose identity is in doubt. Particulars of their parents or other near relatives should always be recorded if available.

The Occupying Power shall not hinder the application of any preferential measures in regard to food, medical care and protection against the effects of war which may have been adopted prior to the occupation in favour of children under fifteen years, expectant mothers, and mothers of children under seven years.

Article 82. The Detaining Power shall, as far as possible, accommodate the internees according to their nationality, language and customs. Internees who are nationals of the same country shall not be separated merely because they have different languages.

Throughout the duration of their internment, members of the same family, and in particular parents and children, shall be lodged together in the same place of internment, except when separation of a temporary nature is necessitated for reasons of employment or health or for the purposes of enforcement of the provisions of Chapter IX of the present Section. Internees may request that their children who are left at liberty without parental care shall be interned with them.

Wherever possible, interned members of the same family shall be housed in the same premises and given separate accommodation from other internees, together with facilities for leading a proper family life.

Article 89. Daily food rations for internees shall be sufficient in quantity, quality and variety to keep internees in a good state of health and prevent the development of nutritional deficiencies. Account shall also be taken of the customary diet of the internees.

Internees shall also be given the means by which they can prepare for themselves any additional food in their possession.

Sufficient drinking water shall be supplied to internees. The use of tobacco shall be permitted.

Internees who work shall receive additional rations in proportion to the kind of labour which they perform.

Expectant and nursing mothers and children under fifteen years of age, shall be given additional food, in proportion to their physiological needs.

Article 94. The Detaining Power shall encourage intellectual, educational and recreational pursuits, sports and games amongst internees, whilst leaving them free to take part in them or not. It shall take all practicable measures to ensure the exercise thereof, in particular by providing suitable premises.

All possible facilities shall be granted to internees to continue their studies or to take up new subjects. The education of children and young people shall be ensured; they shall be allowed to attend schools either within the place of internment or outside

Article 132. Each interned person shall be released by the Detaining Power as soon as the reasons which necessitated his internment no longer exist.

The Parties to the conflict shall, moreover, endeavour during the course of hostilities, to conclude agreements for the release, the repatriation, the return to places of residence or the accommodation in a neutral country of certain classes of internees, in particular children, pregnant women and mothers with infants and young children, wounded and sick, and internees who have been detained for a long time.

Source: Geneva Convention Relative to the Protection of Civilian Persons in Time of War (I-973), August 12, 1949. *Treaties and international agreements registered or filed and recorded with the Secretariat of the United Nations,* vol. 75, 1950, 287. Available at http://

treaties.un.org/doc/Publication/UNTS/Volume%2075/v75.pdf.
Used by permission of the United Nations Publication Board.

1949 Geneva Conventions Common Article 3

This article is found in all four Geneva Conventions and applies to all combatants in noninternational conflicts. Captured child soldiers in noninternational conflicts are entitled to its protections even though they would not be considered prisoners of war.

Article 3. In the case of armed conflict not of an international character occurring in the territory of one of the High Contracting Parties, each Party to the conflict shall be bound to apply, as a minimum, the following provisions:

(1) Persons taking no active part in the hostilities, including members of armed forces who have laid down their arms and those placed hors de combat by sickness, wounds, detention, or any other cause, shall in all circumstances be treated humanely, without any adverse distinction founded on race, colour, religion or faith, sex, birth or wealth, or any other similar criteria.

To this end the following acts are and shall remain prohibited at any time and in any place whatsoever with respect to the above-mentioned persons:

(a) violence to life and person, in particular murder of all kinds, mutilation, cruel treatment and torture;

(b) taking of hostages;

(c) outrages upon personal dignity, in particular humiliating and degrading treatment;

(d) the passing of sentences and the carrying out of executions without previous judgment pronounced by a regularly constituted court, affording all the judicial guarantees which are recognized as indispensable by civilized peoples.

(2) The wounded and sick shall be collected and cared for. An impartial humanitarian body, such as the International Committee of the Red Cross, may offer its services to the Parties to the conflict.

The Parties to the conflict should further endeavour to bring into force, by means of special agreements, all or part of the other provisions of the present Convention.

The application of the preceding provisions shall not affect the legal status of the Parties to the conflict.

Source: Geneva Convention Relative to the Protection of Civilian Persons in Time of War (I-973), August 12, 1949. *Treaties and international agreements registered or filed and recorded with the Secretariat of the United Nations*, vol. 75, 1950, 287. Available at http://treaties.un.org/doc/Publication/UNTS/Volume%2075/v75.pdf. Used by permission of the United Nations Publication Board.

Selections from the Third Convention Relative to the Treatment of Prisoners of War, Geneva, 12 August 1949

Article 4 of the Third Geneva Convention details persons who are entitled to prisoner-of-war status when captured in international conflicts. These persons are generally deemed "lawful combatants," although the Convention does not use this term. Child soldiers, like all soldiers in international conflicts, are presumed to be entitled to the rights of prisoners of war if they meet the criteria of the Convention.

Article 4. A. Prisoners of war, in the sense of the present Convention, are persons belonging to one of the following categories, who have fallen into the power of the enemy:

(1) Members of the armed forces of a Party to the conflict, as well as members of militias or volunteer corps forming part of such armed forces.

(2) Members of other militias and members of other volunteer corps, including those of organized resistance movements, belonging to a Party to the conflict and operating in or outside their own territory, even if this territory is occupied, provided that such militias or volunteer corps, including such organized resistance movements, fulfill the following conditions:
(a) that of being commanded by a person responsible for his subordinates;
(b) that of having a fixed distinctive sign recognizable at a distance;
(c) that of carrying arms openly;
(d) that of conducting their operations in accordance with the laws and customs of war.

(3) Members of regular armed forces who profess allegiance to a government or an authority not recognized by the Detaining Power.

(4) Persons who accompany the armed forces without actually being members thereof, such as civilian members of military aircraft crews, war correspondents, supply contractors, members of labour units or of services responsible for the welfare of the armed forces, provided that they have received authorization, from the armed forces which they accompany, who shall provide them for that purpose with an identity card similar to the annexed model.

(5) Members of crews, including masters, pilots and apprentices, of the merchant marine and the crews of civil aircraft of the Parties to the conflict, who do not benefit by more favourable treatment under any other provisions of international law.

(6) Inhabitants of a non-occupied territory, who on the approach of the enemy spontaneously take up arms to resist the invading forces, without having had time to form themselves into regular armed units, provided they carry arms openly and respect the laws and customs of war.

B. The following shall likewise be treated as prisoners of war under the present Convention:

(1) Persons belonging, or having belonged, to the armed forces of the occupied country, if the occupying Power considers it necessary by reason of such allegiance to intern them, even though it has originally liberated them while hostilities were going on outside the territory it occupies, in particular where such persons have made an unsuccessful attempt to rejoin the armed forces to which they belong and which are engaged in combat, or where they fail to comply with a summons made to them with a view to internment.

(2) The persons belonging to one of the categories enumerated in the present Article, who have been received by neutral or non-belligerent Powers on their territory and whom these Powers are required to intern under international law, without prejudice to any more favourable

treatment which these Powers may choose to give and with the exception of Articles 8, 10, 15, 30, fifth paragraph, 58-67, 92, 126 and, where diplomatic relations exist between the Parties to the conflict and the neutral or non-belligerent Power concerned, those Articles concerning the Protecting Power. Where such diplomatic relations exist, the Parties to a conflict on whom these persons depend shall be allowed to perform towards them the functions of a Protecting Power as provided in the present Convention, without prejudice to the functions which these Parties normally exercise in conformity with diplomatic and consular usage and treaties.

C. This Article shall in no way affect the status of medical personnel and chaplains as provided for in Article 33 of the present Convention.

Article 5. The present Convention shall apply to the persons referred to in Article 4 from the time they fall into the power of the enemy and until their final release and repatriation.

Should any doubt arise as to whether persons, having committed a belligerent act and having fallen into the hands of the enemy, belong to any of the categories enumerated in Article 4, such persons shall enjoy the protection of the present Convention until such time as their status has been determined by a competent tribunal.

Source: Geneva Convention Relative to the Protection of Civilian Persons in Time of War (I-973), August 12, 1949. *Treaties and international agreements registered or filed and recorded with the Secretariat of the United Nations*, vol. 75, 1950, 288. Available at http://treaties.un.org/doc/Publication/UNTS/Volume%2075/v75.pdf. Used by permission of the United Nations Publication Board.

Protocol Additional to the Geneva Conventions of 12 August 1949, and Relating to the Protection of Victims of International Armed Conflicts (Protocol I), 8 June 1977

Article 77 of this treaty details those aspects of the laws of war that apply to child soldiers in internationaal armed conflicts. Among its provisions is that "Parties to the conflict shall take all feasible measures in order that children who have not attained the age of fifteen years do not take a direct part in hostilities." This set the standard for the criminal prohibitions on recruitment of children under age 15 contained in the Rome Treaty of the International Criminal Court.

Article 77. Protection of children

1. Children shall be the object of special respect and shall be protected against any form of indecent assault. The Parties to the conflict shall provide them with the care and aid they require, whether because of their age or for any other reason.

2. The Parties to the conflict shall take all feasible measures in order that children who have not attained the age of fifteen years do not take a direct part in hostilities and, in particular, they shall refrain from recruiting them into their armed forces. In recruiting among those persons who have attained the age of fifteen years but who have not attained the age of eighteen years the Parties to the conflict shall endeavour to give priority to those who are oldest.

3. If, in exceptional cases, despite the provisions of paragraph 2, children who have not attained the age of fifteen years take a direct part in hostilities and fall into the power of an adverse Party, they shall continue to benefit from the special protection accorded by this Article, whether or not they are prisoners of war.

4. If arrested, detained or interned for reasons related to the armed conflict, children shall be held in quarters separate from the quarters of adults, except where families are accommodated as family units as provided in Article 75, paragraph 5.

5. The death penalty for an offence related to the armed conflict shall not be executed on persons who had not attained the age of eighteen years at the time the offence was committed.

Source: Protocol Additional to the Geneva Conventions of 12 August 1949 (I-17512), adopted 8 June 1977. *Treaties and international agreements registered or filed and recorded with the Secretariat of the United Nations*, vol. 1125, 1979, 3. Available at http://treaties.un .org/doc/Publication/UNTS/Volume%201125/v1125.pdf. Used by permission of the United Nations Publication Board.

Protocol Additional to the Geneva Conventions of 12 August 1949, and Relating to the Protection of Victims of Non-International Armed Conflicts (Protocol II), 8 June 1977

Article 4 of this treaty required that children in noninternational armed conflicts "who have not attained the age of fifteen years shall neither be recruited in the armed forces or groups nor allowed to take part in hostilities." The treaty also provides special protections for such children even if, despite prohibitions on recruitment, they become child soldiers and are captured.

Article 4. Fundamental guarantees

1. All persons who do not take a direct part or who have ceased to take part in hostilities, whether or not their liberty has been restricted, are entitled to respect for their person, honour and convictions and religious practices. They shall in all circumstances be treated humanely, without any adverse distinction. It is prohibited to order that there shall be no survivors.

2. Without prejudice to the generality of the foregoing, the following acts against the persons referred to in paragraph I are and shall remain prohibited at any time and in any place whatsoever:
(a) violence to the life, health and physical or mental well-being of persons, in particular murder as well as cruel treatment such as torture, mutilation or any form of corporal punishment;
(b) collective punishments;
(c) taking of hostages;
(d) acts of terrorism;
(e) outrages upon personal dignity, in particular humiliating and degrading treatment, rape, enforced prostitution and any form or indecent assault;
(f) slavery and the slave trade in all their forms;
(g) pillage;
(h) threats to commit any or the foregoing acts.

3. Children shall be provided with the care and aid they require, and in particular:

(a) they shall receive an education, including religious and moral education, in keeping with the wishes of their parents, or in the absence of parents, of those responsible for their care;
(b) all appropriate steps shall be taken to facilitate the reunion of families temporarily separated;
(c) children who have not attained the age of fifteen years shall neither be recruited in the armed forces or groups nor allowed to take part in hostilities;
(d) the special protection provided by this Article to children who have not attained the age of fifteen years shall remain applicable to them if they take a direct part in hostilities despite the provisions of subparagraph (c) and are captured;
(e) measures shall be taken, if necessary, and whenever possible with the consent of their parents or persons who by law or custom are primarily responsible for their care, to remove children temporarily from the area in which hostilities are taking place to a safer area within the country and ensure that they are accompanied by persons responsible for their safety and well-being.

Source: Protocol Additional to the Geneva Conventions of 12 August 1949 (I-17513), adopted 8 June 1977. *Treaties and international agreements registered or filed and recorded with the Secretariat of the United Nations,* vol. 1125, 1979, 609. Available at http:// treaties.un.org/doc/Publication/UNTS/Volume%201125/v1125 .pdf. Used by permission of the United Nations Publication Board.

Articles Relating to Child Soldiers from the Convention on the Rights of the Child (1989)

Article 1 of the Convention on the Rights of the Child, the most important children's rights treaty of the modern era, defines a child as "every human being below the age of eighteen" but in Article 38 requires only that states "refrain from recruiting any person who has not attained the age of fifteen years into their armed forces."

Article 1
For the purposes of the present Convention, a child means every human being below the age of eighteen years unless under the law applicable to the child, majority is attained earlier.

Article 38

1. States Parties undertake to respect and to ensure respect for rules of international humanitarian law applicable to them in armed conflicts which are relevant to the child.
2. States Parties shall take all feasible measures to ensure that persons who have not attained the age of fifteen years do not take a direct part in hostilities.
3. States Parties shall refrain from recruiting any person who has not attained the age of fifteen years into their armed forces. In recruiting among those persons who have attained the age of fifteen years but who have not attained the age of eighteen years, States Parties shall endeavour to give priority to those who are oldest.
4. In accordance with their obligations under international humanitarian law to protect the civilian population in armed conflicts, States Parties shall take all feasible measures to ensure protection and care of children who are affected by an armed conflict.

Source: Convention on the Rights of the Child, entry into force 2 Sept 1990. Available at. http://www2.ohchr.org/english/law/crc. htm. Used by permission of the United Nations Publication Board.

Optional Protocol to the Convention on the Rights of the Child on the Involvement of Children in Armed Conflict (2000)

This treaty is an amendment to the Convention on the Rights of the Child. It is a children's rights treaty that raises the age of recruitment for the armed forces of state parties and even for armed groups that are not parties to the treaty.

The States Parties to the present Protocol,

Encouraged by the overwhelming support for the Convention on the Rights of the Child, demonstrating the widespread commitment that exists to strive for the promotion and protection of the rights of the child,

Reaffirming that the rights of children require special protection, and calling for continuous improvement of the situation of children without distinction, as well as for their development and education in conditions of peace and security,

Disturbed by the harmful and widespread impact of armed conflict on children and the long-term consequences it has for durable peace, security and development,

Condemning the targeting of children in situations of armed conflict and direct attacks on objects protected under international law, including places that generally have a significant presence of children, such as schools and hospitals,

Noting the adoption of the Rome Statute of the International Criminal Court, in particular, the inclusion therein as a war crime, of conscripting or enlisting children under the age of 15 years or using them to participate actively in hostilities in both international and non-international armed conflict,

Considering therefore that to strengthen further the implementation of rights recognized in the Convention on the Rights of the Child there is a need to increase the protection of children from involvement in armed conflict,

Noting that article 1 of the Convention on the Rights of the Child specifies that, for the purposes of that Convention, a child means every human being below the age of 18 years unless, under the law applicable to the child, majority is attained earlier,

Convinced that an optional protocol to the Convention that raises the age of possible recruitment of persons into armed forces and their participation in hostilities will contribute effectively to the implementation of the principle that the best interests of the child are to be a primary consideration in all actions concerning children,

Noting that the twenty-sixth International Conference of the Red Cross and Red Crescent in December 1995 recommended, inter alia, that parties to conflict take every feasible step to ensure that children below the age of 18 years do not take part in hostilities,

Welcoming the unanimous adoption, in June 1999, of International Labour Organization Convention No. 182 on the Prohibition and Immediate Action for the Elimination of the Worst Forms of Child Labour, which prohibits, inter alia, forced or compulsory recruitment of children for use in armed conflict,

Condemning with the gravest concern the recruitment, training and use within and across national borders of children in hostilities by armed groups distinct from the armed forces of a State, and recognizing the responsibility of those who recruit, train and use children in this regard,

Recalling the obligation of each party to an armed conflict to abide by the provisions of international humanitarian law,

Stressing that the present Protocol is without prejudice to the purposes and principles contained in the Charter of the United Nations, including Article 51, and relevant norms of humanitarian law,

Bearing in mind that conditions of peace and security based on full respect of the purposes and principles contained in the Charter and observance of applicable human rights instruments are indispensable for the full protection of children, in particular during armed conflict and foreign occupation,

Recognizing the special needs of those children who are particularly vulnerable to recruitment or use in hostilities contrary to the present Protocol owing to their economic or social status or gender,

Mindful of the necessity of taking into consideration the economic, social and political root causes of the involvement of children in armed conflict,

Convinced of the need to strengthen international cooperation in the implementation of the present Protocol, as well as the physical and psychosocial rehabilitation and social reintegration of children who are victims of armed conflict,

Encouraging the participation of the community and, in particular, children and child victims in the dissemination of informational and educational programmes concerning the implementation of the Protocol,

Have agreed as follows:

Article 1

States Parties shall take all feasible measures to ensure that members of their armed forces who have not attained the age of 18 years do not take a direct part in hostilities.

Article 2

States Parties shall ensure that persons who have not attained the age of 18 years are not compulsorily recruited into their armed forces.

Article 3

1. States Parties shall raise the minimum age for the voluntary recruitment of persons into their national armed forces from that set out in article 38, paragraph 3, of the Convention on the Rights of the Child, taking account of the principles contained in that article and recognizing that under the Convention persons under the age of 18 years are entitled to special protection.

2. Each State Party shall deposit a binding declaration upon ratification of or accession to the present Protocol that sets forth the minimum age at which it will permit voluntary recruitment into its national armed forces and a description of the safeguards it has adopted to ensure that such recruitment is not forced or coerced.

3. States Parties that permit voluntary recruitment into their national armed forces under the age of 18 years shall maintain safeguards to ensure, as a minimum, that:
    (a) Such recruitment is genuinely voluntary;
    (b) Such recruitment is carried out with the informed consent of the person's parents or legal guardians;
    (c) Such persons are fully informed of the duties involved in such military service;
    (d) Such persons provide reliable proof of age prior to acceptance into national military service.

4. Each State Party may strengthen its declaration at any time by notification to that effect addressed to the Secretary-General of the United Nations, who shall inform all States Parties. Such notification shall take effect on the date on which it is received by the Secretary-General.

5. The requirement to raise the age in paragraph 1 of the present article does not apply to schools operated by or under the control of the armed forces of the States Parties, in keeping with articles 28 and 29 of the Convention on the Rights of the Child.

Article 4

1. Armed groups that are distinct from the armed forces of a State should not, under any circumstances, recruit or use in hostilities persons under the age of 18 years.

2. States Parties shall take all feasible measures to prevent such recruitment and use, including the adoption of legal measures necessary to prohibit and criminalize such practices.

3. The application of the present article shall not affect the legal status of any party to an armed conflict.

Article 5
Nothing in the present Protocol shall be construed as precluding provisions in the law of a State Party or in international

instruments and international humanitarian law that are more conducive to the realization of the rights of the child.

Article 6

1. Each State Party shall take all necessary legal, administrative and other measures to ensure the effective implementation and enforcement of the provisions of the present Protocol within its jurisdiction.
2. States Parties undertake to make the principles and provisions of the present Protocol widely known and promoted by appropriate means, to adults and children alike.
3. States Parties shall take all feasible measures to ensure that persons within their jurisdiction recruited or used in hostilities contrary to the present Protocol are demobilized or otherwise released from service. States Parties shall, when necessary, accord to such persons all appropriate assistance for their physical and psychological recovery and their social reintegration.

Article 7

1. States Parties shall cooperate in the implementation of the present Protocol, including in the prevention of any activity contrary thereto and in the rehabilitation and social reintegration of persons who are victims of acts contrary thereto, including through technical cooperation and financial assistance. Such assistance and cooperation will be undertaken in consultation with the States Parties concerned and the relevant international organizations.
2. States Parties in a position to do so shall provide such assistance through existing multilateral, bilateral or other programmes or, inter alia, through a voluntary fund established in accordance with the rules of the General Assembly.

Article 8

1. Each State Party shall, within two years following the entry into force of the present Protocol for that State Party, submit a report to the Committee on the Rights

of the Child providing comprehensive information on the measures it has taken to implement the provisions of the Protocol, including the measures taken to implement the provisions on participation and recruitment.

2. Following the submission of the comprehensive report, each State Party shall include in the reports it submits to the Committee on the Rights of the Child, in accordance with article 44 of the Convention, any further information with respect to the implementation of the Protocol. Other States Parties to the Protocol shall submit a report every five years.

3. The Committee on the Rights of the Child may request from States Parties further information relevant to the implementation of the present Protocol.

Article 9

1. The present Protocol is open for signature by any State that is a party to the Convention or has signed it.

2. The present Protocol is subject to ratification and is open to accession by any State. Instruments of ratification or accession shall be deposited with the Secretary-General of the United Nations.

3. The Secretary-General, in his capacity as depositary of the Convention and the Protocol, shall inform all States Parties to the Convention and all States that have signed the Convention of each instrument of declaration pursuant to article 3.

Article 10

1. The present Protocol shall enter into force three months after the deposit of the tenth instrument of ratification or accession.

2. For each State ratifying the present Protocol or acceding to it after its entry into force, the Protocol shall enter into force one month after the date of the deposit of its own instrument of ratification or accession.

Article 11

1. Any State Party may denounce the present Protocol at any time by written notification to the Secretary-General of the

United Nations, who shall thereafter inform the other States Parties to the Convention and all States that have signed the Convention. The denunciation shall take effect one year after the date of receipt of the notification by the Secretary-General. If, however, on the expiry of that year the denouncing State Party is engaged in armed conflict, the denunciation shall not take effect before the end of the armed conflict.

2. Such a denunciation shall not have the effect of releasing the State Party from its obligations under the present Protocol in regard to any act that occurs prior to the date on which the denunciation becomes effective. Nor shall such a denunciation prejudice in any way the continued consideration of any matter that is already under consideration by the Committee on the Rights of the Child prior to the date on which the denunciation becomes effective.

Article 12

1. Any State Party may propose an amendment and file it with the Secretary-General of the United Nations. The Secretary-General shall thereupon communicate the proposed amendment to States Parties with a request that they indicate whether they favour a conference of States Parties for the purpose of considering and voting upon the proposals. In the event that, within four months from the date of such communication, at least one third of the States Parties favour such a conference, the Secretary-General shall convene the conference under the auspices of the United Nations. Any amendment adopted by a majority of States Parties present and voting at the conference shall be submitted to the General Assembly of the United Nations for approval.

2. An amendment adopted in accordance with paragraph 1 of the present article shall enter into force when it has been approved by the General Assembly and accepted by a two-thirds majority of States Parties.

3. When an amendment enters into force, it shall be binding on those States Parties that have accepted it, other States Parties still being bound by the provisions of the present Protocol and any earlier amendments they have accepted.

Article 13

1. The present Protocol, of which the Arabic, Chinese, English, French, Russian and Spanish texts are equally authentic, shall be deposited in the archives of the United Nations.
2. The Secretary-General of the United Nations shall transmit certified copies of the present Protocol to all States Parties to the Convention and all States that have signed the Convention.

Source: United Nations, *Treaty Series*, vol. 2173, 222; Doc.A/RES/ 54/263; and C.N.1031.2000.TREATIES-82 of 14 November 2000.

Articles Relating to Child Soldiers from the Rome Statute of the International Criminal Court (1998)

The Rome Statute, the treaty that established the International Criminal Court, makes the recruitment of children under age 15 a war crime. See Article 8 (2) (b)(xxvi) and 8(2) (e) (vii). Both the armed forces of state parties and the armed groups of nonstate actors are legally obligated under the laws of war to prohibit such recruitment.

Article 8. War Crimes

1. The Court shall have jurisdiction in respect of war crimes in particular when committed as part of a plan or policy or as part of a large-scale commission of such crimes.
2. For the purpose of this Statute, "war crimes" means:
(a) Grave breaches of the Geneva Conventions of 12 August 1949, namely, any of the following acts against persons or property protected under the provisions of the relevant Geneva Convention:
(i) Willful killing;
(ii) Torture or inhuman treatment, including biological experiments;
(iii) Willfully causing great suffering, or serious injury to body or health;

(iv) Extensive destruction and appropriation of property, not justified by military necessity and carried out unlawfully and wantonly;

(v) Compelling a prisoner of war or other protected person to serve in the forces of a hostile Power;

(vi) Willfully depriving a prisoner of war or other protected person of the rights of fair and regular trial;

(vii) Unlawful deportation or transfer or unlawful confinement;

(viii) Taking of hostages.

(b) Other serious violations of the laws and customs applicable in international armed conflict, within the established framework of international law, namely, any of the following acts:

(i) Intentionally directing attacks against the civilian population as such or against individual civilians not taking direct part in hostilities;

(ii) Intentionally directing attacks against civilian objects, that is, objects which are not military objectives;

(iii) Intentionally directing attacks against personnel, installations, material, units or vehicles involved in a humanitarian assistance or peacekeeping mission in accordance with the Charter of the United Nations, as long as they are entitled to the protection given to civilians or civilian objects under the international law of armed conflict;

(iv) Intentionally launching an attack in the knowledge that such attack will cause incidental loss of life or injury to civilians or damage to civilian objects or widespread, long-term and severe damage to the natural environment which would be clearly excessive in relation to the concrete and direct overall military advantage anticipated;

(v) Attacking or bombarding, by whatever means, towns, villages, dwellings or buildings which are undefended and which are not military objectives;

(vi) Killing or wounding a combatant who, having laid down his arms or having no longer means of defence, has surrendered at discretion;

(vii) Making improper use of a flag of truce, of the flag or of the military insignia and uniform of the enemy or of the United Nations, as well as of the distinctive emblems of the Geneva Conventions, resulting in death or serious personal injury;

(viii) The transfer, directly or indirectly, by the Occupying Power of parts of its own civilian population into the territory it occupies, or the deportation or transfer of all or parts of the population of the occupied territory within or outside this territory;

(ix) Intentionally directing attacks against buildings dedicated to religion, education, art, science or charitable purposes, historic monuments, hospitals and places where the sick and wounded are collected, provided they are not military objectives;

(x) Subjecting persons who are in the power of an adverse party to physical mutilation or to medical or scientific experiments of any kind which are neither justified by the medical, dental or hospital treatment of the person concerned nor carried out in his or her interest, and which cause death to or seriously endanger the health of such person or persons;

(xi) Killing or wounding treacherously individuals belonging to the hostile nation or army;

(xii) Declaring that no quarter will be given;

(xiii) Destroying or seizing the enemy's property unless such destruction or seizure be imperatively demanded by the necessities of war;

(xiv) Declaring abolished, suspended or inadmissible in a court of law the rights and actions of the nationals of the hostile party;

(xv) Compelling the nationals of the hostile party to take part in the operations of war directed against their own country, even if they were in the belligerent's service before the commencement of the war;

(xvi) Pillaging a town or place, even when taken by assault;

(xvii) Employing poison or poisoned weapons;

(xviii) Employing asphyxiating, poisonous or other gases, and all analogous liquids, materials or devices;

(xix) Employing bullets which expand or flatten easily in the human body, such as bullets with a hard envelope which does not entirely cover the core or is pierced with incisions;

(xx) Employing weapons, projectiles and material and methods of warfare which are of a nature to cause superfluous injury or unnecessary suffering or which are inherently indiscriminate in violation of the international law of armed conflict, provided that such weapons, projectiles and material and methods of warfare are the subject of a comprehensive prohibition and are included in an annex to this Statute, by an amendment in accordance with the relevant provisions set forth in articles 121 and 123;

(xxi) Committing outrages upon personal dignity, in particular humiliating and degrading treatment;

(xxii) Committing rape, sexual slavery, enforced prostitution, forced pregnancy, as defined in article 7, paragraph 2 (f), enforced sterilization, or any other form of sexual violence also constituting a grave breach of the Geneva Conventions;

(xxiii) Utilizing the presence of a civilian or other protected person to render certain points, areas or military forces immune from military operations;

(xxiv) Intentionally directing attacks against buildings, material, medical units and transport, and personnel using the distinctive emblems of the Geneva Conventions in conformity with international law;

(xxv) Intentionally using starvation of civilians as a method of warfare by depriving them of objects indispensable to their survival, including willfully impeding relief supplies as provided for under the Geneva Conventions;

(xxvi) Conscripting or enlisting children under the age of fifteen years into the national armed forces or using them to participate actively in hostilities.

(c) In the case of an armed conflict not of an international character, serious violations of article 3 common to the four Geneva Conventions of 12 August 1949, namely, any of the following acts committed against persons taking no active part in the hostilities, including members of armed forces who have laid down their arms and those placed hors de combat by sickness, wounds, detention or any other cause:

(i) Violence to life and person, in particular murder of all kinds, mutilation, cruel treatment and torture;
(ii) Committing outrages upon personal dignity, in particular humiliating and degrading treatment;
(iii) Taking of hostages;
(iv) The passing of sentences and the carrying out of executions without previous judgement pronounced by a regularly constituted court, affording all judicial guarantees which are generally recognized as indispensable.
(d) Paragraph 2 (c) applies to armed conflicts not of an international character and thus does not apply to situations of internal disturbances and tensions, such as riots, isolated and sporadic acts of violence or other acts of a similar nature.
(e) Other serious violations of the laws and customs applicable in armed conflicts not of an international character, within the established framework of international law, namely, any of the following acts:
(i) Intentionally directing attacks against the civilian population as such or against individual civilians not taking direct part in hostilities;
(ii) Intentionally directing attacks against buildings, material, medical units and transport, and personnel using the distinctive emblems of the Geneva Conventions in conformity with international law;
(iii) Intentionally directing attacks against personnel, installations, material, units or vehicles involved in a humanitarian assistance or peacekeeping mission in accordance with the Charter of the United Nations, as long as they are entitled to the protection given to civilians or civilian objects under the international law of armed conflict;
(iv) Intentionally directing attacks against buildings dedicated to religion, education, art, science or charitable purposes, historic monuments, hospitals and places where the sick and wounded are collected, provided they are not military objectives;
(v) Pillaging a town or place, even when taken by assault;

(vi) Committing rape, sexual slavery, enforced prostitution, forced pregnancy, as defined in article 7, paragraph 2 (f), enforced sterilization, and any other form of sexual violence also constituting a serious violation of article 3 common to the four Geneva Conventions;

(vii) Conscripting or enlisting children under the age of fifteen years into armed forces or groups or using them to participate actively in hostilities;

(viii) Ordering the displacement of the civilian population for reasons related to the conflict, unless the security of the civilians involved or imperative military reasons so demand;

(ix) Killing or wounding treacherously a combatant adversary;

(x) Declaring that no quarter will be given;

(xi) Subjecting persons who are in the power of another party to the conflict to physical mutilation or to medical or scientific experiments of any kind which are neither justified by the medical, dental or hospital treatment of the person concerned nor carried out in his or her interest, and which cause death to or seriously endanger the health of such person or persons;

(xii) Destroying or seizing the property of an adversary unless such destruction or seizure be imperatively demanded by the necessities of the conflict;

(f) Paragraph 2 (e) applies to armed conflicts not of an international character and thus does not apply to situations of internal disturbances and tensions, such as riots, isolated and sporadic acts of violence or other acts of a similar nature. It applies to armed conflicts that take place in the territory of a State when there is protracted armed conflict between governmental authorities and organized armed groups or between such groups.

3. Nothing in paragraph 2 (c) and (e) shall affect the responsibility of a Government to maintain or re-establish law and order in the State or to defend the unity and territorial integrity of the State, by all legitimate means.

Source: Rome Statute of the International Criminal Court, 17 July 1998. United Nations, Treaty Series, vol. 2187, 3. Available at http://untreaty.un.org/cod/icc/statute/romefra.htm. Used by permission of the United Nations Publication Board.

Statute of the Special Court for Sierra Leone (2000)

Article 4 of the treaty establishing the Special Court for Sierra Leone also makes criminal the acts of "conscripting or enlisting children under the age of 15 years into armed forces or groups or using them to participate actively in hostilities." After the end of the civil war in Sierra Leone, a number of defendants were convicted of this crime.

Article 1. Competence of the Special Court

1. The Special Court shall, except as provided in subparagraph (2), have the power to prosecute persons who bear the greatest responsibility for serious violations of international humanitarian law and Sierra Leonean law committed in the territory of Sierra Leone since 30 November 1996, including those leaders who, in committing such crimes, have threatened the establishment of and implementation of the peace process in Sierra Leone.

Article 4. Other serious violations of international humanitarian law

The Special Court shall have the power to prosecute persons who committed the following serious violations of international humanitarian law:

a. Intentionally directing attacks against the civilian population as such or against individual civilians not taking direct part in hostilities;
b. Intentionally directing attacks against personnel, installations, material, units or vehicles involved in a humanitarian assistance or peacekeeping mission in accordance with the Charter of the United Nations, as long as they are entitled to the protection given to civilians or civilian objects under the international law of armed conflict;

c. Conscripting or enlisting children under the age of
15 years into armed forces or groups or using them to
participate actively in hostilities.

Source: Statute of the Special Court for Sierra Leone, 2002. Available
at http://www.sc-sl.org/DOCUMENTS/tabid/176/Default.aspx.
Used by permission of the United Nations Publication Board.

African Charter on the Rights and Welfare of the Child (1990)

*The African Charter is a regional children's rights treaty. Article 22 of
the treaty requires parties to the treaty to take "all necessary measures
to ensure that no child shall take a direct part in hostilities and refrain
in particular, from recruiting any child."*

Article 2. Definition of a Child

For the purposes of this Charter. a child means every human
being below the age of 18 years.

Article 4. Best Interests of the Child

1. In all actions concerning the child undertaken by any person or authority the best interests of the child shall be the primary consideration.
2. In all judicial or administrative proceedings affecting a child who is capable of communicating his/her own views, and opportunity shall be provided for the views of the child to be heard either directly or through an impartial representative as a party to the proceedings, and those views shall be taken into consideration by the relevant authority in accordance with the provisions of appropriate law.

Article 5. Survival and Development

1. Every child has an inherent right to life. This right shall be protected by law.
2. States Parties to the present Charter shall ensure, to the maximum extent possible, the survival, protection and development of the child.
3. Death sentence shall not be pronounced for crimes committed by children.

Article 22. Armed Conflicts

1. States Parties to this Charter shall undertake to respect and ensure respect for rules of international humanitarian law applicable in armed conflicts which affect the child.
2. States Parties to the present Charter shall take all necessary measures to ensure that no child shall take a direct part in hostilities and refrain in particular, from recruiting any child.
3. States Parties to the present Charter shall, in accordance with their obligations under international humanitarian law, protect the civilian population in armed conflicts and shall take all feasible measures to ensure the protection and care of children who are affected by armed conflicts. Such rules shall also apply to children in situations of internal armed conflicts, tension and strife.

Cape Town Principle and Best Practice on the Prevention of Recruitment of Children into the Armed Forces and Demobilization and Social Integration of Child Soldiers in Africa (1997)

The Cape Town Principles are not a treaty and are not part of international law. They are a set of principles that frequently guide humanitarian and human rights views about child soldiers.

Adopted by the participants in the Symposium on the Prevention of Recruitment of Children into the Armed Forces and Demobilization and Social Reintegration of Child Soldiers in Africa, organized by UNICEF in cooperation with the NGO Sub-group of the NGO Working Group on the Convention on the Rights of the Child, Cape Town, 30 April 1997

DEFINITIONS
"Child soldier" in this document means any person under 18 years of age who is part of any kind of regular or irregular armed force or armed group in any capacity, including but not limited to cooks, porters, messengers, and those accompanying such groups, other than purely as family members. It includes

girls recruited for sexual purposes and forced marriage. It does not, therefore, only refer to a child who is carrying or has carried arms.

"Recruitment" encompasses compulsory, forced and voluntary recruitment into any kind of regular or irregular armed force or armed group.

"Demobilization" means the formal and controlled discharge of child soldiers from the army or from an armed group.

The term "psycho-social" underlines the close relationship between the psychological and social effects of armed conflict, the one type of effect continually influencing the other. By "psychological effects" is meant those experiences which affect emotions, behaviour, thoughts, memory and learning ability and how a situation may be perceived and understood. By "social effects" is meant how the diverse experiences of war alter people's relationships to each other, in that such experiences change people, but also through death, separation, estrangement and other losses. "Social" may be extended to include an economic dimension, many individuals and families becoming destitute through the material and economic devastation of war, thus losing their social status and place in their familiar social network.

PREVENTION OF CHILD RECRUITMENT
1. Establish 18 as the minimum age for any participation in hostilities and for all forms of recruitment into all armed forces and armed groups.
2. Governments should adopt and ratify an Optional Protocol to the Convention on the Rights of the Child raising the minimum ages from 15 to 18.
3. Governments should ratify and implement pertinent regional and international treaties and incorporate them into national law, namely:
a. The African Charter on the Rights and Welfare of the Child which upon entry into force will establish 18 as the minimum age for recruitment and participation;
b. The two Additional Protocols to the 1949 Geneva Conventions and the Convention on the Rights of the Child, which currently establish 15 as the minimum age for recruitment and participation.
4. Governments should adopt national legislation on voluntary and compulsory recruitment with a minimum age of 18 years and should establish proper recruitment procedures and the

means to enforce them. Those responsible for illegally recruiting children should be brought to justice. These recruitment procedures must include:

a. Requirement of proof of age;

b.Safeguards against violations;

c. Dissemination of the standards to the military, especially the recruiters;

d. Publicization of the standards and safeguards to the civilian population, especially children at risk of recruitment and their families and those organizations working with them;

e. Where the government establishes, condones or arms militias or other armed groups, including private security forces, it must also regulate recruitment into them.

5. A permanent International Criminal Court should be established whose jurisdiction would cover, inter alia, the illegal recruitment of children.

6. Written agreements between or with all parties to the conflict which include a commitment on the minimum age of recruitment should be concluded. The SPLM/Operation Lifeline Sudan Agreement on Ground Rules (July 1995) is a useful example.

7. Monitoring, documentation and advocacy are fundamental to eliminating child recruitment and to informing programmes to this end. Community efforts to prevent recruitment should be developed and supported.

a. Local human rights organisations, the media, former child soldiers, and teachers, health workers, church leaders and other community leaders can play an important advocacy role.

b. Establish a dialogue between government and communities in which children are regarded as adults before the age of 18 about the importance of the 18-year limit for recruitment.

c. Provide children with alternative models to the glorification of war, including in the media;

d. Government representatives, military personnel and former opposition leaders can be instrumental in advocating, negotiating and providing technical assistance to their counterparts in other countries in relation to the prevention of recruitment of child soldiers, as well as their demobilization and reintegration.

8. Programmes to prevent recruitment of children should be developed in response to the expressed needs and aspirations of the children.

9. In programmes for children, particular attention should be paid to those most at risk of recruitment: children in conflict zones,

children (especially adolescents) separated from or without families, including children in institutions; other marginalized groups (e.g. street children, certain minorities, refugees and the internally displaced); economically and socially deprived children.

a. Risk mapping can be helpful to identify the groups at risk in particular situations, including such issues as areas of concentration of fighting, the age and type of children being militarized and the main agents of militarization;

b. Promote respect for international humanitarian law;

c. To reduce volunteerism into opposing armed forces, avoid harassment of or attacks on children, their homes and families;

d. Monitor recruitment practices and put pressure on recruiters to abide by the standards and to avoid forced recruitment.

10. All efforts should be made to keep or reunite children with their families or to place them within a family structure.

a. This can be done for example through warnings (e.g. by radio or posters) of the need to avoid separation, or through attaching identification to young children, except where this would expose them to additional risk. For further ideas, see "Unaccompanied Minors: Priority Action Handbook for UNICEF/UNHCR Field Staff."

11. Ensure birth registration, including for refugees and internally displaced children, and the provision of identity documents to all children, particularly those most at risk of recruitment.

12. Access to education, including secondary education and vocational training, should be promoted for all children, including refugee and internally displaced children.

a. Adequate economic provision or opportunities also need to be considered for children or their families.

13. Special protection measures are needed to prevent recruitment of children in camps for refugees and internally displaced persons.

a. Refugee camps should be established at a reasonable distance from the border, wherever possible;

b. The civilian nature and humanitarian character of camps for refugees and internally displaced persons should be ensured. Where this is a problem, specific educational and vocational programmes for children, including adolescents, are even more critical;

c. Host governments, if necessary with the assistance of the international community, should prevent the infiltration of armed elements into camps for refugees and internally displaced persons, and provide physical protection to persons in such camps.

14. The international community should recognize that children who leave their country of origin to avoid illegal recruitment or participation in hostilities are in need of international protection. Children who are not nationals of the country in which they are fighting are also in need of international protection.

15. Controls should be imposed on the manufacture and transfer of arms, especially small arms. No arms should be supplied to parties to an armed conflict who are recruiting children or allowing them to take part in hostilities.

DEMOBILIZATION

16. All persons under the age of 18 should be demobilized from any kind of regular or irregular armed force or armed group.

a. Direct and free access to all child soldiers should be granted to relevant authorities or organizations in charge of collecting information concerning their demobilization and of implementing specific programmes.

17. Children should be given priority in any demobilization process.

18. In anticipation of peace negotiations or as soon as they begin, preparations should be made to respond to children who will be demobilized.

a. Prepare initial situation analysis/needs assessment of children and their communities;

b. Ensure coordination between all parties to avoid duplication and gaps;

c. Where there is access to governmental and other local structures, incorporate and (where necessary) strengthen existing capacities to respond;

d. Ensure training of staff who will be involved in the process;

e. Organize logistical and technical support in collaboration with agencies responsible for the formal demobilization process;

f. Ensure that the demobilization package is of a long-term, sustaining nature rather than in the form of an immediate "reward," taking into account the implications of the nature of the package for future recruitment of children.

19. The issue of demobilization of children should be included in the peace process from the beginning.

20. Where children have participated in armed conflict, peace agreements and related documents should acknowledge this fact.

21. The demobilization process should be designed as the first step in the social reintegration process.

22. The demobilization process should be as short as possible and take into account the human dignity of the child and the need for confidentiality.

a. Ensure adequate time and appropriate personnel to make children feel secure and comfortable so that they are able to receive information, including about their rights, and to share concerns;

b. Wherever possible, staff dealing with the children should be nationals;

c. Special measures must be taken to ensure the protection of children who are in demobilization centres for extended periods of time;

d. Children should be interviewed individually and away from their superiors and peers;

e. It is not appropriate to raise sensitive issues in the initial interview. If they are raised subsequently, it must be done only when in the best interest of the child and by a competent person;

f. Confidentiality must be respected;

g. All children should be informed throughout the process of the reasons why the information is being collected and that confidentiality will be respected. Children should be further informed about what will happen to them at each step of the process;

h. Wherever possible, communication and information should be in the mother tongue of the children;

i. Particular attention should be paid to the special needs of girls and special responses should be developed to this end.

23. As soon as possible start establishing family tracing, contacts and reunification.

24. Health assessment and treatment should be priorities.

a. As soon as possible during the demobilization process, all children should undergo assessment of their physical health and receive treatment as necessary;

b. Particular responses should be developed for girls;

c. Particular responses are needed for children with special needs, e.g. children with disabilities, child soldiers with children of their own, children with substance abuse problems and sexually-transmitted diseases (HIV/AIDS, etc,);

d. Ensure linkages between the demobilization process and existing programmes which are competent to deal with the health needs of children.

25. Monitoring and documentation of child involvement, as well as advocacy for demobilization and release of children,

should be undertaken throughout the armed conflict. Community efforts to this end should be supported.

26. Children who leave any armed forces or groups during on-going hostilities have special needs for protection which must be addressed.

During on-going hostilities there is rarely any formal demobilization. However, children may leave the army, for example by escaping or as a result of being captured or wounded. This may compromise their security, protection and access to services. Despite difficulties in identifying such children, there must be recognition of their special needs for protection:

a. Efforts should be made for an early start to programmes and family tracing for unaccompanied children;

b. Efforts should be made to ensure that re-recruitment does not occur. The likelihood of re-recruitment can be reduced if: (i) children are returned to their care-givers as soon as possible; (ii) children are informed of their rights not to be recruited; and (iii) where children have been formally demobilized, others are informed of this fact;

c. Any assembly areas must be sufficiently far from the conflict zones to ensure security. Particular problems may include: (i) some children may not be able to go home; (ii) some areas may be inaccessible for tracing; (iii) families of some children may be in camps for refugees or internally displaced persons; and (iv) the risk of the children being placed in institutions.

27. Illegally recruited children who leave the armed forces or armed groups at any time should not be considered as deserters. Child soldiers retain their rights as children.

28. Special assistance and protection measures must be taken on behalf of children and those recruited as children. See for example "Basic Rights Recognized For the Angolan Under-aged Soldiers."

29. Ensure to the extent possible that demobilized children return to their communities under conditions of safety.

30. Ensure that demobilized children are not discriminated against in services and benefits for demobilized soldiers.

31. Ensure that the rights of children involved in the demobilization process are respected by the media, researchers and others.

a. With specific regard to journalists, a code of conduct should be developed in order to prevent the exploitation of child soldiers by the media. Such a code should take account of inter alia the manner in which sensitive issues are raised, the child's right to anonymity and the frequency of contacts with the media.

RETURN TO FAMILY AND COMMUNITY LIFE

32. Family reunification is the principal factor in effective social reintegration.

a. For family reunification to be successful, special attention must be paid to re-establishing the emotional link between the child and the family prior to and following return;

b. Where children have not been reunited with their family, their need to establish and maintain stable emotional relationships must be recognized;

c. Institutionalization should only be used as a last resort, for the shortest possible time, and efforts to find family-based solutions should continue.

33. Programmes should be developed with the communities, built on existing resources, taking account of the context and community priorities, values and traditions.

a. Programmes responding to the needs of the children should be developed. They should seek to enhance the self-esteem of children, promote their capacity to protect their own integrity and to construct a positive life. Activities must take into account the age and stage of development of the child and accommodate the particular requirements of girls and children with special needs;

b. Programmes can only develop through relationships of trust and confidence, require time and a commitment of resources, and will necessitate a close and on-going cooperation between all actors involved;

c. The impact of the conflict on children and their families must be assessed in order to develop effective programming. This should be undertaken through interviews and discussions with the children concerned, the families and the community as well as, where appropriate, the government. The information should be gathered as early as possible to enable preparation and planning;

d. Policies and strategies to address the situation of demobilized child soldiers should be developed and implemented on the basis of such assessments.

34. The capacity of the family and community to care for and protect the child should be developed and supported.

a. Identify and support traditional resources and practices in the community which can support the psycho-social integration of children affected by war;

b. Assess and understand the socio-economic context with specific reference to poverty, and food and nutritional security;

c. Identify and build on the traditional ways of generating income, traditional apprenticeships, credit and money-making schemes;

d. Initiate dialogue with communities to understand their main concerns for their children and their perception of their own roles and responsibilities with regard to the children.

35. Programmes targeted at former child soldiers should be integrated into programmes for the benefit of all war-affected children.

a. Whilst stressing that it is essential to normalize the life of child soldiers, it is important to recognize that all children in a community will have been affected to some degree by the conflict. Programmes for former child soldiers should therefore be integrated into efforts to address the situation of all children affected by the conflict, while ensuring the continuing implementation of specific rights and benefits of demobilized children;

b. The existing health, education and social services within the communities should be supported.

36. Provision should be made for educational activities which reflect: the loss of educational opportunities as a consequence of participation; the age and stage of development of the children; and their potential for promoting development of self-esteem.

37. Provision should be made for relevant vocational training and opportunities or (self-) employment, including for children with disabilities.

a. Upon completion of vocational skills training, trainees should be provided with the relevant tools and, where possible, with start-up loans to promote self-reliance.

38. Recreational activities are essential for psycho-social well-being.

a. Recreational activities should be included in all reintegration programmes for war-affected children. These contribute to the children's psycho-social well-being, facilitate the reconciliation process and form part of their rights as children.

39. Programme development and implementation should incorporate the participation of the children and, with due regard for the context of reintegration, reflect their needs and concerns.

40. Psycho-social programmes should assist children to develop and build those capacities that will facilitate a re-attachment to families and communities.

41. Monitoring and follow-up of the children should take place to ensure reintegration and receipt of rights and benefits. Use community resources for this, e.g. catechists, teachers or others, depending on the situation.

42. In order to be successful, reintegration of the child within the community should be carried out in the framework of efforts towards national reconciliation.

43. Programmes to prevent, demobilize and reintegrate child soldiers should be jointly and constantly monitored and evaluated with communities.

Cape Town, 30 April 1997.

Source: African (Banjul) Charter on Human and Peoples' Rights. Adopted 27 June 1981, OAU Doc. CAB/LEB/67/3 rev. 5, 21 I.L.M. 58 (1982), entered into force 21 October 1986. Available at http://www.africa-union.org/official_documents/treaties_%20conventions_%20protocols/banjul%20charter.pdf.

International Labour Organization Convention 182 Concerning the Prohibition and Immediate Action for the Elimination of the Worst Forms of Child Labour (1999)

The ILO Convention 182 is an international treaty that defines the recruitment of child soldiers as a practice similar to slavery.

Article 1

Each Member which ratifies this Convention shall take immediate and effective measures to secure the prohibition and elimination of the worst forms of child labour as a matter of urgency.

Article 2

For the purposes of this Convention, the term "child" shall apply to all persons under the age of 18.

Article 3

For the purposes of this Convention, the term "the worst forms of child labour" comprises:

(a) all forms of slavery or practices similar to slavery, such as the sale and trafficking of children, debt bondage and serfdom and forced or compulsory labour, including forced or compulsory recruitment of children for use in armed conflict;

(b) the use, procuring or offering of a child for prostitution, for the production of pornography or for pornographic performances;

(c) the use, procuring or offering of a child for illicit activities, in particular for the production and trafficking of drugs as defined in the relevant international treaties;

(d) work which, by its nature or the circumstances in which it is carried out, is likely to harm the health, safety or morals of children.

Source: Convention Concerning the Prohibition and Immediate Action for the Elimination of the Worst Forms of Child Labour (Convention 182, 17 June 1999). International Labour Organization. Available at http://www.ilo.org/public/english/standards/relm/ilc/ilc87/com-chic.htm. Used by permission of the International Labour Organization.

U.S. Legislation

The Child Soldier Prevention Act of 2008

The Child Soldier Prevention Act of 2008 authorizes the secretary of state of the United States to publish a list of countries that recruit child soldiers in violation of the requirements of the Optional Protocol and requires that such countries be denied certain forms of military assistance. The president of the United States may, however, waive the application of the law when such a waiver is deemed in the national interest of the United States.

TITLE IV—CHILD SOLDIERS PREVENTION

SEC. 401. SHORT TITLE.

This title may be cited as the "Child Soldier Prevention Act of 2008, 22 U.S.C. §§ 2370c, 2370c-1, 2370c-2, 4028 (2008).

SEC. 402. DEFINITIONS.

In this title:

(1) APPROPRIATE CONGRESSIONAL COMMITTEES.— The term "appropriate congressional committees" means—

(A) the Committee on Foreign Relations of the Senate;

(B) the Committee on Appropriations of the Senate;

(C) the Committee on Foreign Affairs of the House of Representatives; and

(D) the Committee on Appropriations of the House of Representatives.

(2) CHILD SOLDIER.—Consistent with the provisions of the Optional Protocol to the Convention of the Rights of the Child, the term "child soldier"—

(A) means—

(i) any person under 18 years of age who takes a direct part in hostilities as a member of governmental armed forces;

(ii) any person under 18 years of age who has been compulsorily recruited into governmental armed forces;

(iii) any person under 15 years of age who has been voluntarily recruited into governmental armed forces; or

(iv) any person under 18 years of age who has been recruited or used in hostilities by armed forces distinct from the armed forces of a state; and

(B) includes any person described in clauses (ii), (iii), or (iv) of subparagraph (A) who is serving in any capacity, including in a support role such as a cook, porter, messenger, medic, guard, or sex slave.

SEC. 403. SENSE OF CONGRESS.

It is the sense of Congress that—

(1) the United States Government should condemn the conscription, forced recruitment, or use of children by governments, paramilitaries, or other organizations;

(2) the United States Government should support and, to the extent practicable, lead efforts to establish and uphold international standards designed to end the abuse of human rights described in paragraph (1);

(3) the United States Government should expand ongoing services to rehabilitate recovered child soldiers and to reintegrate such children back into their respective communities by—

(A) offering ongoing psychological services to help such children—

(i) to recover from the trauma suffered during their forced military involvement;

(ii) to relearn how to interact with others in nonviolent ways so that such children are no longer a danger to their respective communities; and

(iii) by taking into consideration the needs of girl soldiers, who may be at risk of exclusion from disarmament, demobilization, and reintegration programs;

(B) facilitating reconciliation with such communities through negotiations with traditional leaders and elders to enable recovered abductees to resume normal lives in such communities; and

(C) providing educational and vocational assistance;

(4) the United States should work with the international community, including, as appropriate, third country governments, nongovernmental organizations, faith-based organizations, United Nations agencies, local governments, labor unions, and private enterprises—

(A) to bring to justice rebel and paramilitary forces that kidnap children for use as child soldiers;

(B) to recover those children who have been abducted; and

(C) to assist such children to be rehabilitated and reintegrated into their respective communities;

(5) the Secretary of State, the Secretary of Labor, and the Secretary of Defense should coordinate programs to achieve the goals described in paragraph (3);

(6) United States diplomatic missions in countries in which the use of child soldiers is an issue, whether or not such use is supported or sanctioned by the governments of such countries, should include in their mission program plans a strategy to achieve the goals described in paragraph (3);

(7) United States diplomatic missions in countries in which governments use or tolerate child soldiers should develop strategies, as part of annual program planning—

(A) to promote efforts to end such abuse of human rights; and

(B) to identify and integrate global best practices, as available, into such strategies to avoid duplication of effort; and

(8) in allocating or recommending the allocation of funds or recommending candidates for programs and grants funded by the United States Government, United States diplomatic missions should give serious consideration to those programs and candidates that are expected to promote the end to the abuse of human rights described in this section.

SEC. 404. PROHIBITION.

(a) IN GENERAL.—Subject to subsections (b), (c), and (d), the authorities contained in section 516 or 541 of the Foreign Assistance Act of 1961 (22 U.S.C. 2321j or 2347) or section 23 of the Arms Export Control Act (22 U.S.C. 2763) may not be used to provide assistance to, and no licenses for direct commercial sales of military equipment may be issued to, the government of a country that is clearly identified, pursuant to subsection (b), for the most recent year preceding the fiscal year in which the authorities or license would have been used or issued in the absence of a violation of this title, as having governmental armed forces or government- supported armed groups, including paramilitaries, militias, or civil defense forces, that recruit and use child soldiers.

(b) IDENTIFICATION AND NOTIFICATION TO COUNTRIES IN VIOLATION OF STANDARDS.—

(1) PUBLICATION OF LIST OF FOREIGN GOVERNMENTS.—The Secretary of State shall include a list of the foreign governments that have violated the standards under this title and are subject to the prohibition in subsection (a) in the report required under section 110(b) of the Trafficking Victims Protection Act of 2000 (22 U.S.C. 7107(b)).

(2) NOTIFICATION OF FOREIGN COUNTRIES.—The Secretary of State shall formally notify any government identified pursuant to subsection (a).

(c) NATIONAL INTEREST WAIVER.—

(1) WAIVER.—The President may waive the application to a country of the prohibition in subsection (a) if the President determines that such waiver is in the national interest of the United States.

(2) PUBLICATION AND NOTIFICATION.—Not later than 45 days after each waiver is granted under paragraph (1), the President shall notify the appropriate congressional committees of the waiver and the justification for granting such waiver.

(d) REINSTATEMENT OF ASSISTANCE.—The President may provide to a country assistance otherwise prohibited under subsection (a) upon certifying to the appropriate congressional committees that the government of such country—

(1) has implemented measures that include an action plan and actual steps to come into compliance with the standards outlined in section 404(b); and

(2) has implemented policies and mechanisms to prohibit and prevent future government or government- supported use of child soldiers and to ensure that no children are recruited, conscripted, or otherwise compelled to serve as child soldiers.

(e) EXCEPTION FOR PROGRAMS DIRECTLY RELATED TO ADDRESSING THE PROBLEM OF CHILD SOLDIERS OR PROFESSIONALIZATION OF THE MILITARY.—

(1) IN GENERAL.—The President may provide assistance to a country for international military education, training, and nonlethal supplies (as defined in section 2557(d)(1)(B) of title

10, United States Code) otherwise prohibited under subsection (a) upon certifying to the appropriate congressional committees that—

(A) the government of such country is taking reasonable steps to implement effective measures to demobilize child soldiers in its forces or in government-supported paramilitaries and is taking reasonable steps within the context of its national resources to provide demobilization, rehabilitation, and reintegration assistance to those former child soldiers; and

(B) the assistance provided by the United States Government to the government of such country will go to programs that will directly support professionalization of the military.

(2) LIMITATION.—The exception under paragraph (1) may remain in effect for a country for more than 5 years.

SEC. 405. REPORTS.

(a) INVESTIGATION OF ALLEGATIONS REGARDING CHILD SOLDIERS.—United States missions abroad shall thoroughly investigate reports of the use of child soldiers.

(b) INFORMATION FOR ANNUAL HUMAN RIGHTS REPORTS.—In preparing those portions of the annual Human Rights Report that relate to child soldiers under sections 116 and 502B of the Foreign Assistance Act of 1961 (22 U.S.C. 2151n(f) and 2304(h)), the Secretary of State shall ensure that such reports include a description of the use of child soldiers in each foreign country, including—

(1) trends toward improvement in such country of the status of child soldiers or the continued or increased tolerance of such practices; and

(2) the role of the government of such country in engaging in or tolerating the use of child soldiers.

(c) ANNUAL REPORT TO CONGRESS.—If, during any of the 5 years following the date of the enactment of this Act, a country is notified pursuant to section 404(b)(2), or a wavier is granted pursuant to section 404(c)(1), the President shall submit a report to the appropriate congressional committees not later than June 15 of the following year. The report shall include—

(1) a list of the countries receiving notification that they are in violation of the standards under this title;

(2) a list of any waivers or exceptions exercised under this title;

(3) justification for any such waivers and exceptions; and

(4) a description of any assistance provided under this title pursuant to the issuance of such waiver.

SEC. 406. TRAINING FOR FOREIGN SERVICE OFFICERS.

Section 708 of the Foreign Service Act of 1980 (22 U.S.C. 4028) is amended by adding at the end the following:

"(c) The Secretary of State, with the assistance of other relevant officials, shall establish as part of the standard training provided for chiefs of mission, deputy chiefs of mission, and other officers of the Service who are or will be involved in the assessment of child soldier use or the drafting of the annual Human Rights Report instruction on matters related to child soldiers, and the substance of the Child Soldiers Prevention Act of 2008."

SEC. 407. EFFECTIVE DATE; APPLICABILITY.

This title, and the amendments made by this title, shall take effect 180 days after the date of the enactment of this Act.

Source: Child Soldier Prevention Act of 2008, 22 U.S.C. §§ 2370c, 2370c-1, 2370c-2, 4028 (2008). Available at http://www.state.gov/documents/organization/135981.pdf.

The Child Soldier Accountability Act of 2008

The Child Soldier Accountability Act of 2008 allows recruiters of child soldiers under age 15 to be criminally prosecuted in the United States.

An Act

To prohibit the recruitment or use of child soldiers, to designate persons who recruit or use child soldiers as inadmissible aliens, to allow the deportation of persons who recruit or use child soldiers, and for other purposes.

Be it enacted by the Senate and House of Representatives of the United States of America in Congress assembled,

SECTION 1. SHORT TITLE.

This Act may be cited as the "Child Soldiers Accountability Act of 2008."

SEC. 2. ACCOUNTABILITY FOR THE RECRUITMENT AND USE OF CHILD SOLDIERS.

(a) CRIME FOR RECRUITING OR USING CHILD SOLDIERS.—

(1) IN GENERAL.—Chapter 118 of title 18, United States Code, is amended by adding at the end the following: 4

"§ 2442. Recruitment or use of child soldiers

"(a) OFFENSE.—Whoever knowingly—

"(1) recruits, enlists, or conscripts a person to serve while such person is under 15 years of age in an armed force or group; or

"(2) uses a person under 15 years of age to participate actively in hostilities; knowing such person is under 15 years of age, shall be punished as provided in subsection (b).

"(b) PENALTY.—Whoever violates, or attempts or conspires to violate, subsection (a) shall be fined under this title or imprisoned not more than 20 years, or both and, if death of any person results, shall be fined under this title and imprisoned for any term of years or for life.

"(c) JURISDICTION.—There is jurisdiction over an offense described in subsection (a), and any attempt or conspiracy to commit such offense, if—

"(1) the alleged offender is a national of the United States (as defined in section 101(a)(22) of the Immigration and Nationality Act (8 U.S.C. 1101(a)(22))) or an alien lawfully admitted for permanent residence in the United States (as defined in section 101 (a)(20) of such Act (8 U.S.C. 1101(a)(20));

"(2) the alleged offender is a stateless person whose habitual residence is in the United States;

"(3) the alleged offender is present in the United States, irrespective of the nationality of the alleged offender; or

"(4) the offense occurs in whole or in part within the United States.

"(d) DEFINITIONS.—In this section:

"(1) PARTICIPATE ACTIVELY IN HOSTILITIES.—The term 'participate actively in hostilities' means taking part in—

"(A) combat or military activities related to combat, including sabotage and serving as a decoy, a courier, or at a military checkpoint; or

"(B) direct support functions related to combat, including transporting supplies or providing other services.

"(2) ARMED FORCE OR GROUP.—The term 'armed force or group' means any army, militia, or other military organization, whether or not it is state-sponsored, excluding any group assembled solely for nonviolent political association."

(2) STATUTE OF LIMITATIONS.—Chapter 213 of title 18, United States Code is amended by adding at the end the following:

"§ 3300. Recruitment or use of child soldiers

"No person may be prosecuted, tried, or punished for a violation of section 2442 unless the indictment or the information is filed not later than 10 years after the commission of the offense."

(3) CLERICAL AMENDMENT.—Title 18, United States Code, is amended—

(A) in the table of sections for chapter 118, by adding at the end the following:

"2442. Recruitment or use of child soldiers.";

and

(B) in the table of sections for chapter 213, by adding at the end the following:

"3300. Recruitment or use of child soldiers."

(b) GROUND OF INADMISSIBILITY FOR RECRUITING OR USING CHILD SOLDIERS.—Section 212(a)(3) of the Immigration and Nationality Act (8 U.S.C. 1182(a)(3)) is amended by adding at the end the following:

"(G) RECRUITMENT OR USE OF CHILD SOLDIERS.—Any alien who has engaged in the recruitment or use of child soldiers in violation of section 2442 of title 18, United States Code, is inadmissible."

(c) GROUND OF REMOVABILITY FOR RECRUITING OR USING CHILD SOLDIERS.—Section 237(a)(4) of the Immigration and Nationality Act (8 U.S.C. 1227(a)(4)) is amended by adding at the end the following:

"(F) RECRUITMENT OR USE OF CHILD SOLDIERS.—Any alien who has engaged in the recruitment or use of child soldiers in violation of section 2442 of title 18, United States Code, is deportable."

(d) ASYLUM AND WITHHOLDING OF REMOVAL.—

(1) ISSUANCE OF REGULATIONS.—Not later than 60 days after the date of enactment of this Act, the Attorney General and the Secretary of Homeland Security shall promulgate final regulations establishing that, for purposes of sections 241(b)(3)(B)(iii) and 208(b)(2)(A)(iii) of the Immigration and Nationality Act (8 U.S.C. 1231(b)(3)(B)(iii); 8 U.S.C. 1158(b)(2)(A)(iii)), an alien who is deportable under section 237(a)(4)(F) of such Act (8 U.S.C. 1227(a)(4)5 (F)) or inadmissible under section 212(a)(3)(G) of such Act (8 U.S.C. 1182(a)(3)(G)) shall be considered an alien with respect to whom there are serious reasons to believe that the alien committed a serious nonpolitical crime.

(2) AUTHORITY TO WAIVE CERTAIN REGULATORY REQUIREMENTS.—The requirements of chapter 5 of title 5, United States Code (commonly referred to as the "Administrative Procedure Act"), chapter 35 of title 44, United States Code (commonly referred to as the "Paperwork Reduction Act"), or any other law relating to

rulemaking, information collection, or publication in the Federal Register, shall not apply to any action to implement paragraph.

(1) to the extent the Attorney General or the Secretary Homeland of Security determines that compliance with any such requirement would impede the expeditious implementation of such paragraph.

Source: Child Soldiers Accountability Act of 2008. Public Law No. 110-340. Available at http://www.govtrack.us/congress/billtext .xpd?bill=s110-2135.

Human Rights Enforcement Act of 2009

The Human Rights Enforcement Act of 2009 allows for the creation of a special unit within the Criminal Division of the Department of Justice for enforcing laws against suspected participants in serious human rights offenses, including the recruitment of child soldiers.

SECTION 1. SHORT TITLE.

This Act may be cited as the "Human Rights Enforcement Act of 2009."

SEC. 2. SECTION TO ENFORCE HUMAN RIGHTS LAWS.

(a) REPEAL.—Section 103(h) of the Immigration and Nationality Act (8 U.S.C. 1103(h)) is repealed.

(b) SECTION TO ENFORCE HUMAN RIGHTS LAWS.— Chapter 31 of title 28, United States Code, is amended by inserting after section 509A the following:

"§ 509B. Section to enforce human rights laws

"(a) Not later than 90 days after the date of the enactment of the Human Rights Enforcement Act of 2009, the Attorney General shall establish a section within the Criminal Division of the Department of Justice with responsibility for the enforcement of laws against suspected participants in serious human rights offenses.

"(b) The section established under subsection (a) is authorized to—

"(1) take appropriate legal action against individuals suspected of participating in serious human rights offenses; and

"(2) coordinate any such legal action with the United States Attorney for the relevant jurisdiction.

"(c) The Attorney General shall, as appropriate, consult with the Secretary of Homeland Security and the Secretary of State.

"(d) In determining the appropriate legal action to take against individuals who are suspected of committing serious human rights offenses under Federal law, the section shall take into consideration the availability of criminal prosecution under the laws of the United States for such offenses or in a foreign jurisdiction that is prepared to undertake a prosecution for the conduct that forms the basis for such offenses.

"(e) The term 'serious human rights offenses' includes violations of Federal criminal laws relating to genocide, torture, war crimes, and the use or recruitment of child soldiers under sections 1091, 2340, 2340A, 2441, and 2442 of title 18, United States Code."

Source: Human Rights Enforcement Act of 2009. Public Law No. 111-122. Available at http://www.govtrack.us/congress/billtext.xpd?bill=s111-1472.

7

Directory of Organizations

Ajedi-Ka/Projet Enfants Soldats
29, Avenue des Pionniers—Uvira /RDC
via BP 1863 Bujumbura
Burundi
Telephone, DRC: 243-994011350
Telephone, USA: 1-847-208-9740
Email: info@ajedika.org
Website: http://www.ajedika.org

Ajedi-Ka/Projet Enfants Soldats operates in the Democratic Republic of the Congo in order to promote and protect the rights of child soldiers and other children affected by armed conflict and child soldiers. It helps to demobilize and reintegrate both boy and girl soldiers and engages in long- term follow-up on their welfare. It also has developed programs to combat the spread of HIV/AIDS among child soldiers and former combatants.

American Friends Service Committee–Youth and Militarism Program
Janine Schwab
1501 Cherry Street
Philadelphia, PA 19102
USA
Telephone: 1-215-241-7176
Email: youthmil@afsc.org
Website: http://www.afsc.org/program/youth-and-militarism
-program

The American Friends Service Committee has youth and militarism programs in the United States and in Asia, Latin America, and the Middle East. In the United States, it provides youth with information about alternatives to military service. Elsewhere, it promotes the involvement of youth in peace-building and reconciliation efforts.

American Jewish World Service
45 West 36th Street
New York, NY 10018
USA
Telephone: 1-212-792-2900, 1-800-889-7146
Fax: 1-212-792-2930
Email: See Website Contact Form
Website: http://ajws.org

American Jewish World Service works to alleviate poverty, hunger, and disease in the developing world. It provides grants to grassroots organizations and engages in advocacy and education. Among the organizations that it supports that deal directly with the issue of the rehabilitation and reintegration of former child combatants are Ajedi-Ka/Projet Enfants Soldats in Burundi and Foro Joven in Colombia.

Amnesty International
International Secretariate
1 Easton Street
London WC1X 0DW
United Kingdom
Telephone: UK 44-20-7413 5500

New York Office
5 Penn Plaza, 16th Floor
New York, NY 10001
USA
Telephone: 1-212-807-8400
Fax: 1-212-627-1451
Email: info@amnesty.org.uk, info@usamnesty.org
Website: http://www.amnesty.org

Founded in 1961, Amnesty International campaigns for internationally recognized human rights. It conducts research and generates action to prevent grave abuses of human rights and to demand justice for those whose rights have been violated. It attempts to exert influence on governments, political bodies, companies, and intergovernmental groups. It publishes reports and studies on the situation of child soldiers in various conflict zones.

Brookings Institution, London School of Economics Project on Internal Displacement
Brookings Institution
1775 Massachusetts Avenue NW
Washington, DC 20036
USA
Telephone: 1-202-797-2477
Fax: 1-202-797-2970
Email: IDP@brookings.edu
Website: http://www.brookings.edu/projects/idp.aspx

London School of Economics and Political Science
Houghton Street
London WC2A 2AE
United Kingdom
Telephone: 41 (31) 631-4838

The project focuses on populations forcibly uprooted within their own countries by armed conflict, large-scale development projects, systematic violations of human rights, or natural disasters and therefore lack predictable structures of support. Currently, there are 27.5 million internally displaced persons in more than 50 countries. The project is designed to promote effective national, regional, and international response to this global problem

CARE
151 Ellis Street NE
Atlanta, GA 30303-2440
USA
Telephone: 1-404-681-2552, 1-800-521-CARE
Fax: 1-404-577-5977
E-mail: See Website Contact Form
Website: http://www.care.org

CARE works to fight global poverty. It places emphasis on working with poor women in the hopes that they can be empowered to help both families and communities escape poverty. Working together with other nongovernmental organizations, CARE has been active in child soldier demobilization and reintegration. Its activities include helping children leave armed forces and groups so as to develop and function within their families and communities.

Caritas Internationalis
Palazzo San Calisto
Vatican City State
V-00120
Telephone: 39 06 698 797 99
Fax: 39 06 698 872 37
Email: caritas.internationalis@caritas.va
Website: http://www.caritas.org

Caritas Internationalis is a network of allied Catholic social service organizations operating across the globe. Caritas's broad-based mission is to build a better world in the poorest places on the planet. It works in key areas such as peace, reconciliation, and economic justice and in providing support for the poor and the oppressed. Caritas has worked in Congo, Sudan, Uganda. and other countries, helping to provide for the livelihood of people and creating and promoting educational, vocation. and peace-building institutions that help reintegrate former child soldiers back into their communities.

Catholic Relief Services
228 West Lexington Street
Baltimore, MD 21201-3443
USA
Telephone: 1-888-277-7575
Email: info@crs.org
Website: http://crs.org

Catholic Relief Services works to assist the poor and vulnerable overseas. In particular, it responds to major humanitarian emergencies, fighting disease and poverty, and attempts to help nurture peaceful and just societies. It frequently partners with Caritas in helping former child soldiers in the process of demobilization and reintegration.

Center for Defense Information
1779 Massachusetts Avenue NW
Washington, DC
USA
Telephone: 1-202-332-0600
Fax: 1-202-462-4559
Email: info@cdi.org
Website: http://www.cdi.org

The Center for Defense Information works to provides analysis in a wide variety of military and defense issues. As part of its work, it provides basic information and analysis of countries affected by the the recruitment and use of child soldiers, on children and small arms, and on developments at the United Nations and international law more generally.

Child Soldier Relief
PO Box 9770
Washington, DC 20016
USA
Telephone: 1-202-905-2519
Email: info@childsoldierrelief.org
Website: http://childsoldierrelief.org

This is an advocacy group that works on behalf of former child soldiers by supporting and creating original multimedia content, maintaining an online repository of data, facilitating information sharing and collaboration within the educational community, and nurturing coalitions to build a global network.

Child Soldiers International (Coalition to Stop the Use of Child Soldiers)
9 Marshalsea Road, 4th Floor
London SE1 1EP
United Kingdom
Telephone: 44 (0)20 7367 4110
Email: info@child-soldiers.org
Website: http://www.child-soldiers.org/home

Child Soldier International is the new name for the organization known for many years as the Coalition to Stop the Use of Child Soldiers). The coalition was formed by a number of humanitarian and human rights groups and played an important role in the negotiation, adoption, and entry into force of the Optional Protocol to the Convention on the Rights of the Child on the involvement of children in armed conflict. It uses its influence on issues that have come before the UN Security Council, the UN Committee on the Rights of the Child, the International Labour Organization, and other international bodies. It publishes the *Child Soldiers Global Report*, which provides country-by-country information on child recruitment, as well as other important publications relevant to the issue of child soldiers.

Child Soldiers Initiative
Office of Lieutenant General Roméo A. Dallaire (Retired)
Ottawa, ON
Canada
Telephone: 1-613-219-9140
Cell: 1-613-219-9140
Email: zayed@peaceoperations.org
Website: http://www.childsoldiersinitiative.org

The Child Soldier Initiative was founded by Lieutenant General Romeo Dallaire, who is widely recognized as the former commander of the peacekeeping force for Rwanda between 1993 and 1994 and for his attempts to stop the genocide in Rwanda. It works to eradicate the use of child soldiers. It attempts to generate the political will needed for enforcing laws that protect children and bring perpetrators to justice. It also works to enhance the technical capacity of military, human rights, and humanitarian organizations, as well as host nation actors, to stop the use of child soldiers.

The Children and Armed Conflict Unit
University of Essex
Wivenhoe Park
Colchester
Essex CO4 3SQ
United Kingdom
Telephone UK: 44 (0)1206 877 936
Fax UK: 44 (0)1206 877 963
Email: vpatti@essex.ac.uk
Website: http://www.essex.ac.uk/armedcon

The Children and Armed Conflict Unit is a project of the Children's Legal Centre, a U.K. registered charity, and the Human

Rights Centre of the University of Essex. It has had projects in Kosovo, Turkey, Sierra Leone, Bosnia. and other areas of the world where it works to enhance children's rights in postconflict zones. The center carries out research and works with governments and nongovernmental organizations to help design and develop institutions, structures, and systems that address children's rights and other issues in postconflict situations.

Children and Youth in Armed Violence
Website: http://www.coav.org.br
Email: Luke Dowdney: luke@vivario.org.br

Children and Youth in Organized Armed Violence is an Internet-based network of international organizations that share research, information, and best practices in ending child participation in organized violence. It focuses primarily on Brazil, Jamaica, El Salvador, Ecuador, Honduras, Philippines, Nigeria, South Africa, the United States, Northern Ireland, and Colombia. Situations that involve children and youth involved in armed violence include drug trade factions, organized criminal gangs, armed ethnic groups, death squads, and vigilante groups. Armed children are also present in postconflict regions where organized crime employs armed groups.

Children's Forum Network of Sierra Leone
Website: http://www.facebook.com/pages/Childrens-Forum
-Network-Of-Sierra-Leone/9034827086

Children's Forum Network of Sierra Leone operates as a Web-based national voice for the children of Sierra Leone. It uses social media to create linkages among the children of war-torn Sierra Leone.

Children's Rights Information Network
East Studio
2 Pontypool Place
London SE1 8QF
United Kingdom
Telephone: 44 20 7401 2257
Email: info@crin.org
Website: http://www.crin.org

The mission of the Children's Rights Information Network is to create a global network for children's rights based on the

Convention on the Rights of the Child. It creates advocacy campaigns and leads international children's rights coalitions in pursuit of these goals. It is a clearinghouse for a wide range of reports and information of the situation of child soldiers in conflict zones.

Cluster Munition Coalition
89 Albert Embankment
London
SE1 7TP
United Kingdom
Telephone: 44 207 820 0222
Website: http://www.stopclustermunitions.org

The Cluster Munition Coalition is an international effort to eradicate cluster munitions, prevent further casualties from these weapons, and put an end for all time to the suffering they cause. Through member efforts, it seeks to change the policy and practice of governments and organizations toward these cluster munitions and to raise public awareness of the problem.

Coalition for Women's Human Rights in Conflict Situations
1001 de Maisonneuve Boulevard E
Suite 1100
Montreal, QC H2L 4P9
Canada
Telephone: 1-514-283-6073
Fax: 1-514 -283-3792
Email: coalition@dd-rd.ca
Website: http://www.coalitiondroitsdesfemmes.org

The Coalition for Women's Human Rights in Conflict Situations helps ensure that crimes committed against women in conflict situations are examined and prosecuted. It attempts to redress the invisibility of women's human rights abuses in conflict situations, to condemn the practice of sexual violence and other inhumane treatment of women as deliberate instruments of war, and to ensure that these are prosecuted as war crimes, torture, crimes against humanity, and crimes of genocide, where appropriate.

Commission for Reception, Truth, and Reconciliation, Timor-Leste
East Timor and Indonesia Action Network

PO Box 21873
Brooklyn, NY 11202-1873
USA
Telephone: 1-718-596-7668
Email: etan@etan.org
Website: http://www.etan.org/news/2006/cavr.htm

The Commission for Reception, Truth, and Reconciliation was formed for the purpose of inquiring into and establishing the truth regarding human rights violations that took place in the context of the political conflicts in Timor-Leste between April 25, 1974, and October 25, 1999. The commission documented 146 cases of child recruitment in the during the conflict and concluded that child recruitment was used mainly during the initial years of the Indonesian occupation.

Control Arms Coalition
PO Box 3795
New York, NY 10163
USA
Telephone: 1-212-682-3086
Email: info@controlarms.org
Website: http://www.controlarms.org

The Control Arms Coalition is an international alliance of nongovernmental organizations working to create a comprehensive arms trade treaty that ends the international trade and transfer of arms and ammunition. It undertakes research and adopts policy positions that the coalition believes will lead to the development of international norms and standards to create a global arms trade treaty.

Crimes of War Education Project
1325 G Street NW, Suite 730
Washington, DC 20005
USA
Telephone: 1-202-638-0230
E-mail: office@crimesofwar.org
Website: http://www.crimesofwar.org

The Crimes of War Education Project is a joint effort of journalists, lawyers, and scholars dedicated to raising public awareness of the application of the laws of war (international humanitarian law) to situations of armed conflict. It promotes the dissemination and understanding of international humanitarian law among journalists, policymakers, and the general public. It goal is to use awareness of international law as a means curbing breaches of the law and to help punish those who commit war crimes and other violations of the laws of war.

Defence for Children International
Rue de Varembe 1
Case Postale 88
CH-1211 Geneva 20
Switzerland
Telephone: 41 22 734 0558
Website: http://www.defenceforchildren.org

Defence for Children International works to promote and protect children's rights on global, regional, national, and local levels. It is dedicated to a rights-based approach in addressing the many challenges facing the world's children. It takes a leadership role in the universal ratification campaign for the Optional Protocols to the Convention on the Rights of the Child.

Doctors Without Borders/Médecins Sans Frontières
333 Seventh Avenue, 2nd Floor
New York, NY 10001-5004
USA
Telephone: 1-212-679-6800
Email: See Website Contact Form
Website: http://www.doctorswithoutborders.org

Doctors Without Borders/Médecins Sans Frontières is an international medical humanitarian organization created by doctors and journalists in France in 1971. It provides medical assistance to more than 60 countries where people are threatened by war, violence, neglect, or catastrophe. It also advocates for improved medical treatments and for the rights of people to have access to medical care. It has provided medical care and mental health care for persons traumatized by violence, including former child soldiers.

Femmes Africa Solidarite
Geneva Office, International Secrétariat
8 Rue du Vieux-Billard

PO Box 5037
1211 Geneva 11
Switzerland
Telephone: 41 22 328 8050
Fax: 41 22 328 8052
Email: info@fasngo.org
Website: http://www.fasngo.org

Femmes Africa Solidarite focuses on fostering, supporting, and promoting women's initiatives in preventing, managing, and resolving conflicts in Africa, with special attention to women's rights. The group also seeks to strengthen women's leadership capacity at the countrywide and local levels so as to foster and restore peace. It endeavors to promote policies, structures, and programs in support of the peace process and the enhancement of human security in Africa.

Gender and Peacebuilding Working Group
1 Nicholas Street, #1216
Ottawa, ON K1N 7B7
Canada
Telephone: 1-613-241-3446
Fax: 1-613-241-4846
Email: info@peacebuild.ca
Website: http://www.peacebuild.ca/work-groups-gender-pb-e.php

The Gender and Peacebuilding Working Group is a Canadian nongovernmental organization that endeavors to promote peace building, human security policy dialogue, and policy development among nongovernmental and governmental agencies and individuals and others. Focuses on developing active collaboration and knowledge exchanges between peace-building organizations and their international counterparts and also facilitates systematic learning, dissemination, and application of knowledge related to peace-building objectives, practices, and outcomes.

Geneva Call
PO Box 334
CH-1211 Geneva 4
Switzerland
Telephone: 41 22 879 1050
E-mail: info@genevacall.org

Website: http://www.genevacall.org/Themes/Children/children
.htm

Geneva Call is a humanitarian organization dedicated to engaging armed nonstate actors toward compliance with the norms of international humanitarian law (the laws of war) and human rights law. The organization focuses on armed groups that operate outside effective state control and are motivated primarily by political goals. It has a particular concern with children who may be recruited (forcibly or otherwise) into armed forces or armed nonstate actors. Geneva Call attempts to improve the compliance of nonstate actors with international norms related to children and armed conflict. It attempts to engage nonstate actors in dialogue on these issues, with the hope of having them comply with existing international norms, and to provide them with a universal and standard mechanism of accountability in order to contribute to the consolidation of international norms on children and armed conflict issues.

Geneva International Centre for Humanitarian Demining
7bis, avenue de la Paix
PO Box 1300
CH-1211 Geneva 1
Switzerland
Telephone: 41 22 906 16 60
Fax: 41 22 906 16 90
Email: info@gichd.org
Website: http://www.gichd.ch

The Geneva International Centre for Humanitarian Demining is an international expert organization that works to eliminate the explosive remnants of war. As long as there is armed conflict, there will be explosive remnants of war, which may affect civilians, and expertise will be required to develop solutions to this problem. The would include bombs, warheads, guided and ballistic missiles, artillery, mortars, rockets, small-arms ammunition, mines, torpedoes, depth charges, and many other forms of ordinance used in war.

Global Witness
6th Floor, Buchanan House
30 Holborn

London EC1N 2HS
United Kingdom
Telephone: 44 207 492 5820
Fax: 44 207 492 5821
Email: mail@globalwitness.org
Website: http://www.globalwitness.org

Global Witness campaigns against natural resource–related conflict and corruption and associated environmental and human rights abuses. It works to expose the brutality and injustice that results from the battles over access and control natural resource wealth and seeks to bring the perpetrators of corruption and conflict to justice. It is particularly interested in armed forces and armed groups that have hijacked the trade in mineral ores while subjecting the civilian population to massacres, rape, extortion, forced labor, and forced recruitment of child soldiers.

Health and Human Rights Info
Kirkegata 5
0153 Oslo
Norway
Telephone: 47 95493248
Fax: 47 22479201
Email: postmaster@hhri.org
Website: http://www.hhri.org

Health and Human Rights Info works to make available professional experiences and resources to health professionals who are working with people exposed to human rights abuses, armed conflict, forced migration, and other human rights violations. It collects and vets key material, such as guidelines, manuals, intervention programs, and tools for assessment and intervention.

Heart and Alliance for Human Needs and Human Rights
208 South LaSalle Street, Suite 1818
Chicago, IL 60604
USA
Telephone: 1-312-660-1300, 1-312-660-1361
Fax: 1-312-660-1500
Email: international@heartlandalliance.org
Website: http://www.heartlandalliance.org

Heart and Alliance works to promote human rights and provide support for poor, isolated, and displaced populations. In Burundi, it focuses on female former child soldier reintegration through the creation of residential rehabilitation centers and by facilitating the development of a program of mentoring and assistance for former combatants. The center offers mental health, medical, vocational, and other services to female ex-combatants.

Human Rights Education Associates
97 Lowell Road
Concord, MA 01742
USA
Telephone: 1-978-341-0200
Fax: 1-978-341-0201
Email: See Website Contact Form
Website: http://www.hrea.org

Human Rights Education Associates works to enhance the teaching and understanding of human rights. It trains activists and professionals, develops educational materials and programming, and supports community building through online technologies. It promotes education and training for human rights and for fostering the emergence of peaceable, free, and just communities. Its website contains a student learning module on the issue of child soldiers as well as additional educational resources.

Human Rights Watch
350 Fifth Avenue, 34th Floor
New York, NY 10118-3299
USA
Telephone: 1-212-290-4700
Email: hrwnyc@hrw.org
Website: http://www.hrw.org

Human Rights Watch is key advocacy group that seeks to investigate and expose human rights abuse and promote respect and compliance with international human rights law. The problem of child soldiers is included as part of its broader human rights mission, and it has published numerous reports on the recruitment of child soldiers across the globe. Members of Human Rights Watch have participated extensively in the criminal trials of persons charged with the recruitment of child soldiers.

Integrated Regional Information Networks
United Nations Office at Nairobi
PO Box 67578
Nairobi, Kenya 00200
Telephone: 254 207 622147
Email: feedback@irinnews.org
Website: http://www.irinnews.org

Integrated Regional Information Networks is the humanitarian news and analysis service of the UN Office for the Coordination of Humanitarian Affairs. It provides up-to-date information on a variety of humanitarian crises, including the use of child soldiers in conflict zones throughout the world.

Interagency Panel on Juvenile Justice
1 rue de Varembé
PO Box 88
CH 1211 Geneva 20
Switzerland
Email: info@juvenilejusticepanel.org
Telephone: 41 22 734 0558
Fax: 41 22 740 1145
Email: See Website Contact Form
Website: http://www.juvenilejusticepanel.org

The Interagency Panel on Juvenile Justice serves to coordinate technical advice and assistance in juvenile justice. The work of the panel is guided by the Convention on the Rights of the Child and other international standards, treaties, and norms on juvenile justice.

It emphasizes the issue of justice for children on the international agenda, including the protection of the rights of children in conflict with the law and of child victims and witnesses of crimes.

Internal Displacement Monitoring Centre
Chemin de Balexert, 7-9
1219 Chatelaine Geneva
Switzerland
Telephone: 41 22 799 0700
Fax: 41 22 799 0701
Website: http://www.internal-displacement.org

The Internal Displacement Monitoring Centre was established in 1998 by the Norwegian Refugee Council. It is the leading international body organization that monitors conflict-induced internal displacement worldwide. It attempts to improve national and international capacities to protect and assist people around the globe who have been displaced within their own country as a result of conflicts or human rights violations. It also maintains an online database providing comprehensive information and analysis on internal displacement in some 50 countries.

International Action Network on Small Arms
Development House
56-64 Leonard Street
London EC2A 4LT
United Kingdom
Telephone: 44 207 065 0870
Fax: 44 207 065 0871
Email: contact@iansa.org
Website: http://www.iansa.org

The International Action Network on Small Arms is a global movement of nongovernmental organizations that works to end the proliferation and misuse of small arms and light weapons. It supports efforts to reduce the demand for such weapons and works for firearm regulation and for strengthening controls over small-arms transfers. Its main activities include raising awareness of the global threat to human rights and human security caused by small arms and promoting efforts to prevent arms proliferation and armed violence.

International Bureau for Children's Rights
2715 Chemin de la Côte-Sainte-Catherine
Montreal, QC H3T1B6
Canada
Telephone: 1-514-932-7656
Fax: 1-514-932-9453
E-mail: info@ibcr.org
Website: http://www.ibcr.org/eng

The International Bureau for Children's Rights is an international nongovernmental organization based in Montreal. Its mission is to contribute to the promotion and respect for the Convention on the

Rights of the Child. Its stated purpose is to ensure that the principles enshrined in the Convention and its optional protocols continue to guide the bureau in its rights-based approach. Among its many child-related concerns are war-affected children, child trafficking, child victims and witnesses of crime, and child sex tourism.

International Campaign to Ban Landmines
9 Rue de Cornavin
CH-1201 Geneva
Switzerland
Telephone: 41 22 920 0325
Email: See Website Contact Form
Website: http://www.icbl.org

The International Campaign to Ban Landmines works to end the use of antipersonnel land mines throughout the world and to help land mine survivors lead fulfilling lives. It was awarded the Nobel Peace Prize through its efforts to bring about the 1997 Mine Ban Treaty. The close civil society–government partnership that it created helped bring about the Mine Ban Treaty and has been cited as a model for addressing other conflict-related issues, such as small arms and child soldiers.

International Centre for Transitional Justice
5 Hanover Square, Floor 24
New York, NY 10004
USA
Telephone: 1-917-637-3800
Fax: 1-917-637-3900
Email: ChildrenTJinfo@ictj.org
Website: http://www.ictj.org

The International Center for Transitional Justice works to help societies grappling with legacies of massive human rights violations build civic trust in state institutions as protectors of human rights and to help them build mechanisms of truth, accountability, and redress for past abuses. The center has reported that although recruiting and using child soldiers is criminal, the increase in visibility of these crimes as a result of international prosecutions may have undermined the formal release or demobilization of child soldiers by armed groups and thereby reduced the children's access to benefits and protection in the short term. The center has raised the issue of whether international prosecutions and the condemnation they bring play a positive role in deterring these crimes.

International Committee of the Red Cross
19 Avenue de la paix
CH 1202 Geneva
Switzerland
Telephone: 41 22 734 60 01
E-mail: webmaster@icrc.org
Website: http://www.icrc.org

The International Committee of the Red Cross (ICRC) is humanitarian organization based in Switzerland that has a unique international status in the protection of victims of armed conflict. The state parties to the 1949 Geneva Conventions and the 1977 Protocols Additional have all agreed that the ICRC shall monitor compliance to the treaties, including the provisions restricting the recruitment of child soldiers. The ICRC also assists in demobilizing child soldiers and provides psychological and other support for reintegrating child soldiers back into society.

International Criminal Court
Maanweg 174
2516 AB, The Hague
Netherlands
Telephone: 31 (0)70 515 8515
Website: http://www.icc-cpi.int

The International Criminal Court was established by the Rome Treaty in 1989 and is the first permanent international criminal court created to help end immunity for the perpetrators of the most serious crimes of concern to the international community, such as war crimes and crimes against humanity. Cases now before the court include individuals charged with recruiting child soldiers.

International Criminal Tribunal for Rwanda
Arusha International Conference Centre PO Box 6016
Arusha
Tanzania
Telephone: 1-212-963-2850 (via New York)
Email: ictrlib@un.org
Website: http://www.ictr.org

Because of the serious violations of humanitarian law that were committed in Rwanda between January 1, 1994, and December 31, 1994, the UN Security Council created the International Criminal Tribunal for Rwanda for the prosecution of persons responsible for genocide and other serious violations of international humanitarian law. The court was also empowered to prosecute Rwandan citizens who were responsible for genocide and other such violations of international law committed in the territory of neighboring states during the same period.

International Criminal Tribunal for Yugoslavia
PO Box 13888
2501 EW, The Hague
Netherlands
Email: press@icty.org
Website: http://www.icty.org

International Criminal Tribunal for the former Yugoslavia was established by the United Nations to try persons responsible for war crimes (violations of international humanitarian law that took place during the conflicts in the Balkans in the 1990s). The tribunal's work became the basis of widely accepted norms of conflict resolution and postconflict development across the globe.

International Labour Organization
4 route des Morillons
CH-1211 Geneva 22
Switzerland
Telephone: 41 (0) 22 799 6111
Fax: 41 (0) 22 798 8685
E-mail: ilo@ilo.org
Website: http://www.ilo.org

Founded in 1919, the International Labour Organization is the international organization charged with developing and implementing international labor standards. It brings together representatives of governments, employers, and labor to collectively shape policies and programs promoting decent work standards. It regards child soldiers as victims of the worst forms of child labor.

International Organization for Migration
17, route des Morillons

CH-1211 Geneva 19
Switzerland
Telephone: 41 22 717 9111
Fax: 41 22 798 6150
Email: hq@iom.int
Website: http://www.iom.int

The International Organization for Migration is one of the key inter-governmental organizations in the field of migration. It works together with governmental, intergovernmental, and nongovernmental partners to promote the orderly and humane management of migration, to encourage international cooperation on migration issues, and to help develop practical solutions to migration problems. It provides humanitarian assistance to migrants in need, including refugees and internally displaced people.

International Programme on the Elimination of Child Labour, International Labour Organization
4 route des Morillons
CH-1211 Geneva 22
Switzerland
Telephone: 41 22 799 8181
Fax: 41 22 799 8771
Email: ipec@ilo.org
Website: http://www.ilo.org/ipec/lang—en/index.htm

The International Labour Organization's International Programme on the Elimination of Child Labour is the world's largest technical cooperation program to end child labor. It helps develop both policies and direct action programs that address the root causes of child labor and provide alternatives for children and their families. Many former child soldiers benefit from its programs, which serve to reintegrate of youth back into civilian life.

International Rescue Committee
122 East 42nd Street
New York, NY 10168-1289
USA
Telephone: 1-212-551-3000
Fax: 1-212-551-3179

Email: advocacy@rescue.org
Website: http://www.rescue.org

The International Rescue Committee works to alleviate the world's worst humanitarian crises and helps people survive and rebuild their lives. It provides lifesaving care and assistance to refugees forced to flee from war or disaster. It provides interim care, rehabilitation, and community reintegration of former child soldiers. It has helped former child soldiers and other children in Nepal return to school or enroll in vocational training programs.

International Women's Tribune Centre
777 United Nations Plaza
New York, NY 10017
USA
Telephone: 1-212-687-8633
Fax: 1-212-661-2704
Email: iwtc@iwtc.org
Website: http://www.iwtc.org

The International Women's Tribune Centre is a nongovernmental organization that provides communication, information, education, and organizing support services to women's organizations and community groups in Africa, Asia and the Pacific, Latin America and the Caribbean, eastern Europe, and western Asia. An important component of the center's work is the Human Rights, Human Security and Peace Building Programme, which makes knowledge and know-how about UN Security Council Resolution 1325 and other legal mechanisms available to women at national and community levels. The center is a founding member of the nongovernmental organization Working Group on Women, Peace, and Security, which advocates on issues related to women in armed conflict and for the full implementation of UN Security Council Resolution 1325, which requires, among other things, that attention be paid to specific protection needs of women and girls in armed conflict.

Invisible Children
1620 5th Avenue, Suite 400
San Diego, CA 92101
USA
Telephone: 1-619-631-0362

Email: Movement@invisiblechildren.com
Website: http://www.invisiblechildren.com

Invisible Children is a nongovernmental organization started by young filmmakers documenting the plight of child soldiers in Uganda. It is named after its documentary film, *Invisible Children: Rough Cut*. It continues to create documentary films of people living in conflict and has also worked to expand education opportunities for Uganda children by providing scholarships and mentoring to secondary school and university students. It has been actively involved in fund-raising and in the rebuilding of secondary schools in war zones in Uganda.

Jesuit Refugee Service
1016 16th Street NW, Suite 500
Washington, DC 20036
USA
Telephone: 1-202-629-5943
Email: communications@jrsusa.org
Website: http://jrsusa.org

The Jesuit Refugee Service is one of the founding members of the Coalition to Stop the Use of Child Soldiers. It works to prevent the recruitment and use of child soldiers and to promote their demobilization, rehabilitation, and reintegration. It also works with children regarded as vulnerable to being recruited as child soldiers as well as with former child soldiers. It has programs in Burundi, Chad, Colombia, Sri Lanka, Thailand, and Venezuela.

The Kimberley Process
KP Secretariat, Namibia
Ministry of Mines and Energy
Room 325, 3rd Floor
No. 1 Aviation Road
Windhoek, Namibia
Telephone: 264 61 284 8234
Fax: 264 61 284 8203
Email: kpcs.namibia@kimberleyprocess.com
Website: http://www.kimberleyprocess.com

The Kimberley Process is a global initiative that links governments, industry, and civil society in an effort to contain and/or end the flow of conflict diamonds: rough diamonds used by rebel movements, many of whom recruit child soldiers, to finance wars against legitimate governments. The trade in these illicit stones has fueled widespread and devastating conflicts in countries such as Angola, Côte d'Ivoire, the Democratic Republic of the Congo, and Sierra Leone, all of which have involved the use of child soldiers. The Kimberley Process Certification Scheme involves an extensive set of requirements imposed on members that allow them to verify and certify that shipments of rough diamonds are "conflict free."

Mines Action Canada
1 Nicholas Street, Suite 1502
Ottawa, ON K1N 7B7
Canada
Telephone: 1-613-241-3777
Fax: 1-613-244-3410
Email: info@minesactioncanada.org
Website: http://www.minesactioncanada.org

Mines Action Canada works to eliminate the humanitarian, environmental, and development consequences of land mines, cluster bombs, and other explosive remnants of war. Its goal is to reduce the impact that these weapons have on the rights, dignity, and well-being of civilian populations. Accordingly, it is deeply involved in public life, supporting domestic and international efforts of its partners and researching and monitoring the performance and compliance levels of disarmament and humanitarian laws.

Multi-Country Demobilization Program
MDRP Secretariat
World Bank
1818 H Street NW
MSN J 7-709
Washington, DC 20433
USA
Telephone: 1-202-473-3328
Fax: 1-202-473-8229
Email: info@mdrp.org
Website: http://www.mdrp.org

The Multi-Country Demobilization and Reintegration Program worked between 2002 and 2009 to facilitate the disarmament, demobilization, and reintegration of ex-combatants in seven countries. The program involved about 300,000 ex-combatants, including child soldiers, in Angola, Burundi, the Central African Republic, the Democratic Republic of Congo, the Republic of Congo, Rwanda, and Uganda.

NGO Group for the Convention on the Rights of the Child
Secretariat
1 rue de Varembé
CH-1202 Geneva
Switzerland
Telephone: 41 (0) 22 740 4730
Fax: 41 (0) 22 740 1145
Email: secretariat@childrightsnet.org
Website: http://www.childrightsnet.org

NGO Group for the Convention on the Rights of the Child is a global network composed of international and national nongovernmental organizations that work to advance the implementation of the UN Convention on the Rights of the Child. It supports a variety of national and international nongovernmental organizations to promote, monitor, and implement the Convention and its Optional Protocols, raising public awareness of children's rights, and developing programs and action plans that help facilitate full implementation.

NGO Working Group on Girls' Rights
UNICEF House
3 UN Plaza
New York, NY 10017
USA
Telephone: 1-212-326-2713
Email: wggs@girlsrights.org
Website: http://www.girlsrights.org

The NGO Working Group on Girls' Rights works to promoting the rights of girls internationally. In particular, the working group seeks to monitor and ensure that national governments implement all commitments to girls' rights made through international agreements. It also advocates for the inclusion and development of girls' rights throughout the activities of the UN systems and structures.

NGO Working Group on Women, Peace, and Security
777 United Nations Plaza, 7th Floor
New York, NY 10017
USA
Telephone: 1-212-557-7298
Email: info@womenpeacesecurity.org
Website: http://www.womenpeacesecurity.org

The NGO Working Group on Women, Peace, and Security collaborates with the United Nations, its member states, and civil society toward full implementation of UN Security Council Resolution 1325 as well as any other Security Council resolutions that address women, peace, and security. It works to ensure the full and equal participation of women in issues relating to peace and security and promotes a gender perspective and respect for human rights in all UN initiatives related to peace and security, conflict prevention and management, and peace building.

Norwegian Initiative on Small Arms Transfers
Hausmannsgate 7
N-0133 Oslo
Norway
Telephone: 47 22 05 4166
Fax: 47 22 05 4040
Website: http://www.prio.no/nisat

The Norwegian Initiative on Small Arms Transfers is a coalition of the Peace Research Institute in Oslo, the Norwegian Red Cross, and Norwegian Church Aid. Its goal is to reduce or prevent armed violence through the control of the proliferation of small arms and light weapons, such as rifles, pistols, shotguns, machine guns, and portable missile launchers. It maintains an online database of international authorized trade in small arms and light weapons and a document library containing more than 28,000 articles on small-arms issues.

Norwegian Refugee Council
PO Box 6758, St. Olavs plass
0130 Oslo

Norway
Telephone: 47 23 10 9800
Fax: 47 23 10 9801
Email: nrc@nrc.no
Website: http://www.nrc.no

The Norwegian Refugee Council is a humanitarian nongovernmental organization that provides assistance, protection, and
durable solutions to refugees and internally displaced persons
worldwide. It promotes and protects the rights of people who
have been forced to flee their countries or their homes within their
countries. It provides humanitarian assistance to refugees, internally displaced persons, and returnees.

Office of the United Nations High Commissioner for Refugees
Case Postale 2500
CH-1211 Geneva 2 Dépôt
Switzerland
Telephone: 41 22 739 8111
Email: See Website Contact Form
Website: http://www.unhcr.org

The Office of the United Nations High Commissioner for Refugees is the UN agency that leads and coordinates international
action to protect refugees and resolve refugee problems worldwide. Its main purpose is to safeguard the rights and well-being
of refugees. In particular, it attempts to ensure that everyone can
exercise the right to seek asylum and find safe refuge in another
state, with the option to return home voluntarily, integrate locally,
or resettle in a third country.

Open Society Justice Initiative
400 West 59th Street
New York, NY 10019
USA
Telephone: 1-212-548-0600
Email: See Website Contact Form
Website: http://www.soros.org/initiatives/justice

The Open Society Justice Initiative is a project of the Open Society
Foundations, which works to build democratic societies in which
governments are accountable to citizens. The justice initiative

actively monitors international war crimes trials, including those of Charles Taylor and Thomas Kubanga Dyilo, who have been tried for the recruitment and use of child soldiers. Coverage can be found at http://www.lubangatrial.org and http://www .charlestaylortrial.org.

Partnership Africa Canada
600-331 Cooper Street
Ottawa, ON K2P 0G5
Canada
Telephone: 1-613-237-6768
Fax: 1-613-237-6530
Email: btaylor@pacweb.org
Website: http://www.pacweb.org

Partnership Africa Canada is a nonprofit organization concerned with building sustainable human development in Africa. It works together with numerous nongovernmental organizations in Africa and Canada and internationally on two key issues: peace and human security and sustainable development. A prime example of its work has been research and public outreach surrounding the issue of conflict diamonds. It has strenuously campaigned to stop or contain armed conflict fueled by the trade in diamonds, many of which have involved the recruitment and use of child soldiers.

Peace Direct
Development House
56-64 Leonard Street
London EC2A 4LT
United Kingdom
Telephone: 44 (0)20 7549 0285
Fax: 44 (0)20 7549 0286
Email info@peacedirect.org
Website: http://www.peacedirect.org

Peace Direct works to support local individuals who are actively involved in conflict resolution activities. It has recently supported Henri Ladyi Ongo, whose Center for Conflict Resolution in the Democratic Republic of Congo has rescued 444 child soldiers and helped 14,000 refugees safely return to their villages.

Penal Reform International
60-62 Commercial Street
London E1 6LT
United Kingdom
Telephone: 44 20 7247 6515
Fax: 44 20 7377 8711
Email: info@penalreform.org
Website: http://www.penalreform.org, http://www.penalreform
.org/themes/juvenile-justice

Penal Reform International is a nongovernmental organization
that promotes penal and criminal justice reform worldwide. Its
approach to juvenile justice is based on the Convention on the
Rights of the Child, which requires that the "best interests of the
child shall be a primary consideration" in juvenile justice. It promotes international standards concerning children that require
detained or imprisoned children to have the same rights as adults
as well as additional measures of care and protection that take
their age into consideration.

Project Ploughshares
57 Erb Street West
Waterloo, ON N2L 6C2
Canada
Telephone: 1-519-888-6541
Fax: 1-519-888-0018
Email: See Website Contact Form
Website: http://www.ploughshares.ca

Project Ploughshares is a Canadian nongovernmental organization working to promote policies and actions that prevent war
and armed violence and build peace. It is a church-based organization whose principles are peace, reconciliation, and justice, but
its research involves careful analyses of facts so as to influence
and shape public policy.

Quaker United Nations Office
777 United Nations Plaza
New York, NY 10017
USA
Telephone: 1-212-682-2745
Fax: 1-212-983-0034

Email: qunony@afsc.org
Website: http://www.quno.org

The Quaker United Nations Office represents Quaker (Society of Friends) concerns at the United Nations. It works in areas such as disarmament, peace building, and the prevention of violent conflict. It also works actively on the issue of child soldiers, especially in the creation of international norms that would prohibit the recruitment and use of persons under age 18 by armed forces and groups. It is particularly interested in the issue of girl soldiers.

Refugee Studies Centre
3 Mansfield Road
Oxford OX1 3TB
United Kingdom
Telephone: 44(1865) 281720
Fax: 44(1865) 281730
Email: rsc@qeh.ox.ac.uk
Website: http://www.rsc.ox.ac.uk

The Refugee Studies Centre at the University of Oxford, United Kingdom, focuses research, teaching, and outreach efforts on understanding of the causes and effects of forced migration on the lives of vulnerable populations. Among its concerns is the support of scholarship from a wide variety of disciplinary and multidisciplinary perspectives on child soldiers.

Refworld Virtual Documentation Centre
Status Determination and Protection Information Section
Division of International Protection Services
UN High Commission for Refugees
Case Postale 2500
1211 Geneva 2 Dépôt
Switzerland
Fax: 41 22 739 396
Email: refworld@unhcr.org
Website: http://www.unhcr.org/refworld/children.html

Refworld is the prime source of information necessary for understanding specific issues of refugee status. It maintains a major collection of reports relating to situations in countries of origin, policy documents and positions, and documents relating to international and national legal frameworks. The information has been carefully selected and compiled from the UN High Commission for Refugees' global network of field offices; governments; international, regional; and nongovernmental organizations; academic institutions; and judicial bodies.

Save the Children Alliance
Cambridge House, 2nd Floor
100 Cambridge Grove
London W6 0LE
United Kingdom
Telephone: 44 208 748 2554
Fax: 44 208 237 8000
Email: info@savethechildren.org
Website: http://www.savethechildren.net

Save the Children works with communities, governments, international authorities, and children themselves to stop violations of children's rights, including the recruitment of children by armed groups. It advocates widely for children's rights and also provides safe spaces and transit centers for former child soldiers.

Say NO—UNiTE to End Violence against Women
220 East 42nd Street
15th Floor
New York, NY 10017
USA
Telephone: 1-212-906-6400
Fax: 1-212-906-6705
Email: saynotoviolence@unifem.org
Website: http://www.saynotoviolence.org

Say NO—UNiTE to End Violence against Women works to end violence against women and girls. Comparative country data available indicate that between 15 and 76 percent of women experience physical or sexual violence at home, work, on the streets, and in schools during peacetime and in conflict. Violence against women and girls has far-reaching consequences, harming families and communities, stunting human development, and undermining economic growth.

Search for Common Ground
1601 Connecticut Avenue, Suite 200
Washington, DC 20009
USA
Telephone: 1-202-265-4300
Fax: 1-202-232-6718
Email: search@sfcg.org
Website: http://www.sfcg.org

Search for Common Ground uses collaborative problem solving to deal with issues of conflict. It works with governments and nongovernmental organizations to find and make us of culturally appropriate means to strengthen societies' capacity to deal with conflicts. In Nepal, it has used Dohiri folk music festivals to help reconcile former child soldiers with parents and communities.

Security Council Working Group on Children and Armed Conflicts
Radhika Coomaraswamy, Undersecretary-General
1 UN Plaza DC1, 627 F
New York, NY 10017
USA
Telephone: 1-212-963-3178
Fax: 1-212-963-0807
Website: http://www.un.org/children/conflict/english/security councilwgroupdoc.html

The Security Council Working Group on Children and Armed Conflict was established by the UN Security Council to systematically deal with issues involving the use of children in armed conflict situations. Representatives from member countries of the United Nations meet to review situations in which the use of children in armed conflict may come before the Security Council. The group reviews the reports of the monitoring and reporting mechanism and reviews progress in the development and implementation of action plans and is supported by the Office of the Special Representative of the Secretary General on Children and Armed Conflict.

Office of the Special Representative of the Secretary-General for Children and Armed Conflict.

Sexual Violence Research Initiative
Gender and Health Research Unit

Medical Research Council, South Africa
Private Bag x385
0001 Pretoria
South Africa
Telephone: 27 12 339-8527
Fax: 27 12 339-8582
Email: svri@mrc.ac.za
Website: http://www.svri.org

The Sexual Violence Research Initiative works to promote research on sexual violence and to generate empirical data that ensures that sexual violence is recognized as a key public health problem. Its work includes the sexual violence children are subject to during armed conflict. The initiative uses an experienced and committed network of researchers, policymakers, activists, and donors to ensure that issues of sexual violence are addressed from the perspective of different disciplines and cultures.

Small Arms Survey
Avenue Blanc 47
1202 Geneva
Switzerland
Telephone: 41 22 908 5777
Fax 41 22 732 2738
E-mail: sas@smallarmssurvey.org
Website: http://www.smallarmssurvey.org

The Small Arms Survey is the prime international source of public information on all aspects of small arms and armed violence. It serves governments, policymakers, researchers, and activists. Among its stated objectives are to serve as a resource for information and research on small-arms and armed violence issues, to be an independent monitor of national and international governmental and nongovernmental policy initiatives on small arms and armed violence, to channel policy-relevant research on small-arms and armed violence issues, and to help develop and disseminate the best-practice measures and initiatives for dealing with small-arms and armed violence issues.

The Special Court for Sierra Leone
Jomo Kenyatta Road
New England, Freetown

Sierra Leone
Telephone: 232 22 297000
Email: scsl-mail@un.org
Website: http://www.sc-sl.org

New York Office:
Chrysler Building
405 Lexington Avenue
5th Floor, Room 5090
New York, NY 10174
USA
Telephone: 1-212-457-1293
Fax: 1-212-457-4059

The Special Court for Sierra Leone was set up jointly by the government of Sierra Leone and the United Nations. It is mandated to try those people who bear the greatest responsibility for serious violations of international humanitarian law and Sierra Leone law committed in the territory of Sierra Leone since November 30, 1996. Almost all cases before the court have involved, among other things, individuals charged with the recruitment of child soldiers. Three cases before the court were heard in Freetown, and the trial of former Liberian president Charles Taylor was heard at The Hague, Netherlands.

Special Rapporteur on Contemporary Forms of Slavery, Its Causes, and Consequences
Office of the United Nations High Commissioner for Human Rights
Palais des Nations
CH-1211 Geneva 10
Switzerland
Fax: 41 22 917 9006
Email: srslavery@ohchr.org
Website: http://www2.ohchr.org/english/issues/slavery/rapporteur/index.htm

The special rapporteur has the mandate of the United Nations to examine, monitor, advise, and publicly report on human rights problems. In particular, the special rapporteur may investigate labor practices that are defined by international law as forms of slavery or practices similar to slavery. These may include sale and trafficking of children, debt bondage and serfdom, and forced or compulsory labor, including forced or compulsory recruitment of children for use in armed conflict.

Special Rapporteur on Trafficking in Persons, Especially in Women and Children
Office of the High Commissioner for Human Rights
United Nations at Geneva
8-14 avenue de la Paix
1211 Geneva 10
Switzerland
Fax: 41 22 917 9006
Email: SRtrafficking@ohchr.org (subject: Special rapporteur on trafficking in persons)
Website: http://www2.ohchr.org/english/issues/trafficking/index.htm

As with other special rapporteurs in the United Nations, the special rapporteur on trafficking in persons, especially in women and children, has a mandate to examine, monitor, advise, and publicly report on human rights problems. The recruitment of child soldiers is sometimes regarded as a form of child trafficking and is included under the rapporteur's mandate.

Terre des Hommes International Federation
1 chemin Franck Thomas
CH-1223 Cologny/Geneva
Switzerland
Telephone: 41 22 736 33 72
Fax: 41 22 736 15 10
Email: info@terredeshommes.org
Web: http://www.terredeshommes.org

Terre des Hommes is one of the founding organizations of the Coalition to Stop the Use of Child Soldiers. It provides support to children, without racial, religious, political, cultural, or gender-based discrimination. Guided by the conceptual framework of the Convention on the Rights of the Child, the organization develops and implement projects designed to improve the living conditions of disadvantaged children in their own environment. It coordinates major campaigns on ending the use of child soldiers and on the issue of child trafficking.

Truth and Reconciliation Commission of Liberia
9th Street, Beach Side
Sinkor, Monrovia
Liberia
Telephone: 231 6 123 456
Email: info@trcofliberia.org
Website: https://www.trcofliberia.org

The Truth and Reconciliation Commission of Liberia was created to promote national peace, security, unity, and reconciliation in Liberia by investigating gross human rights violations and violations of international humanitarian law during the period January 1979–October 14, 2003, including the recruitment and use of child soldiers.

UNICEF
UNICEF House
3 United Nations Plaza
New York, NY 10017
USA
Telephone: 1-212-326-7000
Email: info@unicef.org
Web: http://unicef.org

UNICEF was created by the United Nations to provide humanitarian aid to the world's children. It takes a rights-based approach to children's issues and has been central to international efforts to end the recruitment and use of child soldiers throughout the world. It also plays a major role in reintegrating former child soldiers into society.

UNICEF Innocenti Research Centre
Piazza SS, Annunziata, 12
50122 Florence
Italy
Telephone: 39 39055 20330
Fax: 39 39055 2033220
Email: florence@unicef.org
Website: http://www.unicef-irc.org

The UNICEF Innocenti Research Centre is UNICEF's major research center that produces studies related to neglected areas of child rights and well-being, informing policy and practice in

numerous countries around the world. The website http://www
.childreninarmedconflict.org was developed in connection with
research carried out by the UNICEF Innocenti Research Centre
on the European Network for the Research Agenda on Children
in Armed Conflict.

United Movement to End Child Soldiering
PO Box 21632
Kampala, Uganda
U.S. Office:
PO Box 66296
Washington, DC 20035-6296
USA
Email: info@endchildsoldiering.org
Website: http://www.endchildsoldiering.org

The United Movement to End Child Soldiering works in Uganda to
end child soldiering through grassroots and school-based peace-
building and peace education initiatives to prevent future wars. It
attempts to create joint initiatives between communities and local
and central government to build enduring cultures of peace
through projects that focus on development, agriculture, environmental conservation, education, and the empowerment of women.

United Nations Development Program
Mine Action and Small Arms Advisor
Bureau for Crisis Prevention and Recovery
United Nations Development Program
1 United Nations Plaza
DC1-2016
New York, NY 10017
USA
Telephone: 1-212-906-6974
Website: http://www.undp.org/cpr/we_do/small_arms.shtml

The United Nations Development Program's Mine Action and
Small Arms Advisor works to control and curtail the supply of
arms in conflict zones by arms collection, surplus destruction,
and stockpile management and by enhancing the transfer and
export controls of arms. It also provides assistance for creating
legislative/regulatory provisions for strict control of small arms
and light weapons. The United Nations Development Program

also works to reduce the demand for arms by targeting the root causes of armed violence and community insecurity, and by supporting armed violence prevention and community security programs.

United Nations Disarmament, Demobilisation, and Reintegration Resource Centre
Room S-3035
Peacekeeping Best Practices Section
Department of Peacekeeping Operations Peacekeeping
United Nations
New York, NY 10017
USA
Telephone: 1-917-367-5436
Fax: 1-917-367-2103
Email: info@unddr.org
Website: http://unddr.org/index.php

The center provides resources to promote the disarmament, demobilization, and reintegration (DDR) of former combatants and those associated with armed groups, a common requirement for postconflict stability. It also provides strategic advice to assist the United Nations in improving its work on DDR, maintains and reviews existing sets of UN guidance on DDR, and facilitates the planning of DDR activities.

United Nations Institute for Disarmament Research
Palais des Nations
1211 Geneva 10
Switzerland
Telephone: 41 22 917 3186
Fax: 41 22 917 0176
Email: unidir@unog.ch
Website: http://www.unidir.org/html/en/home.html

The United Nations Institute for Disarmament Research engages in research on disarmament and security in order to assist the international community in promoting disarmament. Its activities include research projects, publications, small meetings, and expert networks to promote innovative approaches to disarmament and security challenges.

United Nations Office for Disarmament Affairs
United Nations Office for Disarmament Affairs
Information and Outreach Branch
United Nations, Room S-3151
New York, NY 10017
USA
Telephone: 1-917-367-5369
Email: UNODA-web@un.org
Website: http://www.un.org/disarmament

The United Nations Office for Disarmament Affairs was established on the recommendation of the UN General Assembly's second special session on disarmament. Among its mandates are disarmament efforts in the area of conventional weapons, especially land mines and small arms, which are especially prominent in modern conflicts. It supports the development and implementation of practical disarmament measures in postconflict zones, including disarming and demobilizing former combatants and helping them reintegrate into civil society.

United Nations Office of the Special Representative of the Secretary-General for Children and Armed Conflict
Radhika Coomaraswamy, Undersecretary-General
1 UN Plaza DC1, 627 F
New York, NY 10017
USA
Telephone: 1-212-963-3178
Fax: 1-212-963-0807
Website: http://www.un.org/children/conflict/english/index
.html

The Office of the Special Representative engages in a variety of humanitarian and diplomatic initiatives to work with both government agencies and nongovernmental organizations to end the recruitment and use of child soldiers and to protect children affected by armed conflict. Among its stated goals are the support of global initiatives to end grave violations of children's rights, the promotion of rights-based protection for children affected by armed conflict, and making the issue of children and armed conflict an integral aspect of peacekeeping and peace building.

United Nations Office on Drugs and Crime
Vienna International Centre
Wagramer Strasse 5
A 1400 Vienna
Austria
Telephone: 43 1 26060
Fax: 43 1 263 3389
Email: See Website Contact Form
Website: http://www.unodc.org/unodc/en/justice-and-prison
-reform/index.html?ref=menuside

The United Nations Office on Drugs and Crime works to fight against illicit drugs and international crime and is dedicated to assisting member states of the United Nations in attempts to combat illicit drugs, crime, and terrorism. It is concerned that former child soldiers may be recruited into crime because of a lack of alternatives, a lack of reintegration schemes, and other difficulties, such as stigmatization, loss of family ties, and drug or alcohol addiction.

United Nations Population Fund
220 East 42nd Street
New York, NY 10017
USA
Telephone: 1-212-297-5000
Fax: 1-212-370-0201
Email: hq@unfpa.org
Website: http://www.unfpa.org/public

The United Nations Population Fund is an international development agency that, among other activities, supports countries in using population data for policies and programs that combat poverty and want. It has directed its concern to the fact that former child soldiers have usually been left out of formal disarmament, demobilization, and reintegration programs, even though their numbers are significant. It has been noted that in Liberia, an estimated 15,000 children served in the war and that in Sierra Leone, children made up 37 percent of the fighting forces in some armed factions. It has also been concerned that even though girls make up about half the children involved with armed groups, they have routinely been ignored.

United Nations Women
304 East 45th Street
15th Floor
New York, NY 10017
USA
Telephone: 1-212-906-6400
Fax: 1-212-906-6705
Email: See Website Contact Form
Website: http://www.unwomen.org

United Nations Women works to promote the recognition that gender consideration are central to human development and human rights. Among its key areas of concern is the use of violence against women and girls, which undermines women's rights and requires the creation of strong laws and stringent enforcement and protective services. United Nations Women also promotes the recognition that women and girls are especially vulnerable in modern-day conflicts, where rape is frequently used as a weapon of war.

United States Institute of Peace
2301 Constitution Avenue NW
Washington, DC 20037
USA
Telephone: 1-202-457-1700
Fax: 1-202-429-6063
Email: See Website Contact Form
Website: http://www.usip.org
Facebook: http://www.facebook.com/usinstituteofpeace

The United States Institute of Peace use analysis, training, and tools to help prevent and end conflicts, promote stability, and professionalize the field of peace building. It views the role of the United States as essential in working with the international community to prevent and resolve conflicts. One of its key goals is the promotion of youth as peace builders.

U.S. Office of Global Women's Issues
U.S. Department of State
2201 C Street NW
Washington, DC 20520
USA

Telephone: 1-202-647-4000
Email: sgwipublic@state.gov
Website: http://www.state.gov/s/gwi

The Office of Global Women's Issues of the U.S. Department of State is led by Ambassador Melanne Verveer. The broad mission of the office is the political, economic, and social empowerment of women. The epidemic of sexual violence in conflict zones around the world is of particular concern to this office, which is deeply concerned with the protection of local populations, especially women and girls, against sexual and gender-based violence.

War Child International
489 College Street W
Suite 500
Toronto, ON M6G 1A5
Canada
Telephone: 1-416-971-7474
Fax: 1-416-971-7946
Email: info@warchild.ca
Website: http://www.warchild.ca

War Child International is a coalition of humanitarian organizations working across the world to help children affected by war. Its fundamental goals are to advance peace through investing hope in the lives of children caught up in the horrors of war. It has numerous on-the-ground projects designed to enhance the protection, development and survival rights for children and young people in conflict and postconflict zones. These include Afghanistan, Burundi, Chechnya, Colombia, the Democratic Republic of the Congo, Ethiopia, Iraq, Israel, Kosovo, Lebanon, Liberia, Sierra Leone, Sri Lanka, Sudan, Uganda, and the Palestinian Territories.

Watchlist on Children and Armed Conflict
c/o Women's Refugee Commission
122 East 42nd Street, 11th Floor
New York, NY 10168-1289
USA
Telephone: 1-212-551-2941

Fax: 1-212-551-3180
Email: watchlist@watchlist.org

Watchlist on Children and Armed Conflict is a network of international nongovernmental organizations that collects and disseminates information on violations against children throughout the world and uses this information to advocate for change. Its mission is to provide the members of the network with support and advice to strengthen their ability to monitor abuses, to advocate on behalf of children in their communities, and to respond to the immediate needs of victims of conflict. It brings its information to key decision makers at the UN Security Council, where it both recommends policy changes and advocates for the adoption and implementation of global child protection policies.

Women Peace and Security Network Africa
68 Onyankle Street
Abelemkpe
Off Olusegun Obasanjo Highway
PMB 36 Osu
Accra
Ghana
Telephone: 233 21 769274, 233 21 920741
E-mail: wipsen@wipsen-africa.org
Website: http://www.wipsen-africa.org/wipsen

The Women Peace and Security Network Africa is a pan-African nongovernmental organization whose goal is to promote women's strategic participation and leadership in peace and security governance in Africa. It developed from the increased involvement of women in peace building in recent years in the violent conflicts in Africa and the widespread mobilization of women seeking solutions to conflict.

Women's Refugee Commission
122 East 42nd Street
New York, NY 10168
USA
Telephone: 1-212-551-3115
Fax: 1-212-551-3180
Email: info@wrcommission.org
Website: http://www.womenscommission.org/programs/youth

The Women's Refugee Commission advocates for laws, policies, and programs that improve the lives and protect the rights of refugee and displaced women, children, and young people, including those seeking asylum—bringing about lasting, measurable change. It makes use of advocacy research and fact-finding field missions to assess and identify best practices and find solutions on critical issues, including those of children who formerly were armed combatants.

World Food Program
C.G. Viola 68
Parco dei Medici
00148 Rome
Italy
Telephone: 39-06-65131
Fax: 39-06-6590632
Email: See Website Contact Form
Website: http://www.wfp.org

The World Food Program is part of the UN system of organizations. Its mission is to fight hunger across the globe. It provides food for communities in emergency situations, including war and other forms of civil conflict. It has been active in the disarmament, demobilization, and reintegration of child soldiers, sometimes exchanging food for arms.

World Health Organization
Avenue Appia 20
1211 Geneva 27
Switzerland
Telephone: 41 22 791 21 11
Fax: 41 22 791 31 11
Email: info@who.int
Website: http://www.who.int

The World Health Organization provides leadership on global health matters. It works to shape the international health research agenda and provides technical support to countries in monitoring and assessing health trends. It supports the development of child and adolescent mental health programs with special attention to sub-Saharan Africa, where problems among displaced children, particularly former soldiers who are unable to integrate into society because of mental health problems, have well-documented social and political consequences. The economic consequences are obvious and are also now well documented.

World Vision
34834 Weyerhaeuser Way S
Federal Way, WA 98001
USA
Telephone: 1-888-511-6548
Email: info@worldvision.org
Website: http://www.wvi.org

World Vision is a Christian international aid and humanitarian organization whose prime focus is combating the root causes of poverty and responding quickly to disasters. World Vision seeks to prevent the recruitment of child soldiers, but most of its focus is on the problems of demobilization and reintegration of former soldiers by providing medical attention and psychological support, coordinating family tracing and reunification, helping child soldiers reintegrate into their communities, and providing them with education and training,

Youth Advocate Program International, Inc.
4000 Albemarle Street NW
Suite 401
Washington, DC 20016
USA
Telephone: 1-202-244-6410
Fax: 202-244-6396
Email: whe@peaceandyouth.org
Web: http://www.yapi.org

Youth Advocate Program International, Inc., is a youth advocacy program centered in Washington, D.C. Its stated mission is to promote and protect the rights and well-being of the world's youth, giving particular attention to children victimized by conflict, exploitation, and state and personal violence. It works to prevent and eliminate the worst forms of child labor, the use of children in armed conflict, the commercial sexual exploitation of children, and the practice of incarcerating children as adults.

8

Resources

Child Soldiers: General Studies

Boothby, Neil, Alison Strang and Michael G. Wessells, eds. *A World Turned Upside Down: Social Ecological Approaches to Children in War Zones*. Sterling, VA: Kumarian Press, 2006.

This edited collection of essays is written by psychologists who have worked with children in war zones in Africa, Asia, Latin America, and Europe. Importantly, the authors generally emphasize the resilience of children in modern conflict zones. Without ignoring the fact that children are often victims of war, the essays in the book stress the need to avoid seeing children only as victims.

Boyden, Jo, and Joanna De Berry, eds. *Children and Youth on the Front Line: Ethnography, Armed Conflict and Displacement*. London: Berghahn Books, 2004.

A very important collection of essays about children in war zones across the globe. The essays emphasize the importance of detailed ethnographic investigations and pay special attention to young people's own descriptions of their experiences as a key means of understanding the impact of war on children's lives. The authors pay special attention to evaluating research methods used in the study of children in conflict zones.

Dupuy, Kendra E., and Krijn Peters. *War and Children: A Reference Handbook*. Santa Barbara, CA: ABC-CLIO, 2010.

A general reference book that provides a broad overview of the different ways in which armed conflict affects children and youth. The book includes discussions of the recruitment of child soldiers, disarmament, demobilization, and the reintegration of demobilized children soldiers into postwar communities.

Machel, Graca. *The Impact of Armed Conflict on Children.* **New York: United Nations, 1996. Accessed at http:/www.unicef.org/ graca/a51-306_en.pdf.**

An influential report developed in response to a request by the UN General Assembly to the UN secretary-general that an expert be appointed to undertake a comprehensive study of the participation of children in armed conflict. The study, by Graca Machel, became one of the most significant UN policy documents on the issue of child soldiers.

Child Soldiers: Studies of Children at War

Bernal, Virginia. "Equality to Die For: Women Guerilla Fighters in Eritrea's Cultural Revolution." *Polar: Political and Legal Anthropological Review* 28 (2000): 61–78.

This article focuses on "women" who fought during the Eritrean War of Independence (1961–1991). Although the article is subtitled "Women Guerilla Fighters," many of the "women" were between the ages of 15 and 18 and would be classified by many today as "child soldiers." Bernal argues that their experience as soldiers endowed them with a critical perspective toward Eritrean society and provided them with skills to engage in collective action. The article provides a good example of the way age categories have shifted so that persons once considered women are now regarded as children.

Cohen, Ilene, and Guy S. Goodwin-Gill. *Child Soldiers: The Role of Children in Armed Conflict.* **Oxford: Clarendon Press, 1994.**

A widely cited and important overview of the child soldier problem. The book describes the recruitment and use of child soldiers in a variety of different armed conflicts and evaluates the ways international law can provide protections to children.

Coulter, Chris. *Bush Wives and Girl Soldiers: Women's Lives through War and Peace in Sierra Leone.* **Ithaca, NY: Cornell University Press, 2009.**

A study of girls soldiers in the Sierra Leone civil war. The girls were abducted generally by rebel forces. Some became fighters, but most became "bush wives" who were pressed into sexual and domestic relations with rebels. Coulter describes the day-to-day experiences of these young girl soldiers, who lived extraordinarily difficult lives in the bush and who were frequently rejected by their families at the war's end. Coulter argues that the productive work of women and girls sustained the rebel forces and that the organization of labor was similar to but far more extreme than the organization of labor in rural prewar Sierra Leone society.

Coundouriotis, Elen. "The Child Soldier Narrative and the Problem of Arrested Historicization." *Journal of Human Rights* **9 (2010): 191–206.**

A comparative analysis of fictional child soldiers' narratives from Africa. Argues that current child soldier narratives remove both historical contexts and agency from children in comparison with those from the colonial and precolonial period.

Courtney, J. "The Civil War That Was Fought by Children: Understanding the Role of Child Combatants in El Salvador's Civil War, 1980–1992." *Journal of Military History* **74 (2010): 523–56.**

This article argues that the Salvadoran civil war (1980–1992) was marked by the warring parties' dependence on child soldiers. The war was between the government of El Salvador and the rebel group known as Farabundo Martí National Liberation Front. Although both sides recruited homeless, orphaned, displaced, and economically impoverished children, the U.S.-supported government troops relied more on forced recruitment than did the guerrilla forces, which adopted a more protective role toward the children.

Denov, Myriam. *Child Soldiers: Sierra Leone's Revolutionary United Front.* **Cambridge: Cambridge University Press, 2010.**

A study of child soldiers in the Revolutionary United Front (RUF), the rebel force in the Sierra Leone civil war (1991–2002), which was infused with an extreme culture of violence designed to break down resistance and insure obedience. The RUF started the civil war, and from the very beginning its soldiers were known for their cruelty to civilians and for abducting children into their forces and treating them with brutality. Despite this, child combatants were still able to exercise agency, even under extreme circumstances in which they seemed to have little control.

Dickson-Gomez, Julie. "Growing Up in Guerilla Camps: The Long Term Impact of Being a Child Soldier in El Salvador's Civil War." *Ethos 30* (2002): 327–56.

Examines the long-term effects on children of having actively participated in guerilla war. The author argues that suffering traumatic experiences in early childhood may destroy trust and interfere with the development of adolescent autonomy.

Murphy, William P. "Military Patrimonialism and Child Soldier Clientalism in the Liberian and Sierra Leonean Civil Wars." *African Studies Review* 46 (2003): 61–87.

Murphy analyzes the recruitment and use of child soldiers as part of patrimonialism, a system of political governance in which power flows from the leader and creates relationships of dependency and exploitation. Murphy tries to show that the use and abuse of child soldiers by armed forces and groups during the civil war in Sierra Leone was similar to the way power relationships were organized in prewar civil life in Sierra Leone.

Peters, Krijn. *War and the Crisis of Youth in Sierra Leone*. Cambridge: Cambridge University Press, 2011.

Based on interviews with more than 1,000 ex-combatants, many of whom were child soldiers, the book examines how combatants interpreted their experiences of war. Interviews were largely with rank-and-file soldiers and made use of rapport developed by the author over a number of years. The interviews provide a powerful insider's view of warfare in a rebel army. The book raises the problem of how so many people, including soldiers, civilians, and child soldiers, could have empathy for an armed group that was so terribly cruel.

Richards, Paul. *Fighting for the Rain Forest: War, Youth and Resources in Sierra Leone.* **Portsmouth, NH: Heinemann, 1996.**

An analysis of the civil war in Sierra Leone that argues that the war was, in part, a competition for the hearts and minds of young people. Richards argues that the civil war in Sierra Leone involved mobilization of youth by groups that were angry at being excluded from a political system that served mining interests in the country. Richards tries to show that many child soldiers fight with the "eyes open"; that is, they are not merely dupes but have well-articulated reasons for participating in war.

Rosen, David M. *Armies of the Young: Child Soldiers in War and Terrorism.* **New Brunswick, NJ: Rutgers University Press, 2005.**

Argues that the presence of children in the military is an age-old phenomenon that must be examined in light of the context in which children are recruited. The book focuses on three very distinctive case studies of child soldiers: Jewish children who joined anti-Nazi resistance groups during the Holocaust, child soldiers in Sierra Leone, and Palestinian children. The author argues that there is no single type of child soldier. In some instances children are abused, in others they can be leaders in setting the agenda for violence, and elsewhere they may be trying to save their lives and communities.

Utas, Mats, and Magnus Jorgel. "The West Side Boys: Military Navigation in the Sierra Leone Civil War." *Journal of Modern African Studies* **46 (2008): 487–512.**

An analysis of the West Side Boys, a splinter militia during the Sierra Leone civil war that recruited a significant number of child soldiers. Argues that the West Side Boys viewed themselves as part of a "youth revolution" that was fighting to take power from a gerontocratic and patronage-based elite.

Veale, Angela. *From Child Soldier to Ex-Fighter: Female Fighters, Demobilisation and Reintegration in Ethiopia.* **Pretoria: Institute for Security Studies, 2003. Accessed at http://www.iss.co.za/ pubs/Monographs/No85/Contents.html.**

This study traces the history of a group of women in the Tigray People's Liberation Front, which was the victorious rebel group in the Ethiopian civil war (1974–1991_. Veale argues that women's experience as fighters during the war strengthened them by emphasizing their competence, ability, and rights to participate as equals in Ethiopian society. When peace came, however, Ethiopian society tried to force them back into their traditional prewar peacetime roles as subservient and second-class members of society.

Vigh, Henrik. *Navigating Terrains of War: Youth and Soldiering in Guinea-Bissau.* **New York: Berghahn Books, 2006.**

Argues that the members of the youth militia Aguentas in Guinea-Bissau, West Africa, were mischaracterized by humanitarian and human rights organizations that all too often tried to characterize them as victimized child soldiers, that is, impoverished children from rural backgrounds who were tricked into military service. The reality was that they were primarily young men and youth from urban backgrounds who well understood the reasons, risks, and rewards of war.

West, Harry G. "Girls with Guns: Narrating the Experience of War in FRELIMO's 'Female Detachment.'" *Anthropological Quarterly* **73 (2000): 180–94.**

Examines the role of female guerrillas, many of whom were child soldiers, in the armed struggle for national liberation in Mozambique in 1975–1992. West shows that most girls and women felt empowered by their participation as soldiers in armed struggle against the Portuguese colonial power and did not regard themselves as exploited or victimized. Many saw their participation in armed struggle as having provided them with the ability to participate as full citizens in Mozambique society.

Policy and Advocacy

Adult Wars, Child Soldiers. **New York: UNICEF 2002. Accessed at http://www.unicef.org/eapro/AdultWarsChildSoldiers.pdf.**

Key policy document published by UNICEF that argues that the child soldier problem stems largely from the unscrupulous exploitation of children by adults. The report attempt to broadly describe the family background of the children involved with armed groups, the manner in which children become child soldiers, their experience as child soldiers, the impact of that experience on their worldviews, and the children's views and thoughts about the future.

"Cape Town Principles and Best Practice on the Prevention of Recruitment of Children into the Armed Forces and on Demobilization and Socialization Reintegration of Child Soldiers in Africa." New York: UNICEF, 1997. Accessed at http://www .unicef.org/emerg/files/Cape_Town_Principles%281%29.pdf.

The NGO Working Group on the Convention on the Rights of the Child and UNICEF conducted a symposium in Cape Town, South Africa, in 1997 to develop strategies for preventing recruitment of children and to try to establishing age 18 as the minimum age at which soldiers could be recruited. The symposium produced the Cape Town Principles and Best Practices, which recommend actions to be taken by governments and communities in affected countries to end the recruitment of child soldiers. They call for a broad definition of child soldiers that would include not only a child who is carrying or has carried arms but any person under 18 years of age who is part of any kind of regular or irregular armed force or armed group in any capacity.

Giroux, Henry. *Hearts of Darkness: Torturing Children in the War on Terror*. Boulder, CO: Paradigm Publishers, 2011.

When President George W. Bush determined that the Geneva Convention was not applicable to captives during the war on terror, he opened the door for the widespread abuse and torture of suspected enemy combatants, including child soldiers. This book examines the systematic abuse and torture of children by the U.S. military.

"Principles and Guidelines on Children Associated with Armed Forces and Armed Groups" ("Paris Principles") New York: UNICEF 2007. Accessed at http://www.un.org/children/ conflict/_documents/parisprinciples/ParisPrinciples_EN.pdf.

This document was produced as a result of UNICEF's tenth-anniversary review of the Cape Town Principles. Reviews the informal ways in which children become involved with armed forces and armed groups and argues that such children should be deemed children "associated" with an armed force or groups and thereby made subjects of international protection.

Singer, Peter W. *Children at War.* New York: Pantheon Press, 2005.

Argues that children's involvement in war, both as victims and as perpetrators of violence, comes from the breakdown of an age-old taboo that distinguishes between civilians and warriors. Portrays that the recruitment of children is a cheap and easy way to obtain recruits without much investment.

Human Rights Reports

Children and Armed Conflict: Report of the Secretary General. General Assembly-Security Council A/64/742–S/2010/181. New York: United Nations, 2010. Accessed at http://www .securitycouncilreport.org/atf/cf/%7B65BFCF9B-6D27-4E9C-8CD3 -CF6E4FF96FF9%7D/CAC%20S%202010%20181.pdf.

Key annual report of the secretary-general of the United Nations that documents measures undertaken to end all violations and abuses committed against children in armed conflict and provides updates on the implementation of the monitoring and reporting mechanism established by the UN Security Council. The report also gives attention to grave violations committed against children. including the recruitment and use of children by armed forces and armed groups.

Children in the Ranks: The Maoists' Use of Child Soldiers in Nepal. New York: Human Rights Watch, 2007. Accessed at http://www.hrw.org/en/reports/2007/02/01/children-ranks-0.

Argues that most children in Maoist ranks were not forcibly recruited. Many children joined as a result of ideological training and as a way out of way out of unemployment and poverty. Lower-caste Nepalis often joined to escape poverty and caste discrimination and because of the promise of freedom from a life of servility. According to the report, children are involved in many different roles with the Maoists. While most are in local militia groups, others hold positions in the Maoists' central military organization, the People's Liberation Army. Children generally receive extensive military and weapons training.

Dangerous Duty: Children and the Chhattisgarh Conflict. **New York: Human Rights Watch, 2008. Accessed at http://www.hrw .org/en/reports/2008/09/05/dangerous-duty-0.**

Argues that the conflict in India's Chhattisgarh state has irreparably damaged children's lives. Details claims that all parties— the Maoist rebels, anti-Maoist vigilante groups, and the government security forces—recruited children in ways that cause their massive displacement and expose them to the risk of injury and death.

Early to War: Child Soldiers in the Chad Conflict. **New York: Human Rights Watch, 2007. Accessed at http://www.hrw.org/en/ reports/2007/07/15/early-war.**

In Chad, the national army, the Chadian national army has been attempting to defeat a Chadian rebel insurgency led by the *Front Uni pour le Changement* (United Front for Change [FUC]). Both the government and the rebels have recruited children under 18 years old. Human Rights Watch reports that children as young as eight serve as fighters, guards, cooks, and lookouts on the front lines of the conflict. While the government has been cooperating with efforts to demobilize child soldiers, to date the vast majority of demobilized child soldiers have come from the FUC and not from Chadian government forces.

Erased in a Moment: Suicide Bombing Attacks against Israeli Civilians. **New York: Human Rights Watch, 2007. Accessed at http://www.hrw.org/en/reports/2002/10/15/erased-moment.**

According to Human Rights Watch, at the time of this report, more than 415 Israeli and other civilians have been killed and more than 2,000 injured by suicide bombings. The majority of these deaths and injuries were the result of suicide terrorist operations carried out by Palestinians. The attacks deliberately targeted civilians in restaurants and other public places. Suicide terrorists typically used bombs packed with nails and pieces of metal in order to sow widespread death and destruction. This report details the recruitment and use of suicide terrorists, including children, in the Israeli-Palestinian conflict, arguing that these attacks are crimes against humanity and that in the context of armed conflict they amount to war crimes.

Global Report 2008. London: Coalition to Stop the Use of Child Soldiers, 2008. Accessed at http://www.child-soldiers.org/library/global-reports.

The coalition was founded by six international nongovernmental organizations and advocates a worldwide prohibition on the recruitment and use of persons under the age of 18 in armed forces and groups. It has published a report every three to four years that documents military recruitment legislation and practice and child soldier use in hostilities by governments and armed groups across the globe in 197 countries. Each individual country report focuses on circumstances and methods of recruitment and the role that children play in armed forces or groups.

"My Gun Was as Tall as Me": Child Soldiers in Burma. New York: Human Rights Watch, 2002. Accessed at http://www.hrw.org/en/reports/2002/10/16/my-gun-was-tall-me.

According to Human Rights Watch, Burma (Myanmar) has more child soldiers than any other nation in the world. In contrast to the situation elsewhere in the world, in Burma the vast majority of child soldiers are recruited by the national army. Human Rights Watch also alleges that Burma's record on child soldiers is the worst in the world. This report reviews the recruitment of child soldiers by the Burmese government as well as that by opposition groups. Those in the government army are reported to be beaten and humiliated during training. As soldiers, they are involved in combat but also participate in human rights abuses against civilians. Child soldiers are also part of the many Burmese rebel groups.

The Omar Khadr Case: A Teenager Imprisoned at Guantanamo. New York: Human Rights Watch, 2007. Accessed at http://www.hrw.org/en/reports/2007/06/01/omar-khadr-case.

This is a background report by Human Right's Watch on the arrest and detention of Omar Khadr, a child imprisoned at Guantanamo Bay by the U.S. government and charged with being an enemy combatant. The report contains allegations of his abuse and mistreatment in violation of both U.S. domestic law and international law, which require governments to provide children (persons under the age of 18) with special safeguards and care, including legal protections appropriate to their age. Human

Rights Watch alleges that Khadr was held in violation of international law, which requires that children be treated in a manner that takes into account children's vulnerability and that emphasis be primarily on rehabilitation and reintegration rather than punishment.

A Review of the FBI's Involvement in and Observations of Detainee Interrogations in Guantanamo Bay, Afghanistan and Iraq. **Washington, DC: Office of the Inspector General, Department of Justice, 2008. Accessed at http://www.justice.gov/oig/special/s0805/final.pdf.**

The FBI investigated interrogations at Guantanamo Bay and elsewhere and described methods of interrogation, including the "frequent-flyer program" used against child detainees by non-FBI interrogators. After this investigation, the FBI determined that it would no longer participate in joint interrogations with other agencies that used these methods.

Stolen Children: Abduction and Recruitment in Northern Uganda. **New York: Human Rights Watch, 2003. Accessed at http://www.hrw.org/en/reports/2003/03/28/stolen-children.**

Documents the abduction of children by the Lord's Resistance Army (LRA) in northern Uganda and the use of children as soldiers, laborers, and sexual slaves. Argues that children have been targets of LRA abductions throughout the conflict between the LRA and the Ugandan government that began in 1986. According to the report, children were abducted in record numbers by the LRA and were subjected to brutal treatment as soldiers, laborers, and sexual slaves.

We'll Kill You if You Cry: Sexual Violence in the Sierra Leone Conflict. **New York: Human Rights Watch, 2003. Accessed at http://www.hrw.org/en/reports/2003/01/15/well-kill-you-if-you-cry.**

There was widespread use of sexual violence during the Sierra Leone civil war (1991–2001). Human Rights Watch reports that thousands of women and girls were abducted by the rebels and subjected to sexual slavery and forced to become the sex slaves of their rebel "husbands." Some abducted women and girls were forcibly conscripted into the fighting forces and given military training. The main perpetrators of sexual violence were the rebel forces of the Revolutionary United Front, the Armed Forces Revolutionary Council, and the West Side Boys, an offshoot of the latter.

Disarmament, Demobilization, and Reintegration

Annan, Jeannie, Christopher Blattman, and Roger Horton. *The State of Youth and Youth Protection in Northern Uganda: Findings from the Survey for War Affected Youth.* New York: UNICEF, 2006. Accessed at http:/chrisblattman.com/documents/policy/sway/SWAY.Phase1.FinalReport.pdf.

A key empirical study by the Survey for War Affected Youth (http://chrisblattman.com/projects/sway) focusing on children and youth in northern Uganda, many of whom were abducted by the Lord's Resistance Army. The report details their exposure to war-related violence, psychosocial well-being, education, economic activities, health, and the challenges of reintegration. Argues that that the psychosocial health of male youth is remarkably robust and that there needs to be a shift in humanitarian aid and assistance away from prioritizing psychosocial care to for ex-combatants and toward prioritizing age-appropriate education and income-generating activities.

Christensen, Maya, and Mats Utas. "Mercenaries of Democracy: The 'Politricks' of Remobilized Combatants in the 2007 General Elections, Sierra Leone." *African Affairs* 107 (2008): 515–39.

During the 2007 postwar general elections in Sierra Leone, political parties remobilized ex-combatants into "security squads" both to protect themselves and to mobilize votes. The authors contend that the ongoing political mobilization of children and youth in postwar Sierra Leone has the potential for cultivating future violence.

Honwana, Alcinda. *Child Soldiers in Africa*. Philadelphia: University of Pennsylvania Press, 2007.

An ethnographic study of child soldiers in the civil wars in Angola and Mozambique. The author asserts that local healing rituals can play an important role in reintegrating demobilized child soldiers back into society and claims that a variety of cleansing or purification rituals functioned to facilitate individual and collective healing and promote social harmony.

Kohrt, Brandon A., Mark J. D. Jordans, Wietse A. Tol, Rebecca A. Speckman, Sujen M. Maharjan, Carol M. Worthman, and Ivan H. Komproe. "Comparison of Mental Health between Former Child Soldiers and Children Never Conscripted by Armed Groups in Nepal." *Journal of the American Medical Association* **6 (2008): 691–702.**

Examines the mental health of former child soldiers among the Maoist rebels of Nepal, matched by age, sex, education, and ethnicity with children in the same conflict zone who were not conscripted. The study demonstrates that differences in mental health between former child soldiers and civilians is concentrated among child soldiers with greater trauma exposure.

Shaw, Rosalind. "Displacing Violence: Making Pentecostal Memory in Postwar Sierra Leone." *Cultural Anthropology* **22 (2007): 66–93.**

Examines how Pentecostal youth in postwar Sierra Leone, many of whom were child soldiers, remember and reimagine the war as having been a "spiritual battle." Shaw argues that "forgetting" the war in a realistic way allows young people to rebuild their lives along a new moral axis that reduces their sense of weakness and dependency.

Shepler, Susan. "The Rites of the Child: Global Discourses of Youth and Reintegrating Child Soldiers in Sierra Leone." *Journal of Human Rights* **4 (2005): 197–211.**

Describes how the Convention on the Rights of the Child and other international child rights instruments, together with humanitarian and human rights workers, help create an understanding of childhood as "innocent" and "apolitical" for strategic purposes and help promote "discourses of abdicated responsibility" in children's narrations of their war experiences.

Wessels, Michael. *Child Soldiers: From Violence to Protection.* **Cambridge, MA: Harvard University Press, 2006.**

Wessels argues for the need to contextualize the understanding of child soldiers: to understand that childhoods outside the West may be shaped by different values so as to avoid either infantilizing child soldiers or sensationalizing their brutality. The book rejects the idea that children who serve in armies are somehow damaged for life.

Child Soldiers in History

Conley, Mary A. *From Jack Tar to Union Jack: Representing Naval Manhood in the British Empire, 1870–1918.* Manchester: Manchester University Press, 2009.

Discusses, among other issues, the case of Jack Travers Cornwall, killed at age 16 in the Battle of Jutland in World War I. Cornwall was a boy sailor aboard the HMS *Chester* during the battle. He was part of a gun crew and stayed at his post while all the members of his gun crew were killed. He was the sole survivor but died of his wounds shortly afterward. He was awarded the Victoria Cross, Britain's highest military honor, and given a hero's funeral attended by thousands, including schoolchildren and Boy Scouts. Conlan argues that the life and death of this humble working-class boy served as a symbol of the democratization of heroism and for the continued endurance of the British Empire.

Cox, Caroline. "Boy Soldiers of the American Revolution: The Effects of War on Society." In *Children and Youth in a New Nation,* edited by James Marten, 13–28. New York: New York University Press, 2009.

Tracking the careers of boy soldiers, Cox argues that there was no single, predictable age-graded path from childhood to adulthood in early America. Accordingly, enlistment in the revolutionary forces was governed not by strict age criteria but by a balance of local norms, family concerns, and young people's desire for adventure.

Drago, Edmund. *Rebel Phoenix: Rebel Children and Their Families in South Carolina.* New York: Fordham University Press, 2008.

Examines the role of South Carolina children during the American Civil War. Children, from the age of seven upward, participated in the war effort. The war transformed children's lives, as youngsters joined the Confederate army, raised money for warships, found personal freedom, replaced adult labor, and came to serve as icons of the Confederate cause.

Marten, James, ed. *Children and War: A Historical Anthology.* **New York: New York University Press, 2008.**

A collection of 21 essays that detail children's engagement with war as soldiers, victims, observers, supporters, and spies and as symbols of national angst, identity, and valor in a wide variety of conflicts. The portraits that emerge are complex, inspiring, and troubling and illustrate the agility and resourcefulness of children in times of terrible danger. Most compelling is the way in which children are engaged and animated by war both in the imagination and in reality. In addition, the book shows the ways in which children are subjected to relentless attempts by society to control and mediate their responses to war, even trying to shape their memories of war.

Mayall, Berry, and Virginia Murrow. *You Can Help Your Country: English Children's Work during the Second World War.* **London: University of London, Institute of Education, 2011.**

A study of English children's work during World War II that examines their participation in the national war effort through activities such as helping with the harvest, raising funds for warplanes and warships, and keeping businesses running while parents were engaged in other war work. Details the roles of children as active social agents during the war. It emphasizes their often ignored participation in the war effort.

Ronald, D. A. B. *Young Nelsons: Boy Sailors during the Napoleonic Wars.* **Oxford: Osprey Publishing, 2009.**

During the Napoleonic Wars, boys as young as 10 or 11 were recruited into the navy in two ways, depending largely on social class. The Marine Society, a charitable organization, channeled boys from poor backgrounds into naval service, while boys from other class backgrounds came in for training and apprenticeship as future officers.

Stargardt, Nicholas. *Witnesses of War: Children's Lives under the Nazis.* **New York: Vintage Press, 2007.**

A powerful historical study of the lives of children in Nazi Germany based on juvenile diaries, letters, and other documents. Details the lives of children across the racial and national divides of Nazi Germany to portray the way in which both the war and German ideals of racial utopianism entered in the lives and imaginations of children.

Van Emden, Richard. *Boy Soldiers of the Great War.* **London: Headline Books, 2005.**

Examines the recruitment of underage soldiers into the British army in World War I. Argues that underage enlistees made up approximately 10 to 15 percent of the army and that there was widespread connivance at all levels of society to evade age restrictions, including by the political elite, the army, the parents of the boys, and the boys themselves.

Child Soldiers and International Law: Key Treaties

"Convention on the Rights of the Child, Nov. 20, 1989." **Accessed at http://www.icrc.org/ihl.nsf/FULL/540?OpenDocument, March 12, 2011.**

The full text of the Convention on the Rights of the Child, which has been signed by virtually all the nations of the world except for the United States and Somalia. It creates an international definition of childhood as beginning at birth and ending at age 18 but permits the recruitment of children into armed forces beginning at age 15. It has been ratified by most of the nations of the world (the United States and Somalia are the only major exceptions). Compliance with the treaty is monitored by the UN Committee on the Rights of the Child.

"Geneva Convention Relative to the Protection of Civilian Persons in Time of War (Fourth Geneva Convention)." 1949. Accessed at http://avalon.law.yale.edu/20th_century/geneva07.asp.

The Geneva Conventions of 1949 consisted of four related treaties. They created the basic international standards for international humanitarian law (the laws of war). The Fourth Convention contains important protections for children relating to their care, treatment by occupying powers in times of war, and their rights to remain connected to their families.

"International Labour Organization Convention (No. 182) concerning the Prohibition and Immediate Action for the Elimination of the Worst Forms of Child Labor of 1999." Accessed at http:/www.ilo.org/ilolex/cgi-lex/convde.pl?C182.

The full text of the International Labour Organization Convention, which categorizes the forced or compulsory recruitment of child soldiers under age 18 in armed conflict as a form of slavery or a practice similar to slavery, such as the sale and trafficking of children, debt bondage, and serfdom.

"Optional Protocol to the Convention on the Rights of the Child on the Involvement of Children in Armed Conflict." 2000. United Nations Treaty Series 2173: 222. Accessed at http:/www2.ohchr.org/english/law/crc-conflict.htm.

A supplementary treaty to the Convention on the Rights of the Child. The state parties to the treaty agree to raise the age of recruitment of children above the age permitted by the Convention. It imposes stricter controls on rebels and insurgents.

"Protocols Additional to the Geneva Conventions of 12 August 1949, and Relating to the Protection of Victims of International Armed Conflicts (Additional Protocol I), June 8, 1977." Accessed at http:/www2.ohchr.org/english/law/protocol1.htm.

The first international treaty to specifically restrict the recruitment of child soldiers in international armed conflict between nation-states. The parties to the treaty agreed to refrain from recruiting children under 15 years old into their armed forces.

"Protocol Additional to the Geneva Conventions of 12 August 1949, and Relating to the Victims of Non-International Armed Conflicts (Additional Protocol II), June 8, 1977." Accessed at http:/www2.ohchr.org/english/law/pdf/protocol2.pdf.

The first international treaty to restrict the recruitment of child soldiers in noninternational conflicts, such as civil wars and insurgencies. The parties to the treaty imposed an absolute ban on the recruitment of children under 15 years old by rebels and other armed groups.

"Rome Statute of the International Criminal Court." 1998. Accessed at http:/untreaty.un.org/cod/icc/statute/romefra.htm.

Full text of the Rome Statute, which provides for the prosecution of a wide variety of war crimes and crimes against humanity under international criminal law. The statute imposes an absolute ban on the recruitment of children under 15 years old by armed forces and armed groups.

International Criminal Tribunals

International Criminal Court. http:/www.icc-cpi.int

The International Criminal Court was established in 2002 at The Hague as the permanent tribunal to try violations of international criminal law, including the recruitment of child soldiers under the age of 15. The website contains the transcripts of trials before the court as well as of the many judicial decisions made in these cases. The first case ever to be tried before the International Criminal Court is that of Thomas Lubanga Dyilo, a former rebel leader from the Democratic Republic of the Congo who was charged with recruiting child soldiers.

Special Court for Sierra Leone. http:/www.sc-sl.org

The Special Court for Sierra Leone was created to try those people most responsible for war crimes during Sierra Leone civil war. Defendants from all the major warring factions were charged with recruiting child soldiers and other war crimes. The website of the Special Court contains the transcripts of all these trials, along with the many judicial decisions made during the course of the trial.

Child Soldiers: Legal Analyses

Frakt, David R. "Closing Argument at Guantanamo: The Torture of Mohammed Jawad." *Harvard Human Rights Journal* 22 (2009): 401–23.

Mohammed Jawad was a child soldier who was tortured and detained at Guantanamo Bay Naval Base in Cuba. His defense attorney made an impassioned argument before a U.S. military tribunal as to why his detention and abuse were unlawful. Major Frakt argued that Jawad was tortured for sport long after it was clear that he had no useful information to provide authorities.

Happold, Matthew. *Child Soldiers in International Law.* **Huntington, NY: Juris Publishing, 2005.**

Basic review of the laws governing the recruitment and use of child soldiers. It also reviews developments in the law related to the criminal culpability of child soldiers who commit war crimes, the treatment of child captives, and the prosecution of recruiters under international law. Contains a strong detailed analysis of the controversies and historical development of the law.

Kelsall, Tim. *Culture under Cross Examination: International Justice and the Special Court for Sierra Leone.* **Cambridge: Cambridge University Press, 2009.**

An anthropological analysis of trials held by the Special Court for Sierra Leone in the aftermath of the Sierra Leone civil war. The book reviews many aspects of the trials at the Special Court that resulted in the conviction and sentencing of key leaders of the warring parties during the war. Argues that the prosecution and the court leveled inappropriate and ethnocentric charges against defendants accused of recruiting child soldiers and other war crimes.

Mann, Howard. "International Law and the Child Soldier." *International and Comparative Law Quarterly* **36 (1987): 32–57.**

Mann reviewed the history and politics surrounded the creation of international law governing the recruitment and use of child soldiers. The article includes very helpful discussions of how age categories became part of international law.

Rosen, David M. "Who Is a Child? The Legal Conundrum of Child Soldiers." *Connecticut Journal of International Law* **25 (1, 2009): 81–118. Accessed at http://www.law.uconn.edu/system/files/private/Rosen+Article+Final.pdf.**

Examines the legal and political controversies surrounding the age at which children may be recruited into armed forces and armed groups and the age at which they may be deemed culpable for the commission of war crimes. Argues for the need to take into account local ideas of justice in framing international law.

Wilson, Richard A. "Children and War in Sierra Leone: A West African Diary." *Anthropology Today* **17 (5, 2001): 20–22.**

Wilson reports on his participation in technical meetings about children's participation in Sierra Leone's Truth and Reconciliation Commission. He describes the development of a consensus among international experts and local professionals, their general hostility toward local standards of law and justice, and their belief that international norms of justice and ideas about childhood must prevail over any local or traditional standards.

Autobiographies and Biographies

Beah, Ishmael. *A Long Way Gone: Memoirs of a Boy Soldier.* **New York: Farrar, Straus and Giroux, 2007.**

A powerful firsthand account by Ishmael Beah, a child soldier, that describes struggles by Beah and his friends to escape the danger and chaos of the civil war in Sierra Leone. He was finally recruited into the Sierra Leone army and later experiences a wrenching and dangerous process of demobilization. He describes his participation in war in a compelling and highly nuanced manner.

Herman, Marek. *From the Alps to the Red Sea.* **Western Galilee: Ghetto Fighters Museum, 1985.**

The author, a Polish Jew, managed to escape from Poland to Italy with the help of members of a garrison of Italian soldiers stationed in Lvov. Although hidden in relative safety in Italy, he rejected safety and joined the 49th Garibaldi Partisan Brigade at age 16 and fought against Italian fascist and German army units in Italy.

Holt, Tonie. *My Boy Jack? The Search for Kipling's Only Son.* **Barnsley: Pen and Sword Books, 2008.**

Rudyard Kipling's (British author of the *Jungle Book* and many other works of fiction) only son John ("Jack") Kipling was commissioned in the Irish Guards in 1915 at age 17. Kipling was a powerful public supporter of war with Germany. Although his son was deemed medically unfit for service, because of his father's influence with the army, Jack was commissioned into the Irish Guards; he was killed in action in September 1915.

Kehoe, Thomas Joseph. *The Fighting Mascot: The True Story of a Boy Soldier.* **London: Blackie and Son, 1918. Accessed at http:/ www.archive.org/details/thefightingmascot00kehouoft.**

The memoir of a 16-year-old boy soldier who enlisted in the 5th Kings Liverpool Regiment by lying about his age. Details his participation in trench warfare in Belgium and France during the war and his subsequent role as a spokesman and fund-raiser for the Red Cross.

Lister, David. *Die Hard, Aby.* **London: Pen and Sword Books, 2005.**

Details the background and events leading to the court-martial for desertion and execution by firing squad of a 17-year-old British boy soldier during World War I. He was one of more than 300 soldiers (including other child soldiers) shot by the British for desertion or cowardice. The book also discusses attempts by members of Parliament to change government and army policy with little effect.

Martin, John Plumb. *Private Yankee Doodle.* **Fort Washington, PA: Eastern National, 2002.**

Originally published in Maine in 1830, Martin's memoir describes his enlistment at age 15 in a regiment of Connecticut troops in 1775 and later in the Continental Army. Considered to be one of the most important primary sources for understanding the daily life of the common soldier. Plumb makes it clear that his family had little ability to affect his decision to enlist and that his young age was no barrier to enlistment.

Quaifem, M. "A Boy Soldier under Washington: The Memoir of Daniel Granger." *Mississippi Valley Historical Review* **16 (4, 1930): 538–60.**

Granger joined the ranks of the rebel forces when he was 13 years old but did not write this memoir until 1848. Granger enlisted when he substituted as a soldier for this older brother who had taken ill. Granger was witness to many of the horrors of war, including the execution of fellow soldiers.

Raban, Havka Folman. *They Are Still with Me.* **Western Galilee: Ghetto Fighter's Museum, 1997.**

Sixteen-year-old Havka was part of the youth resistance movements in the Warsaw Ghetto and served as a courier, transmitting information outside the Ghetto under an assumed Polish identity and helping to organize armed resistance. The memoir details the resistance activity of the youth movements in the Ghetto. Raban was captured by the Germans and sent to Auschwitz-Birkinau but survived the war.

Smith, William B. *On Wheels and How I Came There.* **New York: Hunt & Easton, 1892. Accessed at http://www.archive.org/details/onwheelsandhowi00mccagoog.**

The experiences of a 15-year-old Union army boy soldier who was captured and became a prisoner of war during the American Civil War. Describes his ordeal at Andersonville, a notorious southern prisoner-of-war camp.

Memorial Books

Anonymous. *Jack Cornwall: The Story of John Travers Cornwell, V.C. Boy—1st Class.* **London: Hodder & Stoughton, 1917. Reprint, Uckfield: The Naval and Military Press, 2009.**

Posthumous tribute to the boy hero of the Battle of Jutland in World War I who was killed at age 16 and was the recipient of the Victoria Cross. He was given a hero's funeral at Manor Park Cemetery in London in a ceremony attended by schoolchildren and Boy Scouts. Described by his commander as having remained by his post under heavy fire "with only his own brave heart and God's help to support him."

Bingham, Luther Goodyear. *The Little Drummer Boy, Clarence McKenzie, the Child of the 13th Regiment New York State Militia and the Child of the Mission Sunday School.* **New York: Board of**

Publication of the Reformed Protestant Dutch Church, 1861
Accessed at http:/www.archive.org/details/littledrummerbo00
binggoog.

A hagiographic memorial book celebrating the life and death of
Clarence McKenzie, one of the early casualties of the American
Civil War who died at age 12. McKenzie was celebrated as a mar-
tyr in the cause of abolition.

A Citizen of Alexandria. *Life of Luther C. Ladd, Who Fell in Baltimore, April 19, 1861 Exclaiming All Hail to the Stars and
Stripes.* Concord, NH: PB Cogswell, 1862. Reprint, Farmington,
MI: Thomson Gale, 1969. Accessed at http:/www.archive.org/
stream/lifeoflutherclad00conc/lifeoflutherclad00conc_djvu.txt.

A funeral memorial book that celebrating the life and death of
Luther Ladd, age 15, the first Union soldier to die in the American
Civil War. Ladd was widely hailed as a martyr in the cause of the
abolition of slavery.

Nadal, Bernhard J. *The Christian Boy-Soldier: The Funeral Ser-
mon of Joseph E. Darrow Preached in Sands Street Methodist
Episcopal Church, Brooklyn, on the 27th of October, 1861.* New
York: Steam Printing House, 1862.

Joseph Darrow died of wounds received in the Battle of Bull Run.
The funeral sermon was given by the minister of the church, Bernard Harrison Nadal, who was a confidant of Abraham Lincoln
and a staunch supporter of the Union. Although Darrow was a
boy, Nadal described him as "never a child . . . but an instance of
manly care and thoughtfulness in infantile habiliments."

Child Soldiers in Fiction

Abani, Chris. *A Song for the Night: A Novella.* New York:
Akashic Books, 2007.

This short novel by the well-known Nigerian writer Chris Abani
follows a pattern seen in several other novels about African child
soldiers by setting the conflict in a nameless African country. As
with these other novels, the presumed intent is to create a general
story about the use and abuse of child soldiers. The exploitation
of children is symbolized by the creation of a fictitious mutilation

of the children. The main protagonist, named My Luck, is part of a group of child sappers charged with clearing minefields. All the children are mutilated by having their vocal chords cut to keep them from crying out if they should accidentally step on a live mine. As improbable as this scenario is, it is the basis of a compelling story.

Dongala, Emmanuel. *Johnny Mad Dog.* **New York: Picador Press, 2006.**

Set during a civil war in an unnamed country, this novel is the story of two 16-year-old teenagers. One, Johnny Mad Dog, is the leader of a militia group called the Mata Mata, or Death Dealers. The world that Johnny lives in is devoid of meaningful social and political forms by which the author intends to convey the meaninglessness of war. Partially redeeming this bleak tale is the story of Laokolo, a young girl on the run from the conflict who wheels her crippled mother around in a wheelbarrow. She is a courageous youngster of uncommon intelligence who tries to survive in an insane world.

Forbes, Edna. *Johnny Tremain.* **New York: Yearling, 1987.**

This novel, first published in 1943 during World War II, focuses on Johnny as he grows and develops from a self-centered and arrogant child into a young man who takes up arms on behalf of the American Revolution. The novel opens in 1773, when Johnny is age 14, and he is age 16 when the novel ends in the aftermath of the battles of Lexington and Concord. The novel tracks Johnny as he matures so that his joining the ranks of fighting forces of the rebellion is seen as a sign of his growing maturity and responsibility. It is the ideal of fighting for a cause that allows him to leave the narrow confines of childhood and move into the open vistas of adulthood.

Hugo, Victor. *Les Miserables.* **New York: Alfred Knopf, 1998.**

While this novel is not strictly speaking a book about child soldiers, one of the principal characters in the novel is among the most famous child soldiers in literary history. A major portion of the novel concerns the Paris uprising of 1832. The scenes of revolutionary action on the Parisian street barricades focus on the orphan Gavroche, a street urchin who joins with the rebels and is killed. In popular culture, Gavroche's gallant and heroic death came to represent the French people and their struggle for democracy.

Iwela, Uzodinma. *Beasts of No Nation*. New York: Harper Collins, 2007.

This novel is set in a nameless African country with the idea that the tale speaks to the plight of child soldiers everywhere. It tells the story of Agu, a child soldier who, under the influence of drugs, participates in the most gruesome form of murder and who himself is routinely sexually abused by the commander of his unit. His commander, also nameless, kills for the sake of killing as well as for his own lust and amusement. The novel portrays war as pointless and horrific with child soldiers killing and being killed for nothing.

Jarret-Macauley, Delia. *Moses, Citizen and Me*. London: Granta Publications, 2005.

Julia, the novel's protagonist, comes back to the home of her Aunt Adele and Uncle Moses in Sierra Leone after a 20-year absence. There she encounters "Citizen," an ex–child soldier who has murdered his own grandmother, Julia's aunt. Moses is torn between the grief for his murdered wife and his duty toward his grandson. The theme of the novel is whether "Citizen" can be redeemed.

Kourouma, Ahmadou. *Allah Is Not Obliged*. New York: Anchor, 2007.

This novel by the late Ahmadou Kourouma, an award-winning writer from Côte d'Ivoire, is perhaps the most nuanced of all contemporary novels about child soldiers. The novel does not traffic in stereotypes, and the children are not simply reduced to abused victims of war. Instead, all the characters feel real. The story is narrated by Birahima, a gritty, tough-talking former child soldier who is haunted by *ganmas*, the "shadows" of the innocent people he has killed in war. It is not really not a child's story but an adult story, full of history, understanding, and comic satire, told thorough the voice of a child.

Saro-Wiwa, Ken. *Sozaboy*. London: Longman, 1994.

This important novel was written by the late novelist and activist Ken Saro-Wiwa, who led a nonviolent protest movement in

Nigeria and was later arrested and executed on politically motivated charges. The novel follows the fortunes of Mene, a young recruit at the time of the Biafra War, the civil war in Nigeria. He manages to survive the fortunes of war, only to find his life and his family shattered at war's end.

Film and Video

Adamovich, Ales. *Come and See*. DVD. Directed by Elem Klimov. Moscow: Mosfilm. 1985

The screenplay for this Belarussian film was written by Elem Klimov and Ales Adamovich, the latter of whom was a philosopher and who as a teenager fought with Belarussian anti-Nazi partisans during World War II. Adamovich witnessed the burning of Belarussian villages and the extermination of their inhabitants by the invading Germans. Through a child's eyes, the film depicts Florya, a Belarussian boy who becomes a partisan fighter. It follows his journeys as a young recruit and his transformation as he experiences the atrocities of partisan warfare.

Aduaka, Newton I., and Alain-Michel Blanc. *Ezra*. Film. Directed by Newton I. Aduaka. San Francisco: California Newsreel, 2007. Accessed at http:/newsreel.org/video/EZRA.

This is the story of a young boy abducted into a rebel army in an unnamed country in Africa (although it is clearly Sierra Leone) who was turned into a child soldier. It is the first film to describe the phenomenon of child soldiers through African eyes. One of the strengths of the film is that it focuses its attention on the daily life of child soldiers and tries to avoid stereotypes. The scenes in which Ezra testifies before a Truth and Reconciliation Commission miss the mark. Such testimony by children was not permitted in Sierra Leone.

Bogomolov, Vladimir. *Ivan's Childhood*. DVD. Directed by Andrey Tarkovskiy. Moscow: Mosfilm, 1962. Accessed at http:/www.criterion.com/films/830-ivans-childhood.

This Russian film was produced in Soviet Russia in 1962. It is set on the Eastern Front during World War II as Soviet forces try to repel the Nazi invasion. Ivan is a 12-year-old boy who works as a spy for the Russian army because he is able to cross into German lines without attracting suspicion. He is an orphan whose family was murdered by the Germans, and he is seeking revenge. Some of the soldiers would like to see him returned to civilian life, but he refuses and threatens to join a partisan unit. The officers and other soldiers in his unit care for him even as he is sent on a last spy mission in which he is captured and killed. War is portrayed as a bitter and tragic experience for men, women, and children.

Davidson, Kief. *Kassim the Dream*. DVD. Directed by Kief Davidson. New York: Believe Media, 2008. Accessed at http:/ www.kassimthedream.com.

This documentary is the story of Kassim Oumo, who was a child soldier in the National Resistance Army in Uganda, which ultimately prevailed in a civil war and became the Uganda People's Army. Kassim joined the army boxing team and ultimately became a champion boxer in the United States.

Folorni, Luigi. *Heart of Fire*. Directed by Luigi Folorni. Munich: TV-60 Filmproduktion, 2009.

A compelling film based on the autobiography by Senait Mehari, a young girl who became part of the Eritrean Liberation Front at age six. There is considerable controversy as to whether Mehari actually served as a child soldier and whether many of the events and experiences she described were fictional. The film should be treated as a fictional account of child soldiers.

Forbes, Ester, and Thomas W. Blackburn. *Johnny Tremain*. DVD. Directed by Robert Stevenson. Burbank, CA: Walt Disney Productions, 1957. Accessed at http:/disneydvd.disney.go.com/ johnny-tremain.html.

Based on the novel by Ester Forbes, this film follows the development of Johnny, a teenage silversmith apprentice, in the years leading to the outbreak of the American Revolution. Johnny joined the Sons of Liberty, and it is seen to be a sign of growing personal and political maturity when he finally takes up arms.

Herzog, Werner, and Denis Reichle. *Ballad of the Little Soldier*. Video. Directed by Werner Herzog and Denis Reichle. Stuttgart: Germany Süddeutscher Rundfunk, 1984 Accessed at http:/ www.youtube.com/watch?v=ZaXLPKNRobk.

This documentary film was directed by Werner Herzog, who is considered to be among the greatest of modern German film-makers. It focuses on the Miskito Indians who fought a war of resistance against the Sandinista government of Nicaragua. It is a complex story: the Miskito were one-time allies of the Sandinista National Liberation Front in their efforts to overthrow the Nicaraguan dictator Anastasio Samoza Debayle. However, when the Sandinistas came to power, they began to persecute the native Miskito. Miskito resistance groups, supported by the Central Intelligence Agency in the United States, included many child soldiers. The film is available for viewing on YouTube at the above website.

Ince, Thomas. *The Drummer of the 8th*. DVD. Directed by Thomas H. Ince. New York: Broncho Films, 1913.

This silent film, produced just before the fiftieth anniversary of the American Civil War, tells the story of young Billy, who runs away from home to join the Union army as a drummer boy. Billy is involved in the fighting and is badly wounded and taken prisoner by the Confederate army. During his captivity, he learns of Confederate battle plans. He escapes and transmits the information to his commander but dies of his wounds. This highly romantic and tragic film closes with the scene of Billy's coffin being brought to his home as his family is preparing a welcome-home dinner for him. Available as part of a DVD collection titled *Civil War Films of the Silent Era* at http://www.image-entertainment.com. Also available on YouTube at http://www.youtube.com/watch?v=N2p3zK8iFg0.

Jal, Emmanuel. *War Child*. DVD. Directed by Christian Karim Chrobog. Washington, DC: 18th Street Films, 2008.

War Child is a documentary film about the hip-hop artist Emmanuel Jal, who was a child soldier during the civil war in Sudan. Using documentary footage and Jal's own personal narrative, the film provides a powerfully absorbing story of rescue, exile, and return to his family in southern Sudan.

Johnny: The True Story of a Civil War Legend. **DVD. Directed by R. David Burns. San Antonio, TX: Historical Productions, 2007.**

This film, which is a mix of history and fiction, attempts to reconstruct the real life of Johnny Lincoln Clem—known as the

Drummer Boy of Chickamauga—who ran away from home and joined the 22nd Michigan Volunteer Infantry during the American Civil War. He was not formally enlisted at first but was informally incorporated into the infantry. At age 12, he was promoted to the rank of sergeant because of his heroism and became the youngest noncommissioned officer in the history of the U.S. Army. The film follows his emergence and growing public popularity as an icon of patriotism.

Kohrt, Brandon, and Robert Koenig. *Returned: Child Soldiers of Nepal's Maoist Army.* **DVD. Directed by Robert Koenig. Baltimore: Adventure Production Pictures, 2008. Accessed at http:/ nepaldocumentary.com.**

This award-winning film documents the stories of boys and girls who joined the Maoist army in Nepal. The children volunteered to join in the hopes of ending the intense gender discrimination and sexual violence of the societies they lived in. While the war ended with the Maoists in control of the government, the children had to return to families, villages, and a society that rejected them. The film demonstrates that for many child soldiers, reintegration into postconflict society can be more painful and traumatic than serving as a child soldier.

Leavitt, Charles. *Blood Diamond.* **DVD. Directed by Edward Zwick. Burbank, CA: Warner Brothers, 2006. Accessed at http:/ blooddiamondmovie.warnerbros.com.**

This film, starring Leonardo DiCaprio, is a thriller set during the Sierra Leone civil war that focuses on how diamonds, so-called blood diamonds, were used to fund the rebel insurrection. Fourteen-year-old Kagiso Kuypers plays a child soldier who was abducted and "brainwashed" by rebel forces.

Lord's Children. **Film. Directed by Oliver Stolts and Ali Samadi Ahadi. Arlington, VA: PBS/Wide Angle, 2008. Accessed at http:/ video.pbs.org/video/1168586547.**

This Emmy-nominated documentary follows three children who were former child soldiers in Uganda's Lord's Resistance Army and are living in a rehabilitation center. Jennifer Akelo, Kilama, and Francis were young children when they were abducted by the army and are trying to rebuild their lives after their experiences of violence and terror. Can be viewed at the above website.

Mansour, Carol. *Invisible Children*. DVD. Directed by Bobby Bailey, Laren Pool, and Jason Russell. San Diego: Invisible Children, 2006. Accessed at http://video.google.com/videoplay ?docid=3166797753930210643#.

A film conceived and narrated by three young Americans—Bobby Bailey, Laren Pool, and Jason Russell—who traveled to Uganda and filmed the impact of the rebel army, the Lord's Resistance Army, on the lives of children. The focus is on the children of Gulu who commute every night to the city center to protect themselves from being recruited as child soldiers by the army. The film has been widely screened on college campuses through the auspices of Invisible Children, an organization that attempts to end the use of child soldiers and promote schools and educational programs in Uganda. It can be viewed online at http:// freedocumentaries.org/film.php?id=114.

One Boy. Video. Berkshire: Commonwealth War Graves Commission. Accessed at http://www.cwgc.org/education/ presentation/default.htm.

This film is a remembrance tribute about Horace Iles, a 16-year-old soldier who died on the first day of the Battle of the Somme in 1916. Isles enlisted at age 14 in the Leeds Pals Battalion formed in Yorkshire, United Kingdom, at the beginning of World War I. It is intended for high school students. It can be viewed online or downloaded at the above website. The film can also be obtained, together with another documentary, *Some Go Early*, in a DVD titled *A Debt of Honor*, available as a free publication from the Commonwealth War Graves Commission at http://www.cwgc .org/learningzone/results.aspx?typus=off.

Reintegrating Child Soldiers in Chad. Video. New York: UNICEF Television, 2010. Accessed at http://www.youtube.com/ watch?v=i6y2dqEDC3o&feature=youtube.

A short video produced by UNICEF Television that provides an update on the situation of child soldiers in Chad with special emphasis on their reintegration. According to the video, some children have been forced to fight, while others have joined up in order to escape poverty or to avenge the deaths of relatives.

Samura, Sorious. *Cry Freetown.* **DVD. Directed by Ron McCullagh. London: Insight News Television, 2000. Accessed at http:/www.cryfreetown.org.**

An award-winning documentary based on the film footage taken by Sorious Samura, a Sierra Leone journalist, during the 1999 rebel invasion of Sierra Leone's capital, Freetown. The film depicts the atrocities carried out by the rebels and examines the involvement of child soldiers in the war. The film is widely available on YouTube.

Sauvaire, Jean-Stéphane, and Emmanuel Dongala. *Johnny Mad Dog.* **DVD. Directed by Jean-Stéphane Sauvaire. Paris: MNP Entreprise, 2008. Accessed at http:/www.tfmdistribution.com/ johnnymaddog.**

Based on the novel by Emmanuel Dongala, this dramatic and powerful film is set in Liberia (the novel was set in an unnamed African country but presumably the Republic of the Congo) and traces a band of child soldiers led by Johnny as they kill and pillage the countryside. The film is very violent and difficult to watch, as it follows the anomic carnage of Johnny and his followers.

Schiff, Elliot. *The Making of a Martyr.* **DVD and video. Directed by Brook Goldstein and Alistair Leyland. Ottowa, Canada: a2b Film Productions, 2006. Accessed at http:/www.snagfilms.com/ films/title/making_of_a_martyr.**

This documentary investigates an incident in March 2004 in which 15-year-old Hussam Abdu approaches an Israeli border checkpoint with live explosives strapped around his waist. He did not detonate the bomb but instead surrendered to the Israeli army and was sentenced to prison for attempted murder. The film examines the background to the incident and especially the involvement of Palestinian children in suicide bombing. The film can be seen at the above website.

Some Go Early. **Video. Berkshire: Commonwealth War Graves Commission. Accessed at http:/www.tpyfdigitalarchive.org.uk/30.**

This film is a remembrance tribute to Jack Banks, a 16-year-old soldier who was killed in the invasion of Normandy in 1944 during World War II. Banks enlisted in the 8th Durham Light Infantry in Lancashire, United Kingdom, at age 15. The film can also be obtained, together with another documentary, *One Boy*, in a DVD titled *A Debt of Honor*, available as a free publication from the Commonwealth War Graves Commission at http://www.cwgc.org/learningzone/results.aspx?typus=off.

Suicide Killers. DVD and video. Directed by Pierre Rehov. New York: City Lights Home Entertainment, 2006. Accessed at http:/video.google.com/videoplay?docid=5671220264306422368#.

A striking documentary by French filmmaker Pierre Rehov that makes use of many interviews with failed and now jailed suicide terrorists, including teenagers who speak about their desires to become martyrs. Many still proclaim their desire to kill if given the opportunity. The film also details the mechanism by which suicide terrorists are recruited and the underlying ideology that informs their actions. Available for viewing at the above website.

Waruzi, Bukeni. *A Duty to Protect: Justice for Child Soldiers in the DRC*. DVD and video. Directed by Bukeni T. Waruzi. Brooklyn, NY: Witness: Uvira, 2009. Accessed at http:/www.witness.org/videos/a-duty-to-protect.

A Duty to Protect is a short documentary that focuses on the stories of two girls, Mafille and January, who were recruited as child soldiers in Congo at ages 13 and 10, respectively. Mafille has experienced extreme violence and sexual exploitation and faced many obstacles in returning to civilian life. January, on the other hand, is an even younger girl who revels in her experience as a child soldier in eastern Congo.

Podcasts

Emmanuel Jal: From Child Soldier to Rising Star. **National Public Radio. May 8, 2008. Audio podcast. Accessed at http:/www.npr.org/templates/story/story.php?storyId=90283154.**

National Public Radio's Dave Davies interviews Emmanuel Jal, a former child soldier from Sudan, who has become a well-known hip-hop artist.

Ishmael Beah's Memoirs of a Boy Soldier. **National Public Radio. February 21, 2007. Audio podcast. Accessed at http:/www.npr .org/templates/story/story.php?storyId=7519542.**

National Public Radio's Terry Gross interviews Ishmael Beah, a former child soldier from Sierra Leone and author of the book *A Long Way Gone: Memoirs of a Boy Soldier.*

Rapper Emmanuel Jal's Trip to Peace. **National Public Radio. October 10, 2005. Audio podcast. Accessed at http:/www.npr .org/templates/story/story.php?storyId=4950821.**

Terry Gross interviews Emmanuel Jal about his life during the civil war in Southern Sudan and about his experiences as a child soldier.

UNICEF Internet Radio. Accessed at http:/www.unicef.org/rss/ podcast.xml.

UNICEF has a variety of short podcasts on the issue of child soldiers and related subjects that can be downloaded from UNICEF Internet Radio. These include *Child Soldiers Return Home* (Sudan), *Somalia Child Soldiers on the Rise*, and many others.

Glossary

Armed Conflict   Armed conflict between states is considered to exist when one or more states uses armed force against another state, regardless of the reasons or the intensity of the confrontation. Armed conflict within a state exists when a state must use military force (and not merely the police) to quell a conflict and the nongovernmental dissident group involved has the capacity to sustain military operations under a clear command structure. Armed conflict is different from other internal disturbances, such as riots or acts of banditry.

Armed Forces   The organized military of a state, including militia and volunteer groups that operate under a command responsible to the state for the conduct of its subordinates.

Armed Group   A nonstate military force that uses armed force to achieve political, ideological, or economic objectives and is not under the formal military command and control of the state in which it functions.

Child   Biologically, the term "child" generally refers to any human being between birth and puberty. The Convention on the Rights of the Child, however, defines a child as any person between birth and age 18. Definitions of childhood vary across the globe, and many cultures and societies may have their own definitions.

Child Soldier   A person too young to be lawfully conscripted, recruited or used by an armed force or armed group. International criminal law sets this age as below 15. Many humanitarian and human rights groups would like to increase the age of prohibition to 18.

Children's Rights   The basic human rights that are said to belong to children everywhere. The Convention on the Rights of the Child establishes four basic sets of children's rights: the rights of participation, protection, prevention, and provision. In practice, however, the central focus of political and legal action has been protection and prevention, while participation and provisioning take a distant second place.

Civil Society   The term generally refers to the panoply of voluntary organizations, such as nongovernmental organizations, advocacy groups, charities, social movements, and religious organizations that function outside the formal structures of government. In the international community, they play a particularly important role in framing and influencing policy under the umbrella of the United Nations.

Civil War   Internal armed conflicts. The international legal rules governing internal armed conflicts are far less developed than those for international conflicts. The basic rules are in Article 3 Common to the Geneva Conventions of 1949 and under some conditions Additional Protocol II of 1977. Combatants captured in civil wars do not generally have prisoner-of-war status and may be tried as criminals.

Combatant   An individual who takes a direct part in the hostilities of an armed conflict. *See also* Lawful Combatants, Noncombatants, and Unlawful Combatant or Unprivileged Belligerent.

Common Article 3 of the Geneva Conventions   Article 3 is the only article in the Geneva Conventions repeated in all four Geneva Conventions and is the only article that explicitly applies to internal armed conflicts.

Customary International Law   Binding rules of law that derive from the general practice of states, even if not written down in treaty form. For a rule of law to be considered binding under international customary law, there must be wide acceptance or consensus among nation-states. There must be evidence that states follow this rule of law as a matter of perceived obligation. Finally, there should also be a substantial history of state practice; that is, it must be demonstrated that states have a history of compliance with the rule of law.

DDR (Disarmament, Demobilization, and Reintegration)   The formal and technical process of disarming, demobilizing, and reintegrating combatants that is part of virtually all peacekeeping strategies in conflict zones.

Demobilization   The organized and supervised discharge of soldiers from an armed force or armed group. It may also involve the disbanding of armed forces or armed groups.

Disarmament   In the context of child soldiers, it refers to the formal surrender of arms by armed forces and groups and their collection and destruction.

Enemy Combatant   A new legal concept introduced by the United States during the wars in Afghanistan and Iraq under President Bush and in violation of the Geneva Conventions by which a captured enemy was presumed to be an unlawful combatant and treated as a criminal and not a prisoner of war unless proven otherwise.

International Criminal Court   In international tribunal established in 2002 by the Rome Treaty for the criminal prosecution of individuals charged with genocide, crimes against humanity, and war crimes.

Lawful Combatants   Members of the regular armed forces of a party to an international conflict but may also include other armed groups allied to a party to an international conflict, such as guerillas, paramilitary, and partisan units. In order to be regarded as lawful, combatants must be under responsible command, carry arms openly, wear distinctive signs that enable them to be identified as combatants, and obey the laws of war. Only lawful combatants are entitled to prisoner-of-war status if captured.

Laws of War   Also known as international humanitarian law, the laws of war were first codified in the 1949 Geneva Conventions, although many of these laws long predate the these treaties. The term "laws of war" refers to the rules of conduct in armed conflicts that also authorize individual criminal liability for their violations.

Noncombatants   Under the laws of war, a noncombatant refers to civilians not taking a direct part in hostilities as well as medical personnel and military chaplains who are regular soldiers but are protected because of their special function. It also includes soldiers who are sick, wounded, detained, or otherwise disabled.

Nongovernmental Organization   An organization that operates separately or independently from government in pursuit of political and social goals although usually independent and not connected to political parties. Some may be partly or fully funded by government.

Reintegration   The process of returning and integrating ex-combatants into civilian life.

Straight-18 Position   Based on a universal definition of childhood that begins at birth and ends at age 18. As applied to child soldiers, it is the position of most human rights and humanitarian groups that the recruitment of children under 18 years old into armed forces and groups should be universally prohibited.

Terrorism   Terrorism refers to attacks specifically directed toward civilians in both international and internal armed conflict.

Treaty   A written agreement between two or more nation-states. Treaties are the main source of international law regulating the recruitment and use of child soldiers. Terms such as "convention," "protocol," and "charter" are alternative terms for treaty. The Rome Statute of the International Criminal Court is a body of international criminal law created by treaty.

Unlawful Combatant or Unprivileged Belligerent   Persons who take a direct part in hostilities without being entitled to do so. These include civilians who take up arms and then attempt to fade back into the civilian population to evade detection. Such persons are not classified or treated as lawful combatants, and if they are captured, they cannot claim prisoner-of-war status. Instead, they may be treated criminals.

Vulnerability of Children   The presumed susceptibility of children to physical and emotional injury or attack.

War Crime   A grievous violation of the laws of war, which are also referred to as international humanitarian law.

Writ of Habeas Corpus   A court-issued order requiring authorities to bring a person before a court or judge. The primary purpose of a writ of habeas corpus is to free a person from unlawful custody. A writ of habeas corpus operates not to determine whether a person is guilty or innocent but merely whether a person is being lawfully detained.

Youth   Usually regarded as the life stage between childhood and maturity.

Index

Abani, Chris, 285
Abdu, Hussam, 293
Abu Sayyaf, 2, 125
Achebe, Chinua, 23
Adam, H., 73
Adamovich, Ales, 288
Additional Protocol I to Geneva
    Convention (1977)
  about, 123, 279
  Article 77, 40, 179–80
  child combatants and, 10–12,
    16, 51
  child recruitment and, 10–11,
    33, 51
  civilians in wars of national
    liberation, 36
  combatant status, 36
  full text access, 279
  international and
    noninternational conflicts,
    10–11, 35–36, 51
  United States as state party to,
    7, 38
  wars of national liberation
    and, 35–36
Additional Protocol II to Geneva
    Convention (1977)
  about, 123, 279
  Amended Protocol II (1996), 127
  Article 4, 181–82
  child combatants and, 10–12,
    16, 51

child recruitment and, 12–13,
    33, 51, 181–82
  combatant status, 36
  full text access, 279
  international and
    noninternational conflicts, 10,
    11–12, 36, 51
  United States as state party to, 7
  wars of national liberation
    and, 36
Adulthood, beginning of, 43–46
Adult Wars, Child Soldiers
    (UNICEF), 19, 268–69
Advocacy groups
  directory of, 219–62
  economic power of, 26
Afghanistan
  Bagram Theater Internment
    Facility, 92
  Bush administration orders and
    subsequent history, 94–99, 131
  characterized by U.S. as failed
    state, 95
  child captives in, 91–92
  child soldiers in, 2–3, 163, 166
  Haqqani network, 3, 126
  Hezb-i-Islami, 123
  interrogations in, 273
  Operation Enduring Freedom, 130
  population statistics, 171
  poverty and unemployment
    statistics, 172

Taliban, 2–3, 21–22, 95, 126, 127, 131, 133
Afghan National Police, 2
AFRC. *See* Armed Forces Revolutionary Council
Africa
  child soldier recruitment in, 2
  child soldiers in, 22
  Conradian view of, 23
  traditional societies and age of maturity in, 47–48
  Women Peace and Security Network Africa, 260
  See also under names of individual countries
African Charter on the Rights and Welfare of the Child (1999), 17, 41, 51, 128, 197–98
African National Congress, 36
African states, war crimes warrant for Sudanese President al-Bashir, 38
African Union Peacekeeping Mission on Somalia (AMISON), 91
African Union-United Nations Mission in Darfur (2010), 71
Age
  culpability and, 64–69
  of legal majority, 43, 44–46
Ahmed, Sharif Sheik, 50
Ajedi-Ka/Projet Enfants Soldats, 219
al-Akhrasas, Ayat, 131, 137
Al-Aqsa Martyrs' Brigades, 130, 131
Algerian War of Independence, 35
al-Harakat al-Islamiyya, 125
Al-Khansaa, 154
Allah Is Not Obliged (Kourouma), 287
Allied Democratic Front, 68
al-Qaeda, 3, 95, 125, 132
al-Shebaab, 135
al-Zahrani, Yasser Talal, 67
Amended Protocol II, 127

American Friends Service Committee, Youth and Militarism Program, 219–20
American Jewish World Service, 220
American Revolution
  child soldiers in, 34, 115, 143, 276, 283, 286
  reintegration of veterans, 75
AMISON. *See* African Union Peacekeeping Mission on Somalia
Amnesty International
  about, 220–21
  on child soldiers, 20–21
  economic power of, 26
Angling, John, 118
Angola, 274
Anticolonialist wars, 35
APRD. *'See* People's Army for the Restoration of Democracy
Arab states, war crimes warrant for Sudanese President al-Bashir, 38
Arafat, Yasser, 120, 138
Armed Forces of Liberia, 127
Armed Forces of the Democratic Republic of Congo, 2, 121
Armed Forces Revolutionary Council (AFRC), 54, 127
Armies of the Young: Child Soldiers in War and Terrorism (Rosen), 267
Arms. *See* Munitions
Article 3 (Geneva Conventions). *See* Common Article 3 (Geneva Conventions)
Arusha Peace and Reconciliation Agreement (Burundi), 129
Asia, child soldier recruitment in, 2
Avondo society (Sierra Leone), 57

Baca v. Obama, 104
Bagram Theater Internment Facility, 92, 94, 100
Bailey, Bobby, 292

Ballad of the Little Soldier (video), 289–90

Banks, Jack, 294

Banning use of child soldiers

about, 6–18, 33–34

Additional Protocols I and II to Geneva Convention (1977), 10–12, 16, 51

Cape Town Principles (1997), 52, 127, 198–207, 269

Coalition to Stop the Use of Child Soldiers, 15

Convention on the Rights of the Child (CRC) (1989), 14–15, 18–19, 41, 42, 51, 182–83, 278

customary law, 14

Geneva Conventions (1949), 7–10, 93, 121, 173–76, 177, 179, 278–79

Paris Principles (2007), 52, 61, 134, 269

Rome Statute (1998), 12–13, 34, 51, 127, 190–96, 280

See also International law

Bayer, C. P., 73

Bdeir, Issa, 131

Beah, Ishmael, 125, 138–39, 282, 295

Beasts of No Nation (Iwela), 287

Becker, Jo, 156–57

Beijing Platform for Action, 126

Bellamy, Carol, 43

Bevistein, Abraham (Aby), 119, 139–40, 283

Biafra, 122

Bin Laden, Osama, 125

Blattman, Chris, 72

Blood Diamond (movie), 291

Borquez, Josefina, 151–52

Boumediene v. Bush, 98

Boyes, Duncan Gordon, 118

"Boy Soldiers of the American Revolution: The Effects of War on Society" (Cox), 276

Boy Soldiers of the Great War (Van Emden), 278

"A Boy Soldier under Washington: The Memoir of Daniel Granger" (Quaifem), 283–84

Brima, Alex Tamba, 133

British child soldiers in history, 3, 116, 118, 119, 120, 129, 139, 141–42, 276, 277, 278, 283, 292, 294

Brookings Institution, 221

Bundu society (Sierra Leone), 47, 56

Burma. *See* Myanmar

Bush administration, War Against Terror, 94–99, 131

Bush Wives and Girl Soldiers: Women's Lives through War and Peace in Sierra Leone (Coulter), 265

"Cannon fodder," child soldiers as, 21

Cape Town Principles and Best Practices on the Prevention of Recruitment of Children into the Armed Forces and on Demobilization and Social Reintegration of Child Soldiers in Africa (1997), 52, 127, 198–207, 269

Captured child combatants. *See* Detainees

CARE, 221–22

Caritas Internationalis, 222

Casabianca, Giancomo (Giocanta), 116, 140

Catholic Relief Services, 222

CDF. *See* Civil Defense Forces

Center for Defense Information, 223

Central African Republic

child soldiers in, 124, 163, 166

civil war in, 135

demographic statistics, 171

poverty and unemployment statistics, 172

Central African Republic Bush War, 132

Central Reserve Police (Sudan), 136
Central Reserve Police Force
    (India), 6
Chad
    child soldiers in, 136, 163,
        166, 271, 292
    demographic statistics, 171
    Human Rights Watch Report
        on, 271
    poverty and unemployment
        statistics, 172
    U.S. economic sanctions
        against, 89, 90
Chapman, Nathan Ross, 2, 130
Cheyenne people, age
    of maturity in, 48
Child, definitions of, 4, 14
    Additional Protocols I and II to
        Geneva Convention, 10–12
    African Charter on the Rights
        and Welfare of the Child
        (1999), 17, 41, 51, 197–98
    age at which person moves
        from childhood to adulthood,
        43–46
    Convention on the Rights of the
        Child (CRC) (1989), 14–15, 18,
        41, 42, 51, 182–83, 278
    international law and, 43–44
    local definitions, 43–44
    Optional Protocol on the
        Involvement of Children in
        Armed Conflicts to the
        Convention on the Rights of
        the Child (2000), 15–17, 41,
        51–52, 67, 85, 92, 183–90, 279
    "Straight-18," 15–17, 41
    universal definition, 41–42
    Worst Forms of Child Labor
        Convention of the
        International Labor
        Organization (1999), 17, 41
    See also Childhood; Children;
        Children's rights; Child
        soldiers

Child captives. *See* Detainees
Childhood
    cross-cultural views on, 42,
        47–50
    "Straight-18" position, 15, 41
    views on, 4, 14, 24, 42
Children
    between age 15 and 18, 14
    age of legal majority, 43, 44
    age of majority, 15
    culpability of, 64–69
    and the law, 45
    seen as vulnerable, 19–20
    See also Child, definitions of;
        Childhood; Child soldiers
*Children and Armed Conflict:
    Report of the Secretary General*
    (United Nations), 270
The Children and Armed Conflict
    Unit, 224–25
*Children and War: A Historical
    Anthology* (Marten, ed.),
    276, 277
*Children and War in Sierra Leone:
    A West African Diary*
    (Wilson), 282
Children and Youth in Armed
    Violence, 225
*Children and Youth on the Front Line:
    Ethnography, Armed Conflict
    and Displacement* (Boyden &
    De Bedry, eds.), 263
Children at War (Singer), 270
*Children in the Ranks: The Maoists'
    Use of Child Soldiers in
    Nepal* (Human Rights
    Watch), 270
Children's Forum Network of
    Sierra Leone, 225
Children's rights
    African Charter on the Rights
        and Welfare of the Child
        (1999), 17, 41, 51, 197–98
    Cape Town Principles (1997),
        52, 127, 198–207, 269

Convention on the Rights of the Child (CRC) (1989), 14–15, 18–19, 42, 51, 182–83, 278
Paris Principles (2007), 52, 61, 134, 269
Children's Rights Information Network, 225–26
Child Soldier Accountability Act of 2008 (CSAA) (U.S.), 50, 88, 89, 91, 213–16
"The Child Soldier Narrative and the Problem of Arrested Historicization" (Coundouriotis), 265
Child Soldier Prevention Act of 2008 (CSPA) (U.S.), 88, 89, 136, 208–13
Child soldier recruitment. *See* Recruitment of child soldiers
Child Soldier Relief, 223
Child soldiers
    as abused and exploited, 19–22
    assumptions about, 19–24
    autobiographies and biographies, 282–84
    as "cannon fodder," 21
    captured child combatants, 37, 40–41
    counseling for, 22, 73
    definitions of, 34, 50–52
    dehumanization of, 21–22
    in fiction, 285–288
    film and video about, 288–295
    forcible recruitment, 54–55
    historical timeline, 115–136
    in history, 1, 6, 161–72, 276–78
    literature about, 263–85
    mental health outcomes, 73–75
    in modern India, 6
    modern statistics for, 1, 6, 161–72
    "programmed to kill," 21–22
    rehabilitation of, 22
    "Straight-18" position, 15, 41
    voluntary enlistment, 11, 40, 54–55

war crimes committed by, 13, 62–69
wars of national liberation, 36
    See also Banning use of child soldiers; International law; Recruitment of child soldiers
Child Soldiers: From Violence to Protection (Wessels), 275–76
Child Soldiers: Sierra Leone's Revolutionary United Front (Denov), 265–66
Child Soldiers: The Role of Children in Armed Conflict (Cohen & Goodwin-Gill), 264
Child Soldiers in Africa (Honwana), 274–75
Child Soldiers in International Law (Happold), 281
Child Soldiers Initiative, 224
Child Soldiers International, 223
China, International Criminal Court at The Hague and, 38
The Christian Boy-Soldier: The Funeral Sermon of Joseph E. Darrow (Nadal), 285
Chui, Mathieu Ngudjolo, 53, 134
Church, Albert, 101
Civil Defense Forces (CDF) (Sierra Leone), 49, 54, 55, 56, 125
Civilians, under Geneva Conventions, 7–8
Civil society, 25, 46–47
Civil War (U.S.)
    child soldiers in, 3–4, 116–18, 140–41, 147–48, 149, 170
    literature and media works on, 276–77, 284, 285, 290–91
Civil wars
    Additional Protocol II of the Geneva Conventions, 11–12
    See also Wars of national liberation
"The Civil War That Was Fought by Children: Understanding

the Role of Child Combatants in El Salvador's Civil War, 1980–1992" (Courtney), 265

Claus, John, 106, 107

Claus, Joshua R., 100

Clem, John Lincoln, 117, 140–41, 290–91

"Closing Argument at Guantanamo: The Torture of Mohammed Jawad" (Frakt), 280–81

Cluster Munitions Coalition, 226

Coalition for Women's Human Rights in Conflict Situations, 226

Coalition to Stop the Use of Child Soldiers, 15, 25, 41, 88, 128, 223–24

Colombia
child soldiers in, 2, 163, 166
demographic statistics, 171
poverty and unemployment statistics, 172

Combatant Status Review Tribunals (CSRT), 97

Come and See (DVD), 288

Commission for Reception, Truth, and Reconciliation, Timor-Leste, 226–27

Common Article 3 (Geneva Conventions), 9, 67, 93, 95, 96, 176–77

"Comparison of Mental Health Between Former Child Soldiers and Children Never Conscripted by Armed Groups in Nepal" (Kohrt et al.), 275

Confederate forces (U.S.), child soldiers in, 3–4

Confessions, 105–6

Congress for the Defense of the People (Congo), 2

Conrad, Joseph, 23

Conscription of child soldiers, 55, 61

See also Recruitment of child soldiers

Control Arms Coalition, 227

Convention of Patriots for Justice and Peace, 135

Convention on the Rights of the Child (CRC) (1989)
about, 14–15, 18–19, 41, 42, 51, 125, 182–83, 278
definition of childhood, 43
United States as state party to, 7
See also Optional Protocol on the Involvement of Children in Armed Conflicts to the Convention on the Rights of the Child (2000)

Cook, John, 117

Coomaraswamy, Radhika, 107–8, 157

Cornwall, John Travers (Jack; Boy Cornwall), 119, 141–42, 276, 284

Côte D'Ivoire
child soldiers in, 163, 166
civil wars in, 131, 136
demographic statistics, 171
poverty and unemployment statistics, 172

Counseling, for child soldiers, 22, 73

Courts, national courts, 67–69

CRC. *See* Convention on the Rights of the Child

Crimes of War Education Project, 227–28

Criminal law, treating juveniles as adults, 44

Cry Freetown (DVD), 293

CSAA. *See* Child Soldier Accountability Act of 2008

CSPA. *See* Child Soldier Prevention Act of 2008

CSRT. *See* Combatant Status Review Tribunals

Culpability, of children, 64–69

Culture under Cross Examination: International Justice and the Special Court for Sierra Leone (Kelsall), 281
Customary law, 13–14, 39–40

Dangerous Duty: Children and the Chhattisgarh Conflict (Human Rights Watch), 271
Darfur conflict, 71, 122, 130, 133, 136
Darfur Liberation Front, 131
Darfur Peace Agreement (2006), 71
Dayan, Moshe, 119, 142
DDR. *See* Disarmament, demobilization, and reintegration of child soldiers
Death penalty
under Additional Protocols, 40
under Geneva Conventions, 9, 10
Defence for Children International, 228
Dellaire, Romeo, 157–58
Demobilization
of child soldiers, 69
See also Disarmament, demobilization, and reintegration of child soldiers
Democratic Forces for the Liberation of Rwanda, 2, 129–30
Democratic Republic of the Congo
captured child combatants, 37
child soldiers in, 124, 136, 163, 167, 294
criminal sanctions against child recruiters, 53
demographic statistics, 171
execution of child soldiers, 68
Front for Patriotic Resistance of Ituri, 131
Mai-Mai Patriotic Resistance, 2, 128
modern history of, 121–22

poverty and unemployment statistics, 72, 172
recruitment in, 2
Second Congo War, 128
U.S. economic sanctions against, 89, 90
Demon Forces, 91
Detainees (captured child combatants), 37, 40–41
Bagram Theater Internment Facility, 92, 94, 100
Common Article 3 (Geneva Conventions), 9, 67, 93, 95, 96, 176–77
confessions, 105–6
"frequent-flyer program" (Guantanamo Bay), 102, 145, 273
Guantanamo Bay, 67, 92, 94, 100, 130–31, 145, 146–47, 272, 273
Jawad, Mohammed, 103, 135, 145, 280–81
juvenile detainees detained by U.S. since 2002, 134
Khadr, Omar, 62, 67, 92, 99, 100, 104–10, 136, 146–47, 272
War Against Terrorism, 93–94
Die Hard, Aby (Lister), 140, 283
Dilawar, 100, 106
Dinka society (Sudan), 48, 124
Disarmament
of child soldiers, 69
United Nations Disarmament, Demobilisation, and Reintegration Resource Centre, 255
United Nations Institute for Disarmament Research, 255
United Nations Office for Disarmament Affairs, 256
Disarmament, demobilization, and reintegration of child soldiers (DDR), 69–76
advocacy groups, 255, 256

"Displacing Violence: Making Potentecostal Memory in Postwar Sierra Leone" (Shaw), 275

Doctors Without Borders, 228

"Drummer Boy of Chickamauga," 141, 291

The Drummer of the 8th (DVD), 290

Durbin, Richard J., 90

A Duty to Protect: Justice for Child Soldiers in the DRC (DVD and video), 294

Dyilo, Thomas Lubanga, 53, 136, 153–54

Early to War: Child Soldiers in the Chad Conflict (Human Rights Watch), 271

East Africa, traditional societies and age of maturity in, 48

East Timor, 66–67, 226–27

Eliminating use of child soldiers, *See also* Banning use of child soldiers

El Salvador, literature on, 265, 266

Emmanuel, Charles McArther, 91

Emmanuel Jal: From Child Soldier to Rising Star (podcast), 294

"Enemy combatants," 94–95 *See also* Unlawful combatants

England, child soldiers in history. *See* British child soldiers in history

Enlistment of child soldiers. *See* Voluntary enlistment of child soldiers

"Equality to Die For: Women Guerilla Fighters in Eritrea's Cultural Revolution" (Bernal), 264

Erased in A Moment: Suicide Bombing Attacks against Israeli Civilians (Human Rights Watch), 271

Eritrean War of Independence, 122, 264

Ethiopian civil war, 267–68, 289

Executions, under Geneva Conventions, 9

Ex post facto laws, 39

Ezra (movie), 288

"Facts about Child Soldiers" (U.S. State Department), 20

FARC. *See* Fuerzas Armadas Revolucionarias de Colombia

Farhat, Maryam Mohammad Yousif, 154

Fatah, 126

Federal Torture Statute (1994) (U.S.), 91

Femmes Africa Solidarite, 228–29

Fighting for the Rain Forest: War, Youth and Resources in Sierra Leone (Richards), 267

The Fighting Mascot: The True Story of a Boy Soldier (Kehoe), 283

First Liberian Civil War, 125

Fitzgibbon, Andrew, 116

Flynn, Thomas, 116

Fofana, Moinina, 55, 132–33, 134

Forbes, Edna, 286, 289

Forces de Résistance Patriotique d'Ituri, 131, 134

Forces patriotiques pour la libération du Congo, 133

Fourth Geneva Convention, 7, 9, 94, 173–76

Frakt, David, 102–3

Franklin, Benjamin, 4–5

FRELIMO. *See* Front for the Liberation of Mozambique

"Frequent-flyer program" (Guantanamo Bay), 102, 145, 273

From Child Soldiers to Ex-Fighter: Female Fighters, Demobilisation and Reintegration in Ethiopia (Veale), 267–68

From Jack Tar to Union Jack: Representing Naval Manhood

in the British Empire
(Conley), 276
From the Alps to the Red Sea
(Marek), 282
Front for Patriotic Resistance
of Ituri, 131
Front for the Liberation of
Mozambique (FRELIMO),
158, 268
Fuerzas Armadas Revolucionarias
de Colombia (FARC), 122

Gallegos v. Colorado, 105–6
Gbao, Augustine, 133, 135
Gender and Peacebuilding
Working Group, 229
Geneva Call, 229–30
Geneva Conventions (1949)
about, 7–10, 93, 121, 278–79
child soldiers and, 9, 10
Common Article 3, 9, 67, 93,
95, 96, 176–77
Fourth Convention, 7, 9, 93,
173–76
Third Convention, 7, 177, 179
United States as state party to, 7
See also Additional Protocols
I and II (1977)
Geneva International Centre for
Humanitarian Demining, 230
Girls. *See* Women and girls
"Girls with Guns: Narrating the
Experience of War in
FRELIMO's "Female
Detachment" (West), 268
Giza, Joseph N., 21
Global Witness, 230–31
Gould, Benjamin, 3
Great Britain, child soldiers in
history. *See* British child
soldiers in history
Group for the Convention on the
Rights of the Child, 242
"Growing Up in Guerilla Camps:
The Long Term Impact of

Being a Child Soldier in El
Salvador's Civil War"
(Dickson-Gomez), 266
Guantanamo Bay, 67, 92, 94, 100,
130–31, 145, 146–47, 272, 273
Guerilla forces, as lawful or
unlawful combatants under
Geneva Conventions, 8
Guinea-Bissau (West Africa), 268

Habeas corpus, 97, 103
Habibullah, Mullah, 100
Haganah, 119, 142
The Hague. *See* International
Criminal Court
Hague Convention of 1899, 118
Hague Convention of 1907, 118
Haley v. Ohio, 105
Hamas, 3, 124
Hamdan v. Rumsfeld, 98
Hamdi v. Rumsfeld, 97
Haqqani network, 3, 126
Harakat al-Shabaab Mujahideen
(Somalia), 49
Hazb-i-Islami, 3
Health and Human Rights
Info, 231
Heart and Alliance for Human
Needs and Human Rights,
231–32
The Heart of Darkness (Conrad), 23
Heart of Fire (movie), 289
*Hearts of Darkness: Torturing
Children in the War on Terror*
(Giroux), 269
Hemans, Dorothea, 116, 140
Henley, Stephen, 103
Here's to You, Jesusa
(Poniatowska), 152
Herzog, Werner, 290
Hezb-i-Islami, 123, 133
Hitler Youth, 119, 120
Hizbul Islam, 135
Hollat, George, 117
Horsfall, William, 118

Howe, Orion P., 117
Humanitarian organizations
    directory of, 219–62
    economic power of, 25–26
Human rights
    Convention on the Rights of the
        Child (CRC) (1989), 14–15,
        18–19, 41, 42, 51, 182–83, 278
    Geneva Conventions (1949),
        7–10
    international law and, 42
    reports on, 270–74
Human Rights Education
    Associates, 232
Human Rights Enforcement Act of
    2009 (U.S.), 88–89, 216–17
Human Rights Watch, 26, 124,
    232, 270–73
Huvelle, Ellen Segal, 103–4

ICC. *See* International Criminal
    Court
ICRC. *See* International Committee
    of the Red Cross
Iles, Horace, 292
Illicit drugs, United Nations Office
    on Drugs and Crime, 257
ILO. *See* International Labor
    Organization
*The Impact of Armed Conflict on
    Children* (Graca for United
    Nations), 127, 158, 264
India
    child soldiers in, 163, 167
    demographic statistics, 171
    International Criminal Court at
        The Hague and, 38
    Maoist insurgency in, 6, 37,
        122, 271
    poverty and unemployment
        statistics, 172
    Salwa Judum, 136
Insurgents
    Geneva Conventions and, 9–10
    as illegitimate actors, 5

Integrated Regional Information
    Networks, 233
Interagency Panel on Juvenile
    Justice, 233
Internal Bureau for Children's
    Rights, 234–35
Internal conflicts
    Additional Protocol I and, 35–36
    Additional Protocol II and,
        11–12, 36
    Geneva Conventions and, 10
Internal Displacement Monitoring
    Centre, 233–34
International Action Network on
    Small Arms, 234
International armed conflicts
    Additional Protocol I (1977), 10–
        11, 35, 35–36, 51, 123, 179–80
    Additional Protocol II (1977),
        10, 11–12, 36, 51, 123,
        181–82
    Geneva Conventions, 7–10
    wars of national liberation
        categorized as, 35
International Campaign to Ban
    Landmines, 235
International Centre for
    Transitional Justice, 235–36
International Committee of the
    Red Cross (ICRC)
    about, 236
    on Optional Protocol Article
        38, 16
    on recruitment of child
        soldiers, 11
International Committee on the
    Rights of the Child, 36
International crime, United
    Nations Office on Drugs and
    Crime, 257
International Criminal Court
    (ICC), 12, 34, 38, 49, 236, 280
    See also Rome Statute (1998)
International Criminal Tribunal
    for Rwanda, 126, 236–37

International Criminal Tribunal
for Yugoslavia, 237
International customary law, 13–
14, 39–40
International Labour
Organization, 17, 41, 123, 128,
237, 238, 279
International law
binding nature of treaties,
6–7, 34
customary law, 13–14, 39–40
definitions of childhood and,
43–44
human rights and the realities
of, 42
national sovereignty and, 5–6
non-state armed groups and, 5
rebels under, 5
state parties to, 7, 13
See also Additional Protocols I
and II; Banning use of child
soldiers; Convention on the
Rights of the Child; Geneva
Conventions; Optional
Protocol on the Involvement
of Children in Armed
Conflicts to the Convention
on the Rights of the Child;
Rome Statute
"International Law and the Child
Soldier" (Mann), 281
International Organization for
Migration, 237–38
International Programme on the
Elimination of Child
Labour, 238
International Rescue Committee,
238–39
International Women's Tribune
Centre, 239
Invisible Children (film), 292
Invisible Children (organization),
239–40
Iraq
al-Qaeda, 3, 95, 125, 132

child soldiers in, 3, 91–92,
164, 167
demographic statistics, 171
interrogations in, 273
poverty and unemployment
statistics, 172
Iraq War, 131
*Ishmael Beah's Memoirs of a Boy
Soldier* (podcast), 295
Islamic Jihad, 3, 22, 124
Islamic Resistance Movement. *See*
Hamas
Israel, Haganah, 119, 142
Israeli-Palestinian conflict, 3, 22,
122, 124, 137, 138, 168, 271, 293
Ituri, 131
Ivan's Childhood (DVD), 288–89
Izz ad-Din al-Qassam Brigade, 124

*Jack Cornwall: The Story of John
Travers Cornwell, V.C. Boy—
1st Class* (anonymous), 284
Jackson, Andrew, 34, 115, 143–44
Jal, Emmanuel, 144–45, 290,
294, 295
Jamat Sunat al-Dawa Salafia, 3
Janjaweed militia, 71
Jawad, Mohammed, 103, 135, 145,
280–81
Jesuit Refugee Service, 240
Joan of Arc, 115, 146
*Johnny: The True Story of a Civil War
Legend* (movie), 141, 290–91
Johnny Mad Dog (Dongala),
286, 293
Johnny Mad Dog (DVD), 293
Johnny Tremain (Forbes), 286
Johnny Tremain (movie), 289
Johnston, William "Willie," 117
Justice and Equality Movement, 130

Kachin Independence Army, 122
Kallon, Morris, 133, 135
Kamajors (Sierra Leone), 55–57, 58
Kamara, Brima Bazzy, 133

Kamara, Ibrahim, 66
Kanu, Santigie Borbor, 133
Kaplan, Robert, 23
Karen Buddhist Army, 126
Kareni National People's
    Liberation Front, 124
Karen National Liberation Army
    (Myanmar), 2, 121, 126
Karen National Union
    (Myanmar), 121
Karenni Army (Myanmar), 2,
    121, 123
Kassim the Dream (DVD), 289
Katanga, Germain ("Simba"),
    53, 131, 134
Kenya, Mau Mau Rebellion,
    35, 121
Khadr, Ahmed Said, 104
Khadr, Omar, 62, 67, 92, 99, 100,
    104–10, 136, 146–47, 272
*Khadr v. The Prime Minister
    of Canada*, 108
Khansaa Falastin, 154
Kilmer, George, 3–4
The Kimberley Process, 240–41
King, Charles, 4
Kipling, Rudyard, 282–83
Klasen, F., 73
Kohrt, B. A., 74, 75
Kondewa, Allieu, 55, 57–58,
    132–33, 134
Kony, Joseph, 49, 53, 154–55
Kountz, John, 117
Kourouma, Ahmadou, 287

Ladd, Luther C., 116, 147–48, 285
Langbein, Julius, 117
Lawful combatants
    defined by Additional Protocols
        I and II, 35–36
    defined by Geneva
        Conventions, 8, 95, 177
    punishment for, 62
Laws of war, 7, 95, 117, 118
    See also Geneva Conventions

(1949); International law;
    Rome Statute (1998)
Law to end use of child soldiers. *See*
    Banning use of child soldiers
League of Nations, 119
Legislation (U.S.). *See* United
    States legislation
Les Miserables (Hugo), 286–87
Liberation Tigers of Tamil Eelam
    (LTTE), 123
Liberia
    child soldiers in, 163, 167, 257
    Demon Forces, 91
    history of civil war, 125, 127,
        128, 132
    literature and media on, 266, 293
    poverty statistics, 72
    Truth and Reconciliation
        Commission of Liberia, 252
Liberians United for
    Reconciliation and
    Democracy, 126
Lieber Code, 117
*Life of Luther C. Ladd, Who Fell in
    Baltimore, April 19, 1861* (A
    Citizen of Alexandria), 285
*The Little Drummer Boy, Clarence
    McKenzie, the Child of the 13th
    Regiment New York State
    Militia and the Childe of the
    Mission Sunday School*
    (Bingham), 284–85
"Little Drummer Boy of
    Brooklyn," 116, 149
Lomé Peace Accord, 128, 129
*A Long Way Gone: Memoirs of a Boy
    Soldier* (Beah), 125, 138, 282
Lord's Children (film), 291–92
Lord's Resistance Army (LRA), 2,
    21, 22, 23, 49, 53, 124–25, 273,
    291–92
Lost Boys of Sudan, 124
LTTE. *See* Liberation Tigers of
    Tamil Eelam
Lucas, Jack, 120, 148–49

Maasai society, age of maturity in, 48
Machel, Graca, 127, 158–59
Machon, James, 117–18
Mackenzie, Clarence, 116, 149, 284–85
Magee, William, 118
Mai-Mai Patriotic Resistance, 2, 128
The Making of a Martyr (DVD), 293
Maoist rebels
    in India, 6, 37, 122, 271
    in Nepal, 74, 75, 126, 127, 270, 275, 291
Mau Mau Rebellion, 35, 121
McCune, Emma, 144
Mehari, Senait, 289
Mende people (Sierra Leone), age of maturity in, 47–48
Mental health outcomes, child soldiers, 73–75
"Mercenaries of Democracy: The "Politricks" or Remobilized Combatants in the 2007 General Elections, Sierra Leone" (Christensen and Utas), 274
Mexican revolution, soldaderas, 119, 151–52
Middle East, child soldier recruitment in, 2, 3
Militants, Geneva Conventions and, 9–10
Military Commissions Act (2006), 67, 92, 98
"Military Patrimonialism and Child Soldier Clientalism in the Liberian and Sierra Leonean Civil Wars" (Murphy), 266
Mines Action Canada, 241
Miskito Indians, 124
Moro Islamic Liberation Front, 2, 37, 124

Moses, Citizen and Me (Jarret-Macauley), 287
Moshe Dayan: The Story of My Life (Dayan), 142
Movement for Democracy in Liberia, 132
Mozambique, 35, 158, 268, 274
Mozambique War of Independence, 35, 122, 268
Multi-Country Demobilization Program, 241–42
Munitions
    humanitarian organizations, 227, 230, 233–34, 241, 243, 254–55
    small arms used by child soldiers, 170
Murphy, Audie, 120, 149–51
Murphy, Robinson Barr, 118
Muslim Youth Organization, 3
Myanmar (Burma)
    child soldiers in, 2, 121, 164, 167, 272
    history of insurgency, 121, 125–27
    U.S. economic sanctions against, 89
Myanmar Armed Forces, 121
Myanmar National Democratic Alliance Army, 125
My Boy Jack? The Search for Kipling's Only Son (Holt), 282–83
"My Gun Was as Tall as Me": Child Soldiers in Burma (Human Rights Watch), 272

Nadal, Joseph, 285
Namibia War of Independence, 36
"Naming and shaming," 34, 42
Napoleonic Wars, child soldiers in, 277
Nationalist and Integrationalist Front (Rwanda), 2, 131

National Liberation Army
(Colombia), 2, 122
National Patriotic Front of
Liberia, 125
Nation-states
on actions of rebel and militant
groups, 5
national sovereignty and,
5–6
as parties to international
treaties, 7, 13
Native American tribes, age of
maturity in, 48
*Navigating Terrains of War: Youth
and Soldiering in Guinea-Bissau*
(Vigh), 268
Nazis, children under the Nazis,
119, 120, 277–78, 284, 288
Nepal
child soldiers in, 74, 75, 164,
167, 291
demographic statistics, 171
history of insurgency, 127
literature on, 270, 275
Maoist rebels in, 74, 75, 126, 127,
270, 275, 291
poverty and unemployment
statistics, 172, 270
Unified Communist Party of
Nepal (Maoist), 37, 126
"New Barbarism," 22–24
New People's Army (Philippines),
2, 123
Nicaragua, 124, 290
Nigeria-Biafran Civil War,
122, 151
9/11 event, unlawful combatants
and, 93–94
Non-governmental organizations
(NGOs)
economic power of, 25–26
as third-party government, 46
Noninternational conflicts
Additional Protocol I, 35–36, 51,
123, 179–80

Additional Protocol II, 10,
11–12, 36, 51, 123, 181–82
treaties and, 9–10
Non-state armed groups
international law and, 5
recruitment of child soldiers by,
2–3
Norwegian Initiative on Small
Arms Transfer, 243
Norwegian Refugee Council,
243–44
Ntaganda, Bosco, 53

Obama, Barack, 90, 136
Odhiambo, Okot, 53
Office of the United Nations
High Commissioner for
Refugees, 244
Okafor, Ben, 151
*The Omar Khadr Case: A Teenager
Imprisoned at Guantanamo*
(Human Rights Watch),
272–73
One Boy (video), 292
Ongwen, Dominic, 53
On Wheels and How I Came There
(Smith), 284
Open Society Justice Initiative,
244–45
Operation Enduring Freedom, 130
Optional Protocol on the
Involvement of Children in
Armed Conflicts to the
Convention on the Rights of
the Child (2000)
about, 15–17, 41, 51–52, 67, 92,
129, 183–90, 279
Article 38, 16
United States as state party to, 7,
85, 86–88
Organization of American States,
129
Organizations, directory of, 219–62
Ottawa Treaty, 127
Otti, Vincent, 53

Otunnu, Olara A., 159
Oumo, Kassim, 289

Pakistan, Haqqani network, 3, 126
Palestinian child soldiers, 3, 22, 124
Palestinian conflict, 3, 22, 122, 124,
    126, 130, 137, 138, 168, 271, 293
Pankhurst, Sylvia, 139
Paris Commitments, 134
Paris Principles and Guidelines on
    Children Associated with
    Armed Force and Armed
    Groups (2007), 52, 61, 134, 269
Participation
    as child right under CRC, 18
    in rehabilitation process, 22
Partisans, 120, 282, 288
Partnership Canada Africa, 245
Patrimonialism, 266
Peace Direct, 245
Peck, Oscar, 117
Penal Reform International, 246
People's Army for the Restoration
    of Democracy (APRD), 132
Philippines
    Abu Sayyaf, 2, 125
    child soldiers in, 2, 123,
        164, 168
    demographic statistics, 171
    Moro Islamic Liberation Front,
        2, 37, 123, 124
    poverty and unemployment
        statistics, 172
Pool, Laren, 292
Popular Front for the Liberation of
    Palestine, 122
Population
    demographic statistics
        of nations, 171
    United Nations Population
        Fund, 257
Poro people (Sierra Leone),
    47–48, 56
Posttraumatic stress disorder
    (PTSD), 74

Prevention, as child right
    under CRC, 18
Prisoner of war status, Geneva
    Conventions, 8, 9, 10,
    177, 179
Private Yankee Doodle (Martin), 283
"Privileged belligerents," 8
    See also Lawful combatants
Project Ploughshares, 246
Prosecutor v. Bosco Ntaganda, 53
Prosecutor v. Brima, 54
Prosecutor v. Charles Taylor, 63
Prosecutor v. Fofana, 55, 57, 58, 60
*Prosecutor v. Germain Katanga and
    Mathieu Ngudjolo Chui*, 53
*Prosecutor v. Joseph Kony, Vincent
    Otti, Okot Odhiambo and
    Dominic Ongwen*, 53
Prosecutor v. Norman, 40
Prosecutor v. Omar Al Bashir, 38
Prosecutor v. Sesay, 54
*Prosecutor v. Thomas Lubanga
    Dyilo*, 53
"Protected persons," 40
Protection, as child right
    under CRC, 18
Protocol against the Illicit
    Manufacturing of and
    Trafficking in Firearms, Their
    Parts and Components and
    Ammunition (2001), 130
Protocols, Additional I and II.
    See Additional Protocols I
    and II
Protocol V Explosive Remnants
    of War, 132
Provisioning, as child right under
    CRC, 18
Psychological counseling, for child
    soldiers, 22, 73
PTSD. *See* Posttraumatic stress
    disorder

Quaker United Nations Office,
    246–47

Raban, Havka Folman, 284
Rape, 45, 62, 70, 73, 107
Rasul v. Bush, 97
Rebellion, 5, 36
Rebel Phoenix: Rebel Children and their Families in South Carolina (Drago), 276–77
Rebels
  as criminals, 5
  Geneva Conventions and, 9–10
  as illegitimate actors, 5
Reck v. Pate, 105
Recruiters of child soldiers, criminal and political sanctions against, 37, 52–53
Recruitment of child soldiers
  about, 1–2, 4, 33–34
  abuse and exploitation of child soldiers, 20–22
  Additional Protocol I to Geneva Convention (1977), 10–11, 33, 36, 51, 123, 179–80
  Cape Town Principles (1997), 52, 127, 198–207, 269
  children as "cannon fodder," 21
  Convention on the Rights of the Child (CRC) (1989), 14–15, 18–19, 41, 42, 51, 182–83
  customary law, 14
  International Committee of the Red Cross (ICRC) on, 11
  by non-state armed groups, 2, 12
  Paris Principles (2007), 52, 61, 134, 269
  Rome Statute, 12–13, 34, 51, 127, 190–96, 280
  Special Court for Sierra Leone, 14
  voluntary enlistment vs. forcible recruitment, 11, 40, 54–55
  worldwide modern hotbeds for, 2–3
Refugee Studies Centre, 247
Refworld Virtual Documentation Centre, 247–48

Rehov, Pierre, 294
Reintegrating Child Soldiers in Chad (video), 292–93
Reintegration
  advocacy groups, 241–42, 255
  of child soldiers, 22, 69
  literature and video on, 292, 294–95
  See also Disarmament, demobilization, and reintegration of child soldiers
Republic of Sierra Leone Armed Forces, 122
Retroactive punishment, 39
Returned: Child Soldiers of Nepal's Maoist Army (film and DVD), 75, 291
A Review of the FBI's Involvement in and Observations of Detainee Interrogations in Guantanamo Bay, Afghanistan and Iraq (U.S. Office of the Inspector General), 273
Revolutionary Armed Forces (Colombia), 2, 122
Revolutionary United Front (RUF) (Sierra Leone), 22, 23, 54, 63, 125, 129, 265–66
"The Rites of the Child: Global Discourses of Youth and Reintegrating Child Soldiers in Sierra Leone" (Shepler), 275
Rome Statute (1998), 12–13, 34, 38, 51, 127, 190–96, 280
RUF. *See* Revolutionary United Front
Russell, Jason, 292
Rwanda
  child soldier recruitment in, 2
  Democratic Forces for the Liberation of Rwanda, 2, 129–30
  genocide in, 126
  International Criminal Tribunal for Rwanda, 126, 236–37

Nationalist and Integrationalist
Front, 2, 131

Salwa Judum (India), 136
Samburu society (Africa), age of
maturity in, 48
Sam Hinga, Norman, 132–33, 134
Samura, Sorious, 293
Sande society (Sierra Leone), 47, 56
Sandinistas, 124, 290
Save the Children Alliance, 248
Say NOUNiTE to End Violence
against Women, 248
Scott, Julian, 118
Search for Common Ground, 249
Second Congo War, 128
Second Côte d'Ivoire Civil War, 136
Second Liberian Civil War, 126, 128
Second Sudanese Civil War, 124
Security Council Resolutions
Resolution 1261, 128
Resolution 1306, 129
Resolution 1314, 129
Resolution 1315, 64
Resolution 1325, 129, 135
Resolution 1379, 130
Resolution 1820, 135
Resolution 1882, 135
Resolution 1888, 135
Resolution 1889, 135
Resolution 2002, 136
Security Council Working Group
on Children and Armed
Conflicts, 249
Sesay, Issa Hassan, 133, 135
Sexual violence, 70, 73, 106, 135,
193, 226, 249–50, 259,
273, 291
literature on, 274–75
Sexual Violence Research
Initiative, 249–50
Shan State Army, 122
Shepler, Susan, 46, 70, 275
Sierra Leone
advocacy groups, 225

Armed Forces Revolutionary
Council (AFRC), 54, 127
child soldiers in, 22, 23, 138–39,
164, 168, 257, 282, 295
child soldiers, statistics, 164
Civil Defense Forces (CDF), 49,
54, 55, 56, 125
customary law and, 39–40
demographic statistics, 171
diamond fields of, 129
economy of, 26
history of civil war, 125–28, 133
initiation rites, 47–48, 56
literature and media on, 265–66,
267, 273, 274, 275, 280, 281,
282, 287, 288, 293, 295
NGOs and access to
resources, 26, 46
poverty and unemployment
statistics, 72, 172
reintegration of children,
70–71
Republic of Sierra Leone Armed
Forces, 122
Revolutionary United Front
(RUF), 22, 23, 54, 63, 125, 129,
265–66
sexual violence in civil war,
273–74
Special Court for Sierra Leone,
14, 39, 53–62, 125, 127,
250–51, 280, 281
Special Court Statute, 54, 130,
196–97
traditional societies and age of
maturity, 47–48
West Side Boys, 267
"Simba." *See* Katanga, Germain
Sinia Brigade, 53
Sioux people, age of maturity
in, 48
The Slavery Convention, 119
Small arms, 170, 250
Small Arms Survey, 250
Snedden, James, 118

Social change, civil society and, 46–47
Soldaderas, 119, 151–52
Soldiers
   defined by Geneva Conventions, 7–9
   treatment of according to Geneva Conventions, 8–9
   See also Child soldiers
Somalia
   arms embargo on, 90–91
   child soldier recruitment in, 2
   child soldiers in, 168
   civil war in, 126, 135
   demographic statistics, 171
   poverty and unemployment statistics, 172
   Transitional Federal Government (TFG), 49–50
   U.S. economic sanctions against, 89
Some Go Early (video), 293–94
A Song for the Night: A Novella (Abani), 285–86
South Africa, African National Congress, 36
South America, child soldier recruitment in, 2
South-central Asia, child soldier recruitment in, 2
Sozaboy (Saro-Wiwa), 287–88
Sparrow, Robert, 22
Special Court for Sierra Leone
   about, 14, 39, 53–62, 127, 250–51, 280
   culpability of children, 64–69
   literature about, 281
   testimony, 57–60, 61, 63
   Witness TF2–021, 57–60
   Witness TR1–012, 61
Special Court Statute, 54, 196–97
Special Rapporteur on Contemporary Forms of Slavery, Its Causes, and Consequences, 251–52

Special Rapporteur on Trafficking in Persons, Especially in Women and Children, 252
Speer, Christopher, 104
SPLA. *See* Sudanese People's Liberation Army
Sri Lanka
   child soldiers in, 123, 164, 168
   civil war, 124
   demographic statistics, 171
   poverty and unemployment statistics, 172
The State of Youth and Youth Protection in Northern Uganda: Findings from the Survey for War Affected Youth (UNICEF), 274
State parties, 6, 7
Statute of the International Criminal Tribunal for Rwanda, 126
Statute of the Special Court for Sierra Leone, 54, 130, 196–97
Steed, R. V., 120
Stolen Children: Abduction and Recruitment in Northern Uganda (Human Rights Watch), 273
"Straight-18" position, 15, 41
Sudan
   child soldiers in, 2, 124, 136, 169
   demobilization and reintegration of children, 72
   demographic statistics, 171
   Lost Boys of Sudan, 124
   media coverage of Jal, 290, 294, 295
   poverty and unemployment statistics, 172
   Second Sudanese Civil War, 124
   traditional societies and age of maturity, 47–48
   U.S. economic sanctions against, 89

war crimes warrant for
President al-Bashir, 38
Sudanese Civil War, 124
Sudanese People's Liberation
Army (SPLA), 2, 38, 124, 144
Sudan Liberation Movement
Army, 71, 131
Suicide bombing, 22, 137, 271, 293
Survey of War Affected Youth, 22, 274
Sweden
demographic statistics, 171
poverty and unemployment
statistics, 172

Taliban, 2–3, 21–22, 95, 126, 127,
131, 133
Tamil Tigers, 123
Tanzim, 126
Tatmadaw-Kyi, 121
Taylor, Charles Ghankay (father),
63, 126, 127, 132, 133, 136,
155–56
Taylor, Chuckie (son), 91
Teh, Alex, 63
Terre des Hommes International
Federation, 252
TFG. *See* Transitional Federal
Government
They Are Still with Me (Raban), 284
Third Geneva Convention, 7,
8, 177, 179
Third-party government, 46
Tigray People's Liberation
Front, 267
Tora Bora Front, 3, 133
Torture
confessions and, 105–6
Federal Torture Statute (1994), 91
"frequent-flyer program"
(Guantanamo Bay), 102,
145, 273
Jawad, Mohammed, 103, 135,
145, 280–81
Khadr, Omar, 62, 67, 92, 99, 100,
104–10, 136, 146–47, 272

Traditional societies, age of
maturity in, 47–50
Transitional Federal Government
(TFG) (Somalia), 2,
49–50, 90
Treaties
declarations, 86
meaning of ratification, 86
nonsignatories bound by, 38
parties bound by, 6–7, 34
reservations to, 86
understandings, 86
See also International law
Trials
age and culpability in U.S.
courts, 67–69
for children, 62–76
of child soldier recruiters, 37,
52–53
under Geneva Conventions, 9
for war crimes committed by
child soldiers, 13, 62–69
See also Special Court for Sierra
Leone
Truth and Reconciliation
Commission of Liberia, 252
Truth and Reconciliation
Commission of Sierra
Leone, 129
Tsam, Herzl Yankl, 152
Tungwar, Lam, 152–53

Uganda
child soldiers in, 21, 22, 23, 124,
164, 169, 291–92
criminal sanctions against child
recruiters, 53
demographic statistics, 171
literature and DVDs on, 273,
274, 289
poverty and unemployment
statistics, 172
trials of child soldiers, 68
United Movement to End Child
Soldiering, 254

UKSIA. *See* United Karenni States
    Independence Army
Umm Nidal, 154
UNICEF
    about, 253
    on child soldiers, 19, 22–23, 43
    Internet radio, 295
    published documents of,
        268–69, 274
    review of Cape Town
        Principles, 52
UNICEF Innocenti Research
    Centre, 253–54
Unified Communist Party of
    Nepal (Maoist), 37, 126
Union des Patriotes Congolais, 133
Union of Democratic Forces for
    Unity, 132
United Karenni States
    Independence Army
    (UKSIA), 121
United Movement to End Child
    Soldiering, 254
United Nations
    about, 121
    insurgency treated as internal
        civil issue, 37
    NGOs and, 46
    Office of the United Nations
        High Commissioner for
        Refugees, 244
    Quaker United Nations Office,
        246–47
    reintegration of children,
        69–70
    reports by, 270
    Special Rapporteur on
        Contemporary Forms of
        Slavery, Its Causes, and
        Consequences, 251–52
    Special Rapporteur on
        Trafficking in Persons,
        Especially in Women and
        Children, 252
    war crimes warrant for

    Sudanese President
        al-Bashir, 38
    work of, 25, 37
    See also Security Council;
        UNICEF
United Nations Development
    Program, 254–55
United Nations Disarmament,
    Demobilisation, and
    Reintegration Resource
    Centre, 255
United Nations High
    Commissioner for
    Refugees, 121
United Nations Institute for
    Disarmament Research, 255
United Nations Office for
    Disarmament Affairs, 256
United Nations Office of the
    Special Representative of the
    Secretary-General for
    Children and Armed
    Conflict, 256
United Nations Office on Drugs
    and Crime, 257
United Nations Population
    Fund, 257
United Nations Transitional
    Administration in East Timor
    (UNTAET), 66–67
United Nations Women, 258
United States
    age and culpability in domestic
        courts, 67–69
    child soldiers in history, 3–4,
        171, 276–77
    child soldiers problem in recent
        history, 85–110
    continued child soldier
        recruitment between 2004
        and 2007, 88
    demographic statistics, 171
    involvement in Somalia, 50
    juvenile detainees since
        2002, 134

military support of nations with child soldier issues, 90–91

as non-state party to Additional Protocol I, 7, 13, 38

Optional Protocol (2000), 7, 85, 86–88, 92–93

poverty and unemployment statistics, 172

and Rome Statute, 38

as state party to various treaties, 7, 13

traditional societies and age of maturity, 48

treating juveniles as adults under criminal law, 44

See also United States legislation

United States Institute of Peace, 258

United States legislation, 85, 88–91

Child Soldier Accountability Act of 2008, 50, 88, 89, 91, 213–16

Child Soldier Prevention Act of 2008, 88, 89, 136, 208–13

Federal Torture Statute (1994), 91

Human Rights Enforcement Act of 2009, 88–89, 216–17

Military Commissions Act (2006), 67, 92, 98

United States v. Mohammed Jawad, 103

United States v. Omar Ahmed Khadr, 100, 106, 107, 108

United Wa State Army, 125

Unlawful combatants

defined by Additional Protocols I and II, 35–36

defined by Geneva Conventions, 8–9, 95

punishment for, 62

War Against Terror, 93–94

"Unprivileged belligerents," 8–9

See also Unlawful combatants

UNTAET. *See* United Nations Transitional Administration in East Timor

U.S. Office of Global Women's Issues, 258–59

U.S. State Department, on child soldiers, 20

Veterans, reintegration of, 75–76

Voluntary enlistment of child soldiers, 11, 40, 54–55

defined, 61

Special Court of Sierra Leona, 58–62

War

Geneva Conventions, 7–10

laws of war, 7

neo-Conradian vision of, 24

"New Barbarism," 22–24

See also Civil wars; Rebellion; Wars of national liberation

War Against Terrorism, 94–99

War and Children: A Reference Handbook (Dupuy & Peters), 263–64

War and the Crisis of Youth in Sierra Leone (Peters), 266

War Child (DVD), 290

War Child International, 259

War crimes

committed by child soldiers, 13, 62–69

defined by Rome Statute, 12, 34, 127, 190–96, 280

retroactive punishment for, 39

See also Special Court for Sierra Leone

War of 1812, child soldiers in, 116

Warsaw Ghetto, 120, 284

Wars of national liberation, 35–37

Watchlist on Children and Armed Conflict, 259–60

We'll Kill You if You Cry: Sexual Violence in the Sierra Leone Conflict (Human Rights Watch), 273–74

Wessels, Robert, 72, 73

West Side Boys, 267

"The West Side Boys: Military Navigation in the Sierra Leone Civil War" (Utas & Jorgel), 267

Whitney, Addison, 147

"Who Is a Child? The Legal Conundrum of Child Soldiers" (Rosen), 281–82

Wilberforce Trafficking Victims Protection Reauthorization Act of 2008, 89

Witnesses of War: Children's Lives under the Nazis (Stargardt), 277–78

Women and girls
advocacy groups for, 124, 226, 238–39, 243, 248, 252, 257, 258, 259, 260–61
Beijing Platform for Action, 126
as child soldiers, 21, 47, 56, 70, 135, 151, 198, 203, 204
literature about, 24, 254, 265, 267–68, 273, 291
rape or sexual abuse of, 71, 73

Women Peace and Security Network Africa, 260

Women's Refugee Commission, 260–61

Working Group on Girls' Rights, 242–43

Working Group on Women, Peace, and Security, 243

World Conference on Human Rights (1995), 126

World Food Program, 261

World Health Organization, 261–62

A World Turned Upside Down: Social Ecological Approaches to Children in War Zones (Boothby & Wessels, eds.), 263

World Vision, 262

World War I
child soldiers in, 3, 4, 119, 139, 141–42, 276, 278, 283, 284, 291
reintegration of veterans, 75

World War II, child soldiers in, 7, 120, 148–51, 277, 288–89, 294

Yemen
child soldiers in, 136
U.S. economic sanctions against, 89, 90

You Can Help Your Country: English Children's Work during the Second World War (Mayall & Murrow), 277

Young Nelsons: Boy Sailors during the Napoleonic Wars (Ronald), 277

Youth Advocate Program International, Inc., 262

Yugoslavia, International Criminal Tribunal for Yugoslavia, 237

Yurlova, Marina, 153

About the Author

David M. Rosen is professor of anthropology at Fairleigh Dickinson University in Madison, New Jersey, where he teaches courses in anthropology and law. He has carried out field research in Sierra Leone, Kenya, Israel, and the Palestinian Territories. He is the author of *Armies of the Young: Child Soldiers in War and Terrorism* (Rutgers University Press, 2005). His recent articles include "Child Soldiers, International Humanitarian Law, and the Globalization of Childhood" in the *American Anthropologist* (2007), "Who Is a Child? The Legal Conundrum of Child Soldiers" in the *Connecticut Journal of International Law* (2009), and "The Child Soldier in Literature or How Johnny Tremain Became Johnny Mad Dog" in Maartje Abbenhuis and Sara Buttersworth (eds.), *Restaging War in the Western World: Non-Combatant Experience* (Palgrave Macmillan, 2009). He received his PhD from the University of Illinois, Urbana–Champaign, and his JD from Pace University School of Law. He is admitted to the bar in the state of New York.